THAILAND'S FAR SOUTH

Engaging the Difficult Realities in a Recurring Conflict

In *Thailand's Far South*, Kee Howe Yong sheds light on the Malay Muslims in Thailand's far south. The book focuses on the relationship between the construction of minorities – and thus majority – and issues of engaging with the difficulties of their realities: loss, violence, history, memory, livelihood, fear and paranoia, and political formations.

The book explores the ways in which regimes of fear affect the way minorities relate to one another and to those in authority. It reveals how Muslim identities in southern Thailand are produced – under what constraints and structures, and by what technologies and force. Drawing on methodologies of narrative theory, performative aspects of language, and questions of history and memory, Yong demonstrates the ways the conflict was and is differently engaged by Malay Muslim interlocutors. The book addresses the generally ignored topic of the varied positions of the Malay Muslims at the borderland of Thailand's far south and the implications of these positions in understanding the meaning of the current insurgency for the heterogeneous Malay Muslim population. In doing so, *Thailand's Far South* provides an invaluable contribution to the southern Thai conflict, fieldwork in conflict zones, and the literature on violence, political science, history, security studies, and philosophies of violence.

KEE HOWE YONG is an associate professor of anthropology at McMaster University.

Thailand's Far South

*Engaging the Difficult Realities
in a Recurring Conflict*

KEE HOWE YONG

UNIVERSITY OF TORONTO PRESS
Toronto Buffalo London

© University of Toronto Press 2024
Toronto Buffalo London
utorontopress.com

ISBN 978-1-4875-5612-9 (cloth) ISBN 978-1-4875-5615-0 (EPUB)
ISBN 978-1-4875-5614-3 (PDF)

Library and Archives Canada Cataloguing in Publication

Title: Thailand's far south : engaging the difficult realities in a recurring conflict / Kee Howe Yong.
Other titles: Far south
Names: Yong, Kee Howe, 1960– author.
Description: Includes bibliographical references and index.
Identifiers: Canadiana (print) 20240347455 | Canadiana (ebook) 20240347536 | ISBN 9781487556129 (cloth) | ISBN 9781487556150 (EPUB) | ISBN 9781487556143 (PDF)
Subjects: LCSH: Muslims – Thailand, Southern. | LCSH: Violence – Thailand, Southern. | LCSH: Insurgency – Thailand, Southern. | LCSH: Thailand, Southern – Politics and government.
Classification: LCC DS570.M85 Y56 2024 | DDC 305.6/9709593 – dc23

Cover design: Heng Wee Tan
Cover image: Courtesy of the author

We wish to acknowledge the land on which the University of Toronto Press operates. This land is the traditional territory of the Wendat, the Anishnaabeg, the Haudenosaunee, the Métis, and the Mississaugas of the Credit First Nation.

University of Toronto Press acknowledges the financial support of the Government of Canada, the Canada Council for the Arts, and the Ontario Arts Council, an agency of the Government of Ontario, for its publishing activities.

Printed and bound by CPI Group (UK) Ltd, Croydon, CR0 4YY

 Canada Council for the Arts Conseil des Arts du Canada

 ONTARIO ARTS COUNCIL
CONSEIL DES ARTS DE L'ONTARIO
an Ontario government agency
un organisme du gouvernement de l'Ontario

Funded by the Government of Canada   Financé par le gouvernement du Canada    Canada

Contents

Acknowledgments vii

Introduction: Ethnographic Beginning, *Biasa* 3

1 The Violent Historical Debris 22

2 Militarized and Islamified 46

3 The *Mak Pasar* 60

4 Households and Marital Unions, the Subject of Insecure Existence 89

5 Hiding the Clouds with the Palms of Your Hands 113

6 Are We *Kon* Thai? 132

7 War on Terror? 158

8 The "Halalness" of Things 184

Notes 205

Bibliography 229

Index 247

Acknowledgments

It can be overwhelming to list all the experiences through which I have journeyed for this book to materialize. I can only hope to make a few gestures of appreciation and acknowledgment here. Allow me to offer my sincere apologies in advance if I have left out any individuals in my acknowledgments. This project began when I made my reconnaissance trip to Muang Pattani back in 2005 and met Ajarnn Wattana Sugunasil and Srisompob Jitpiromsr at Prince of Songkhla University, Pattani campus (PSU). That was slightly over a year after the horrific 2004 tsunami, after more than two decades of relatively *corrupted peace* in Thailand's far south, and after the escalation in 2004 of the current recurring conflict in Thailand's far south. I can still recall how in 2005 Ajarnn Wattana and Srisompod were talking to each other, and to me, about what was going on in the region. There was a lot of speculation, and I mostly listened. And here we are, almost twenty years later, and the end of violent conflict in the region is nowhere in sight.

As I returned again and again to the capital township of Muang Pattani and beyond over the course of several years (mostly Canadian summer months) to conduct ethnographic fieldwork, I met and worked with many *ajarnn* at PSU and other individuals who generously shared ideas, reasons, leads, and connections. Saroja, Srisompod, Suraiya, Alisah, Jason, Bordin, Worawit, Pi Soong, Sumree, Faosee, and Abdullah, to name just a few, were invaluable to my project's development. It was they who enabled me in so many ways to attempt bolder forays and receive critiques. I hope the product of this project in some way reflects well on their encouragement and critiques, their generosity and hospitality.

Obviously, to my interlocutors who took the time and risk to work with me in such sensitive and tumultuous settings, I would like to record my deepest thanks. As an anthropologist, I shall forever remain indebted to them for their gifts. For fear of reprisals against those concerned, I am unable to reveal the names of the interlocutors who worked with me, often at no little risk to themselves. I trust that they will recognize who they are and understand the depth of my gratitude should any of them ever happen to read this study.

This project would not have been possible without the financial support I received for my research. I am grateful for a Canadian SSHRC Standard Research Grant and to a McMaster University Arts Research Board Research Grant. I am also grateful for and have learned a lot from the anonymous reviewers' comments and engaged criticism of my manuscript. Thanks go to the staff at the University of Toronto Press, especially to acquisition editor Jody Lewchuk for bringing it to closure, during a COVID-19 pandemic and the concomitant videoconferencing fatigue. I would also like to thank editorial director Jennifer DiDomenico, associate managing editor Janice Evans, and copy editor Angela Wingfield for their assistance.

My gratitude goes to McMaster University's Department of Anthropology – especially Harvey Feit – that supported this project and steered it through the final passage of its voyage. To my undergraduate students who took my "Anthropology and the Other(ed)" and "The Secret of the Gift" courses, thank you so much. Thanks go also to the graduate students who took my "Politics of Desire" course. I also thank the editors of various journals for permission to use, in certain chapters, a version of articles published by them.

Lastly, my deepest gratitude goes to the *mak pasar* (mothers of market) food vendors and others in Muang Pattani, some mentioned in this book, some not, who received me in their open-air markets, talked to me, and let me talk to them. I am forever grateful to them for their stories, their laughter, their smiles, and their hospitality. I hope that the books manage to convey my debt to them, and much more – their gifts to me that I can never fully reciprocate. Naturally, none of those named here bears any responsibility for any aspect of the contents of this book, the onus of which rests on me alone.

THAILAND'S FAR SOUTH

Introduction

Ethnographic Beginning, *Biasa*

If there was one encounter that in many ways colours my research project in Thailand's far south, it happened on 29 May 2009, and it had to do with a particular word, *biasa*. This was on the very first day of my return to the region since my reconnaissance trip in 2005. I was at a central bus station, where I met Hanisah, a Malay Muslim woman.[1] When I asked her how to get to Muang Pattani (the capital district of the province of Pattani), Hanisah gave me a puzzling look as if to ask, "Why are your heading there?" She was pleasantly surprised that I could speak Malay fluently even though I was conversing in Malaysian Malay, which is not the same as Pattani Malay. Hanisah could also speak English. She said that if only Thais (in Thailand's far south) could speak some Malay, they would have a better chance of understanding each other: "*Muafakat*. We would have *muafakat*." She went on to elaborate: "If different *bangsa* [races or ethnic groups] could speak each other's languages, even a little, we would not only understand each other and live together but also carry each other's burdens in difficult times. That way we would have *muafakat*." She smiled and I smiled at her smiles.[2] I told her I could understand what she said, but I did not elaborate. We had just met.

Hanisah led me to the booth to buy a ticket for Muang Pattani. However, just when the van was about to leave, I found out that it was already full of passengers. I would have to take the next one. At that instant Hanisah literally snatched my ticket from me to swap it with that of another passenger, apparently someone she knew. Handing the ticket to me, she said, "We will be on the same van." Not only was I grateful that the other passenger was willing to swap her ticket, but also I was glad that I now had Hanisah to talk to on the journey to Pattani, someone with whom I could, anthropologically speaking, begin my ethnographic fieldwork sooner than I had expected.

Twelve of us, including the driver, were on the van. Two women, whom I believed to be non-Malays, were sitting on the front seat next to the driver. There were three passengers in each of the second, third, and fourth rows. Hanisah, a man, and I were in the third row. The women in the second and fourth rows were Malay Muslims, judging from their *tudongs* (headscarves). There were three women in front of us. The one on the right sat with her face turned towards the window and her chin held in the cushion of her right hand. Besides her sat a young girl and what appeared to be her grandmother. The man who sat in our row, next to Hanisah, was also looking out of the window. Very soon, everybody appeared to be asleep – except Hanisah and I.

After I had introduced myself as a professor from a Canadian university, she told me she was pursuing a master's degree in hospitality service at Prince of Songkhla University, Hatyai campus.[3] She also told me she had worked for two years at a hotel in Kuala Lumpur, Malaysia, after obtaining her baccalaureate degree in business administration from Mahidol, a prestigious university in Bangkok. Along the journey Hanisah asked me again why I was heading to Muang Pattani. As she put it, "Muang Pattani is not exactly a place *farangs* [foreigners] would want to visit, not since the violence has erupted again [short pause]. Are you not afraid?" She smiled, which made me slightly uncomfortable, before continuing: "Okay, I get it. You are not the typical *farang* but still you are an outsider. Once you open your mouth, people will know …" She continued to smile and look at me with her big brown eyes. Her expression, I felt, was not only a look but also inquisitorial and evaluative. It made me uneasy, I confess. I was a newbie to the place I was heading, a place that outsiders would avoid. Back then I knew very little about Thailand's far south or what I was getting into. I knew I wanted to do some research on the current conflict, but I did not know what kind of research on violence I even wanted to pursue and with whom I would work.

Hanisah gave me a blank look when I told her I was a sociocultural anthropologist and that I wanted to find out how the latest conflict was affecting the lives and livelihoods of ordinary civilians. She continued to give me a blank look and gentle smiles of scepticism as to the plausibility of my research interests or that my concerns even mattered to her. I made a mental note: To whom does it matter? Do those to whom it matters, matter? She then asked, "Anthropology?" And when I said, "Social science," she immediately responded, "Ah! You mean poli science … or sociology." As I tried to further explain what sociocultural anthropology was, Hanisah gave me this nonplussed but somewhat annoyed look, before asking: "Ajarnn [Professor],[4] why are there so many outsiders interested in the latest conflict? Why should they be interested?" She said it was quite common to come across *farangs* in Hatyai asking questions about the latest conflicts. "But Hatyai is not Pattani. Those *farangs* would never head to where you are going ... you *sangat berani* [very brave]," she said, laughing, which made me felt even more uncomfortable, if not embarrassed. As if teasing me, she said, "You know, you might be the only *orang luar* [outsider] in Pattani. *Tak takut?* [Not scared?] Don't worry, *lah.* Just stay in Muang Pattani. Stay away from the village, *lah.*[5] If you need to go there, make sure someone accompany you. No, make sure a Malay accompany you and don't go too *dalam* [deep] into the villages. And never after sunset." I had some idea what she was alluding to when she advised me to make sure I had a Malay accompanying me and to not venture too deep into the villages, and never after sunset.

In a pensive tone she asked: "But what can you do for us? What can you all do for us?" Without waiting for my response (not that I had any), she continued: "You and other researchers who come here and ask all sorts of questions, you have the luxury of coming and going. For you to come here and then leave, you may see violence, even witness shootings or experience bombing. I hope that will not happen to you, *inshallah!*" I smiled but kept quiet. After a long pause she offered a lengthy, albeit somewhat fatalist, description of the violence's history and realities: "For those of us who grew up here, who live here, who are stuck here, we see them as well, but they have become *biasa* [normal] for us. This is not the first time the region has seen violence. We have heard about past violence our entire life. Our entire life we grew up *menunggu* [waiting] for it to happen again, *menunggu* for violence to erupt once again." And then in Malay she said: "Bagi kita yang tinggal di tiga wilayah, ... ini pertentangan yang berulangan [For those of us who live in the three provinces, in Patani, this is a recuring conflict]. The question is, Where do you go when you have nowhere to go, no way out? It's like living in a *penjara* [prison]," she forced a smile. "We can't just leave. We are fed up. Sometimes I want to leave but I can't. My families are here. This is our land. We are stuck. We are stuck in this nightmare we cannot wake up from. It's like ..." She did not finish the sentence. She then scanned across the van, front and back, to see if anyone was listening, before closing her eyes.

At that moment I scribbled down the following notes, however ironic, paradoxical, or even optimistic they may sound: Taking recourse to the *longue durée, menunggu* might describes the Malay Muslims' disposition and psychology in Thailand's far south. Since the days of the Haji

Sulong struggles and the expression of autonomy in the late 1940s, can the series of struggles be seen as progress for the Malay Muslims in Thailand's far south? In other words, to do something instead of being docile subjects, or worse, of being complicit with the state. Paradoxically, building on this line of ambiguous analysis, suppression of such expression of autonomy can lead to a sense of agency for the Malay Muslims, but also agony if one takes into consideration that Thailand's far south has been inflicted, if not conscripted, with the recurring expression of autonomy and its accompanying violence since the late 1940s. This sense of ambivalence might be the key to unpacking the puzzle of their common response in a blasé manner: they are used to it, ... no way out, just can't leave, might as well get used to it, *biasa*.

In many ways the difficulties of reality for the Malay Muslims in the far south can be seen as their being stuck in a certain history that is perceived as a nightmare from which they cannot awake – which reminds me of James Joyce's *Ulysses*: "history is a nightmare from which I am trying to wake." Or of Eugene O'Neill: "there is no present or future, only the past, happening over and over again, now." These quotes suggest the enormous burden of the past on the present and the enormous force that past events still have in the present. Hanisah and those of her generation who were born after the Haji Sulong era have heard about the various recurring struggles and their concomitant violence; as failures they have become unusable past. This generation senses that it is only a matter of time before their desire for a better future, their struggles for more respect and an expression of autonomy, will resurface and, with it, the accompanying violence. They are subjects caught in a paradox. Perhaps my notes then play on this level of ambiguity: that in the process of scribbling down my feelings then, and now upon reflection, I found myself, like Hanisah and others I later met, still *menunggu* in an uneasy silence for the conflict not to reoccur (as it already had) but to end. This reminds me of what Adam Schwarz (1994) writes about Indonesians during the thirty-three years of Suharto's era, from 1965 to 1998: a population waiting not only for democracy, freedom, and employment but also for violence. However, unlike the Indonesians, I am not entirely sure that the Malay Muslims in Thailand's far south are waiting for democracy so much as for freedom, and most definitely for employment because the far south remains one of the backwaters of Thailand.

Looking back over my scribbled notes, I now ponder the optimism, the naivety, and even the imprecision I had back then, and perhaps have even now. What does it mean when I write *waiting*, and waiting for what? And just what is the meaning of *violence*? What does it mean to write of this optimism, naivety, and imprecision as opposed to feeling them? I think of Taussig's decades of experience and reflection on violence in Colombia: "it's not 'violence' per se – whatever that means – but experiencing violence transfigured by the law absorbing the violence and magnifying it" (2003, 47). Similar to the situations in Colombia and other sites of forever conflict, will there ever be, if this is even an appropriate term to use, an *end* to the waiting in Thailand's far south

I ask because the history of the Malay Muslims in Thailand's far south is, as many have remarked, indissociable from the history of struggles against the modern Thai Buddhist kingdom (Che Man 1990; Bradley 2009; Askew 2010c). And as long as the conflict is contained within the far south, Bangkok is never concerned about how long it lasts or how often it reoccurrs (Abuza 2009). I turn to the markers of this continuous history of expression of autonomy to explain in their own terms the Malay Muslims' response to suppression. It is important to note that each period of expression of autonomy was not the same in terms of its ideologies, practices, and religiosity. Each was led by different groups of actors. The collective history of the Haji Sulong movement was one of a modern reformist Islam but with more religious elements. Later, the struggles from the 1960s to the mid-1980s were class oriented and led by the educated elites and the aristocrats.[6] As with the current insurgency, one cannot be sure who are the leaders of the shadow insurgency and their nameless violence. All in all, it is as if time no longer "flows" but rather freezes the future, if there is to be any future at all. Perhaps I am being too pessimistic, even nihilist. With the situation reaching a stalemate, a quagmire, another forever conflict, perhaps my earlier pessimism was warranted.

To come back to Hanisah, I sensed she was trying to tell me that the locals and us outsiders (or tourists) experienced the conflict differently because of our differently situated bodies, nationalities, and (not to forget) passports. Perhaps growing up in the region and feeling as she did about the continuum of violence, she had recourse to this blasé response: *biasa*. Seconds later, in a pensive tone, she continued: "As locals, we are tired of it, tired of thinking or talking about it. You might even say we are used to the conflict." She forced a smile before continuing: "We need to live the lives we are born into … and try to be happy through our faith. *Inshallah!*" At that moment her phone rang, and she answered: "Yeah mak, sekarang baru lepas Hatyai" (Yeah, Mom, we have just left Hatyai). In the interim I thought of talking with the male passenger sitting next to Hanisah when he looked in my direction. I was sure he had overheard what Hanisah had said to me. However, he instantly looked away and shut (or was pretending to shut) his eyes. Soon he was snoring quite loudly, perhaps dreaming of somewhere peaceful. The rest of the other passengers were also napping.

Hanisah and I did not talk about the conflict for the rest of the way. However, she was all too happy to ask me about Canada and the United States, especially New York City when I told her I used to live there. Soon she and I too fell asleep (as the warm air blowing from the supposedly air-conditioned registers above our heads always had the effect of making one sleepy), only to wake up moments later when I sensed that the van was slowing down. We were approaching a military checkpoint. The rest of the passengers woke up as well. We waited in silence as two soldiers armed with semi-automatic rifles (that over the years I would come to recognize as M16s) slid open the van door to check on us. Both soldiers' gaze swept across us, albeit seemingly politely, before they slid shut the van door and asked the driver to move on. I thought to myself that they were just doing their job.[7]

From the van I could see signs in Thai and English on both sides of the road: "Welcome to the Province of Pattani." I immediately made a mental note that Malay, the written and spoken language of the Malay Muslim communities in the far south, was not on those signs.[8] After we journeyed past the initial military checkpoint, I counted a total of eight more checkpoints before the van finally arrived at the service apartments where I was staying in Muang Pattani. Hanisah gave me her phone numbers, and as we said our goodbyes I had this uncanny feeling. I forced a smile, thinking to myself: "Welcome to Pattani. There is no turning back now. But unlike Hanisah and others, I can always leave." I held onto this acknowledgment as the van drove away. Anthropologists, as Das et al. put it well, are "after all only fleeting presences in the lives of [our] interlocutors ... whose separateness [we] accept as a condition of [our] being anthropologists" (2014, 20).

A Recurring Conflict

> Keadaan di sini kalang kabut, semakin susah ... tapi kami sudah biasa, cakapan bahasa Jawi. [The situation here is chaotic, getting more and more difficult ... but we are used to it, *biasa*, as we say in Malay.]
> – Mariyei, a woman food vendor in an open-air market

The Malay Muslim–majority provinces of Pattani, Yala, and Narathiwat in Thailand's far south – formerly known as the Sultanate of Patani (*Patani* with one *t*) – has seen an archaeology of violence resonating through the ebbs and flows of conflict since the late 1940s.[9] They have been a hotbed for separatist movements, and the conflict has been not only the longest running but also the least known in Southeast Asia (Bajunid 1984, 2005; Che Man 1990; Askew 2010a; McCargo 2012). Although the region was relatively *quiet* from the early 1980s to the late 1990s under an atmosphere of "corrupt peace," an apt description by Kasian Tejapira (2006),[10] more than seven thousand lives (and counting) have been lost since the escalation of violence in January 2004.

To be sure, allegations of abuse and violation tar all sides of the latest conflict. Images of the military siege at the historic Krue Se Mosque circulating among Facebook users; video footage on YouTube and other social media of male Malay Muslim bodies stacked on top of each other in army trucks at the horrific Tak Bai incident; the abduction and disappearance of human rights lawyer Somchai Neelaphaijit and other Malay Muslim suspects; the insurgents' targeting of military personal and *soft* targets (Buddhist monks, government schoolteachers, civil servants, Malay village chiefs and their deputies, Malay civil defence volunteers); and ordinary civilians killed or injured while simply going about their daily activities – these have become a spectre for those living in the region. To be sure, the haunting has to do less with the number of deaths than with the fact that the reasons for the violence are still contested and at times seem incomprehensible to most Malay Muslims with whom I worked.[11] Similarly, state agents' reports, news reporting, and the seemingly scholarly and non-scholarly accounts of the conflict at the never-ending series of conferences and workshops reflect this endemic uncertainty of the violence, and, as Abraham and Nakaya point out, "often [lead] to divergent and inconsistent recommendations for its mitigation" (2007, 2304).

As with other conflict sites, civilian deaths amount to 90 per cent of the casualties in the latest conflict in Thailand's far south, including women and children.[12] Despite this statistic, what remains missing from most media and governmental broadcasts are the voices of ordinary civilians who find themselves, once again, dealing with heightened uncertainties, fear, paranoia, and the militarization of their lives. To be sure, such silences, when it comes to reporting the precarious feature of civilian daily lives, are not unique to Thailand's far south. When it comes to war stories, images of war tend to feature their heroic soldiers, sailors, and pilots. The reality is that civilian stories, or refugee stories, are also war stories. Perhaps they are not sensational enough for the news media, best-selling novels, and Hollywood movies. There is neither power nor glory in the stories of civilians killed or maimed, forced to flee, or orphaned by war. But the truth is that it is in civilian experiences that we truly find war stories. They are part of the human toll that continues to grow for years after the official end of a war – or, in the case of Thailand's far south, if the current conflict will ever end. And if it does, when will the next conflict reoccur?

In her work on Sri Lanka and parts of Africa, Carolyn Nordstrom points out that even though civilian casualties have "become fairly obvious ... it is often overpowered by the myth that war equals soldier equals male" (2004, 33). It is as if civilian casualties, lost dreams, lost hopes, devastations, and so on are drifting through the socio-political and media realms like lost fragments. It is as if ordinary civilians, as individuals far removed from power, are crying out for an institutional face to right a wrong, and are answered with silence. As anthropologists, we need to humanize the face of the conflict so that stories from ordinary civilians can fit into the larger picture of the conflict. As emphasized by Kleinman, Das, and Lock more than twenty years ago, our work is critical because "the production of the subject in conditions of violence is largely invisible to public commissions and judicial inquiries about violence" (1997, 13).

I made my reconnaissance trip to Thailand's far south in June 2005. Then I conducted ethnographic fieldwork from 2009 to 2016 (except 2011) during the summer months of June to August, as well as from October 2015 to February 2016 at Muang Pattani. Over this period I began to make friends and acquaintances. My interlocutors included the Malay Muslim *mak pasar* (mothers of market) food vendors at three open-air markets,[13] a few professors at a local university and their students, Islamic religious schoolteachers and their students, the staff at the service apartment building where I lived, street food vendors, and strangers I met during the course of my fieldwork. My engagement with these ordinary civilians allowed me to uncover life at violent sites by seeking to find out not who was killing whom and why, but, following Veena Das's work on the India-Pakistan partition (2007), violence's descent into their ordinary lives.

Besides analysing violence as a set of discrete events that are unfolding in the ongoing conflict, I seek to focus on the violence embedded in institutions and structural patriarchy, the violence that is multiple and mundane in the quotidian aspects of life, and especially for the *mak pasar*. To be sure, concerns for women's rights and liberation have often been used by the West to justify military intervention in many conflict zones, especially of late in Muslim countries. However, the degree to which this intervention is translated into actual support for women remains an empirical question. Furthermore, the media and the academy have paid scant attention to the plight of women despite the fact that they often bear the hardships of maintaining family life under difficult circumstances (see, for example, Herring and Rangwala 2006; Al-Ali 2010). The *mak pasar* with whom I worked fit this description. Where a lack of security goes hand in hand with the difficulties of reality that they must endure and engage, their top priority is livelihoods and safety and fulfilling all the petty obligations of day-to-day living within a complex social, economic, and political system that remains indifferent to their plights.

The book hopes to give voice to these *mak pasar* and other ordinary civilians in order to address the generally ignored topic of the varied positions of the Malay Muslim population of Thailand's far south borderland, and the implications of this in understanding the meaning of the current insurgency to the heterogeneous Malay Muslim population – in other words, how the varied Malay Muslim identity structures are produced, under what constraints, and by what technologies of affect and force. Their subjectivities are never outside the discursive practices that constitute them; their identities are never fixed or immutable; and the boundaries of their communities are not given but constructed, if not conscripted by various factions that include multiple agents of the state (courts, schools, media, police, and the army), the competing Muslim religious authorities, the Malay elites, and the indelible imprints of the recurring conflicts that have been plaguing Thailand's far south.

The originality of this project lies in its nuanced approach to the question of *Muslimness*, both historically and in the historical present. The larger notion of social stereotyping identities and the relationship between that stereotyping and politics, which is an important issue, is here reduced to a very manageable size, one that will allow the researcher to treat it in subtle detail in order to present the diversity among these Malay Muslim communities and thereby counter the accusations of "banditry," terrorism," and "militia" activities that are divisive to the Malay Muslim communities and the Thai societies at large.[14]

Most of the questions that guide the labour of my research are equally pertinent in the investigation of conflict situations across the world where disenfranchised minorities clamour for recognition, especially after 9/11 as we witness a shift to the Islamist register as a marker of common solidarity among these diverse Malay Muslim communities. The book hopes to contribute to the literature on the ethnography of the state and the pervasiveness of violence in modern societies that question the naturalness of the nation-states and their transformation in neoliberal globalization's long-standing blind eye towards it, both theoretically and practically. Indeed, what can one learn from investigating the lives and livelihoods of minorities in threatening circumstances – issues in which the state has significant interests – and about the kind of state power in Thailand? What might that suggest about the very concept of "the state"? Do we find the state as a ragged and miscellaneous collection of resources whose invocation in local struggles produces and reifies it? Indeed, who and what is the state in Thailand? My research argues that Siam's annexation of the Sultanate of Patani under the language of modernity requires a revised history that brings the country's Malay Muslims centrally and integrally into the history of modern Buddhist Thailand. Given the kingdom's propensity to use the trope of fragility to manufacture unity and patriotism, the Malay Muslims are in fact not at the margins but one of the key problems for Thai nationalism, one that provides a pretext for the continuing exercise of state power and violence in Thailand's far south.

The Frontier Provinces of Thailand's Far South

It is commonly taken for granted that the pasts that haunt the public imaginations in Southeast Asia and elsewhere are national pasts: moments in which individual lives converged on national histories. This is signalled in Hegel's commentary that it is the state itself which first presents a subject matter that is entirely appropriate to the prose of its history. In other words, the state creates its history as it creates itself. Or, to put it slightly differently, the state does what the state theorizes by putting into practice specific bureaucratic policies and battles to shape institutionally the political, social, and economic world of itself. Indeed, nation-states, the building blocks of politics, have for centuries been politically organized and empowered by states that deliver the institutions for governance and security, the capacity to coordinate the economy, forging commonality, and so forth. The notion of the nation-state also involves a strong sense of sovereignty and territoriality and a national distinctiveness between citizens and foreigners, or even between friends and foes (Schmitt 2010). This one-to-one correspondence between a nation and the state's exclusive sovereign territory has achieved almost theological force, as if it were the only natural way to divide the world.

I have always worried about such privileging of the state when these projects often use divergent national dreams against each other. My previous work on the silencing of communism in Borneo stirs my dissatisfaction with this concession, even as I see no clear alternative (Yong 2006, 2013). But the nation-state is not dead, and it deserves constant troubling. One kind of troubling that is worthwhile to conjure is the spaces between nations (the frontier provinces) whereby the ghost of the past simultaneously interrupts and empowers the naturalness of the nation as the frame in which we tell our personal, political, and ethical stories.

Joining with critics of anthropology's tendency that favour representations of contained people, places, and identities (Gupta and Ferguson 1992; Clifford 1992), my research calls for understanding frontier provinces from the standpoint of contestation: as sites of displacement through unequal access to economic and political power, and of the multiplicities of voices that have been shaped by shared, yet separate, histories of involvement in local, national, regional, and global events (see, for example, Blu 2001; Navaro-Yashin 2002; Das and Poole 2004; Reeves 2014; Johnson 2020). By conceptualizing frontier provinces from the standpoint of their contestations, we can better capture the dynamics, which are always projects in the making, of the moving zones of state control and often ecologically unsound resource extraction that have continued to make such regions sites of intense securitization and conflict.

An understanding of these dynamics – which are unstable and in flux – will help clarify both the shifting processes that are shaping and reshaping the geopolitics of the region and reformatting people's relationship to their land, and, as echoed by Feld and Basso more than two decades ago, "the now acute world conditions of exile, displacement, diasporas, and inflamed borders" (1996, 3). In the context of Thailand, this will help determine whether national boundaries in its far south articulate well with projects of national security, sovereignty, and state formation, or in fact remain porous, underlying a coterminous cultural zone that contributes to, among many other things, the imagined affinities of its Malay Muslims with the Malay Archipelago. Indeed, is the formulation of the category "Malay Muslims" in Thailand's far south influenced by a homogeneous notion of culture that is essentially modern, if not national, in origin?

Theoretical Discussion

Hobbes, Marx, Benjamin, Arendt, Schmitt, Derrida, Agamben, Rancière, and many others have acknowledged the violent dimensions of the modern nation-state: first, the violence of the legitimate state, a state that has the backing of the nation and can speak in the name of its people; second, violence that is not merely transitional, a birthmark, or a departure but also a much more general and continuous aspect of modern life. As emphasized by Benjamin (1968), these are the social, political, and economical forms of violence that are linked to, and not separated from, the workings of the state's legal apparatus. Violence as such is seen as one that Marcel Mauss ([1950] 1990) would call a total social phenomenon. Mauss was of course writing about the dynamics of the gift exchanges that involve the totality of society and its institutions. In essence, however, we can also think along with Mauss in recognizing violence not only in its most spectacular, explosive, and visible moments but also in its most disguised forms – in our day-to-day behaviour, the way we construct and respond to neighbours as well as strangers, and the conversations and silences in which we participate – in other words, in the routine violence involved in the construction of nations, of communities and histories, and the so-called cultures of minorities, and thus majorities (Pandey 2005). This ethnography will continue with the discussions brought on by the literature.

In developing an adequate analysis to understand and appreciate the diverse identities and experiences of the current conflict among the Malay Muslims in Thailand's far south, the first task is to recognize their comments, their refrains, and their laments as dialogical social utterances (Bakhtin 1981) whereby "meanings" are constructed in interactional processes that connect historical moments to each other in social life as they circulate through society and through time (Agha 2005). Such a dialogical concept of utterances brings into analysis a subject's biographical history that shapes one's ability to use and construe utterances to index identities, historical, and contemporary events. They also alert us to the fact that all social utterances are, to a certain extent, ideologically informed, providing ways of thinking about authority and power in speech and identity.

In this book I focus on the production of social utterances to bring into focus the performance and subtlety at work in everyday uses of language. In terms of certain Malay Muslim male interlocutors, their social utterances indexed not only their identities but also the historical and contemporary events that allegedly "legitimated" their tradition. We will ask: How does the way in which an individual or a community subverts its usage of *the past* and *tradition* in idiomatic and nuanced ways highlight a deep equivocation towards the systematic political installations of the state and its military power to which the individual or community is circumscribed? I want to invoke what David Scott emphasizes: to understand "'tradition' in a far more critical sense, following Alasdair MacIntyre (1984), we have to remember the contradictions within any tradition, namely and simultaneously that 'tradition cannot have a life without density, without conflict, without alteration, without intensity, and without instability'" (D. Scott 1999, 9). Following such critical emphasis on tradition, how do these Malay Muslim men practice remembrance and how are they socially organized? How is this remembrance associated with a distinctive and disjunctive temporality and spatiality, indeed distinctive and disjunctive politics and economy? How is this temporality and spatiality conceptualized, constructed, and marked out publicly? How and who among these Malay Muslim subjects manipulate and generate their own essentialism through engaging with the embodied representations of their morality and tradition?

By grounding my analysis in a concern for the moral context in which remembering and forgetting are important functions for subjects to live sanely in an unjust world, I am also touching on an epistemological issue: our ability to recognize and understand the production of certain utterances and silences within subaltern groups so that we may be provoked into thinking of more inclusive ways of embodying the experience of human practices within particular cultural, political, economic, and militaristic frames of reference. Perhaps it is in listening to and telling of the cacophony of the troubled stories of deaths, dispossession, marriage and family break-ups, and the concerns and anxieties for their children and grandchildren, that we might encounter the hopes in facing the challenges of the present for subjects engaging with precarious survival. This ethnography tells a few such stories in all their messiness.

Shadow Insurgency

Vladimir Ilyich Lenin once famously said, "There are decades where nothing happens, and there are weeks where decades happen." Sometimes decades become condensed into one month that changes dramatically the political dynamics of a region. January 2000 was one such month for Thailand's far south. The current conflict has been simmering since that time. In April 2002 – a matter of weeks after the then prime minister Thaksin had returned from Washington, DC – the Bangkok-based government replaced the leadership of the Fourth Army in the far south with many newcomers to the region, and many local contacts within the intelligence network were exposed or killed (Abuza 2011). On January 2004 the violence escalated when militants attacked and stole over three hundred weapons from the Ratchanakarin military camp in Narathiwat province; on the same day, twenty schools were set on fire (Askew 2010b).[15] Thaksin responded by declaring martial law, giving the *tahann* (military armed forces) a wide range of extrajudicial power.[16] To be sure, the origins of the conflict lie in historical grievances stemming from systematic state discrimination against the ethnic Malay Muslim population over the last century (Bajunid 2005; McCargo 2009). Armed and non-armed groups calling for greater autonomy and/or independence have operated in the region, and their activities have ebbed and flowed since 1948. But unlike the past when various separatist groups would acknowledge their actions, not a single group has taken credit for the outbreaks since the escalation of conflict in 2004, which is why the current conflict is sometimes called the shadow insurgency.[17] Indeed, *fighting with ghosts* is a common metaphor used by the *tahann* and police commanders in describing their dealings with the perpetrators of violence (Askew 2010a; Liow and Pathan 2010).

But who exactly are these "ghosts"? Moreover, is all the violence in the current conflict ideologically driven, carried out in the name of achieving autonomy and/or independence? As Askew points out, "the 'ghosts' behind the turbulence goes beyond the mysterious insurgents and its purportedly ideologically driven insurgency, and although the public 'text' on the shadow insurgency is undoubtedly insurgent-centered, a mix of pragmatic political business motivations and other conflicts lie behind many of the killings and attacks" (2010a, 117). If so, even though there now appears to be a consensus that the situation of violent unrest in Thailand's far south constitutes an insurgency, what does naming the situation *insurgency* precisely mean in the politics of the twenty-first century, especially after 9/11? In response to the complex challenges confronting US and allied forces in Afghanistan and Iraq, many counter-insurgency specialists have questioned the Cold War convention that defined *insurgency* as an organized movement seeking to undermine the authority of an established state through subversion and guerrilla warfare, and with the inherent or explicit objective of replacing the state with a new form of government (Record 2007, ix). As Chris North (2008, 117) points out, insurgencies now include "extremists, tribes, gangs, militias, warlords, and combinations of these," and with different aims. Some are networked with loose objectives and simply aim to enhance their survival, and many do not actually seek the overthrow of established governments. North thus prefers an open-ended definition of *insurgency* as "a violent struggle among state and non-state actors for legitimacy and/or influence over the relevant populations" (117).

It is also important to note that linguistically there is no corresponding term in Thai vocabulary for *insurgency*. As Askew (2010a) points out, the instability caused by the conflict is officially called *khwam mai sangop* (turbulence or disturbance) and its instigators *phu ko khwam mai sangop* (disturbance makers). Key words applying to contests for state power are *kabot*, a Malay word for "illegitimate rebellion or chaos"; *ratprahan*, a Thai word for "a successful seizure of state power"; and *batiwat*, a Thai word for "revolution." Interestingly, when the current conflict erupted in January 2004, the term *separatism* was not explicitly used in Thai state or media discourse, though its implication was there. It was only four years after the current conflict had escalated in 2004 that a few Thai security academics, army staff college personnel, and commanders referred to the conflict as that of *kan ko khwam mai sangop* (making disturbance) in order to explicitly match the English expression *insurgency*, that is, to mean politically or ideologically inspired irregular warfare aiming to subvert state authority (Askew 2010a). Yet, *kan ko khwam mai sangop* does have the capacity to describe forms of turbulence that are driven by non-ideological interests because there has been a long history of fomented and disguised disturbances and violence in the far south. The current wave of violence is no exception to this pattern, making a narrow (or casual) use of the English-language term *insurgency* inadequate to define the totality (and banality) of the violence. Something more than an insurgency is going on in the current mix of violent events.

As such, Askew (2010a) prefers "insurgency-centred turbulence" or "insurgency-driven violence" to encompass a situation in which a comprehensive disorder is being experienced in a chronically disordered borderland, a borderland that is exploited by drug dealers, the *tahann*, the police, and other vested interest groups. In other words, they are confusing overlaps between the shadow insurgents, drug dealers, criminals, and competing local political and business groups, with each group having its own vested, opportunistic-violence interest in parallel with insurgent aggression towards a weakened frontier-states and enforcement structure.

Numbers and Statistics

In contradistinction to the complexity of the current conflict, as in a host of other conflict sites, is the politics of number. As if we value a statistical life, the quantification of deaths and casualties and coming up with the corresponding statistics have become as important as the quest to give meaning to the violence in Thailand's far south. Colluding with the state, analysts commonly introduce their accounts of the violence by citing the total number of deaths and/or casualties, and its corresponding statistics, thereby giving the impression that these were all related to the insurgency. As in other conflict sites, the tendency to inflate the number of deaths functions as a gesture towards the enormity of the violence and, in the case of Thailand's far south, to not only satisfy the need of so-called terror experts (Connors 2009), but also construct the state as the only agent of order. Some counter-insurgency experts have even claimed that Thailand's far south has the most intense insurgency after Iraq and Afghanistan (see, for example, Kilcullen 2009; Abuza 2011).

Make no mistake, the Thai government will broadcast the statistics, and they will be reported by the local newspapers as and when there is a drop in fatalities or casualties in any one month, period of months, or from one year to the next. The Thai government has been using the declining numbers of attacks and deaths of late (and here I want to emphasize *of late* as in a bracketed number of days or weeks as there is no telling if the declining numbers of attacks and deaths will last much longer) as an indication of some form of rapprochement. But most of my interlocutors, including myself, know that this is just sheer hallucination. Such discrepancies between two different realities – between the government's hallucination and the reality on the ground – is not uncommon in Thailand's far south.[18] For example, with regard to Colombia, Taussig asks: "Is it not the case that such hallucinatory uncertainty (with the numbers expressed with hallucinatory certainty) reflects a world in which truth, like justice, is forever hostage and, what is more, everyone knows that ... [of] fighting fire with fire?" (2018, 117).

Ironically, if the politics of number and its corresponding labelling of violence have arrived in Thailand's far south, the treatments have not. Besides, the number of deaths tell only one story. The brutal manner of some of the insurgents' killings is quite another, their being especially nifty with beheading their victims, amputating and setting the corpses on fire, using a chilling execution style – sometimes of both husband and wife – in broad daylight at convenience stores, in roadside ambushes, or by motorcycle pillion riders, and killing monks and teachers, sometimes in front of their traumatized students or, should I say, children, and leaving behind a growing number of orphans. The killings have become a spectre for those living in the region. Indeed, the targeting of government schoolteachers and Buddhist monks is the most troubling for the government as it not only attracts national media coverage but also tends to encourage Buddhists to leave the region (Abuza 2011).

Askew (2010a) and others have pointed out that even though the actual number of insurgency-related deaths is much lower than reported, and even if we were to reduce the figure, the human suffering and loss that informed the meaning of their lives cannot be elucidated through numbers. During fieldwork it was not uncommon to hear my interlocutors talking about the reasons behind certain deaths that often contradicted both state and media accounts: deaths as consequences of political and business rivalries; retaliation by drug dealers after each drug bust; or personal vendettas (Jerryson 2009). In other words, these figures and statistics do not disaggregate private, political, or business-motivated killings, or those that materialized out of retaliation by drug dealers.[19] In fact, the proportion of personal, political, and business killings, as well as those from retaliations by drug dealers, may be higher than identified in police statistics. There have been cases that were classified as "security-related" even though clear evidence was unavailable to demonstrate cause or culprit. Shooting cases initially determined as "private" by the police, however, were sometimes switched to the "security-related" category following appeals from victims' relatives who were seeking state compensation payments. Some police commanders privately suggested to Marc Askew (2007) that personally, politically, or business-motivated killings could be responsible for as much as 40 to 50 per cent of total civilian deaths, and Askew also notes that some of these unattributable shootings might include cases of clandestine assassination by police and army hit squads.

In short, the regional politicians and/or business rivalries and crime networks criss-cross with ideologically motivated groups in varied and confusing ways in the current conflict. And just to elaborate on this point, the much-publicized bombing of C.S. Pattani, one of the luxury hotels in the township of Pattani, if not the entire far south, was initially claimed by journalists as marking an escalation in insurgency violence. Subsequently, even though evidence unearthed by police confirmed that the bombing was undertaken by insurgent bomb makers, information about the vehicle used in this attack (and a simultaneous, but failed, car-bomb attack in Yala) points to the involvement of a prominent local Malay Muslim suspected of having sought revenge against the son of the hotel owner, Anusart Suwanmongkol. The latter, also a senator and a member of Thailand's military-installed national assembly, had supported the suspect's political rival in a provincial election. Interestingly, when the same hotel was bombed again, in 2012, as was the owners' Honda showroom, no Thai newspapers reported the incidents as being related to the insurgency. In addition, an insurgent gunman, who also happened to be a police informant, assassinated a local politician in the Thamuang sub-district of Thepa and confessed that the instruction had come from the president of Thamuang Council.

Then there is the drug-related violence. In retaliation for a drug bust in 2008, a leading drug trafficker hired some insurgents to carry out a firestorm of counter-attacks that included a major bombing outside the police headquarters in Sungai Kolok (Kolok River). On top of all these, the leaving of leaflets to disguise attacks as insurgent-related is also common. There are many more that I will have the chance to talk about in this ethnography. To reiterate, even though the shadow insurgents are the driving core of the current instability afflicting Thailand's far south, the current violence is multifaceted, nested within an existing disorder, and reflecting the character of the endemically weak frontier provinces and the generic features of a violent society.

As the latest insurgency in Thailand's far south reached a stalemate and took on a life of its own, a complex web of structures of violence has emerged wherein various groups are carrying out acts of political and business violence while the majority of the victims and targets in the conflict are civilians. Fuelled by a political economy of vested power interests buttressed by fundamentalist and nationalist rhetoric, the conflict dynamics have created an environment of lawlessness and insecurity for the entire population in the region. To make the matter worse, the government has adopted some heavy-handed tactics since the start of the violence in 2004, one of which was to *oum* (carry away) suspects. The widely circulated rumour among concerned parents at that time was that if their sons or grandsons were taken away by the *tahaan*, there was still a chance they might make it back. However, if they were *oum* by the police, their disappearance (read "death") was a foregone conclusion (Thanet Aphornsuvan 2004). On top of this, many attacks remain unresolved while confusion regarding the identity of the perpetrators lingers on. Meanwhile, as the government continues to ignore or address historical grievances, hard-line military and police measures adopted since 2004 have further heightened the sense of injustice and oppression among the diverse Malay Muslims.

Book Layout

Besides the introduction, chapter 1 touches on the violent historical debris of Thailand's far south, what I consider to be the urhistory of the recurring conflict inthe area.

Chapter 2 touches on the beginnings of my ethnography and on a certain word, *biasa*, that haunted as well as guided me throughout my ethnographic enterprises. The chapter also touches on my interlocutors' forms of life and asks if the shadow insurgency lies at the forefront of their concerns or if the issues relating to livelihoods affected by the conflict are much more salient. The chapter looks into words for traces of meaning, along with other non-verbal actions, all of which are a mix of subjective pragmatic moves within my interlocutors' cultural assumptions and political tensions.

Chapters 3, 4, and 5 touch on my interactions with the *mak pasar* at the open-air markets and the ways in which they engaged their difficulties of reality. These chapters touch on the resources – both physical and mental – that they drew upon in order to live sanely in a precarious world. The chapters also address the violence that these *mak pasar* habitually experience, which is intertwined with the other forms of violence that have held sway in Thailand's far south as well as in other contexts in which the manifold forms of oppression against women arise from multiple institutional and structural patriarchies.

Chapter 6 talks about Thainess as a degree of citizenship. The chapter also touches on the literature on Islam and Muslims since 9/11 that has sought to locate the basis of Muslimness in some essentialist cultural value. In addition, it touches on the fact that essentialism, especially tradition, is a discursive element within the Malay Muslim societies in Thailand's far south, something that is imminently violent towards some of the country's own subjects.

Chapter 7 provides a different picture from that commonly portrayed about the *ponoks* (Muslim boarding schools) as being rigidly strict and pious or the playground for radical Islam. It provides a glimpse into the bonding between the *ponoks* and the communities they serve, the kind of kinship that is built upon the state of being poor and having pain, loss, love, humiliation, and survival.

The concluding chapter, chapter 8, talks about the harvesting of funding to the region and the materialization of what I call the *talking task industry* – non-governmental organizations (NGOs), security experts, think tanks, and local elites – with its endless meetings and conferences under the rubric of reconciliation, peace, development, security, and compensation. The chapter also talks about Halal Industrial Park as part of the development project and its violent aftermath. The book will end with the word that followed me all along my ethnographic enterprise, *biasa*.

Chapter One

The Violent Historical Debris

The wounds of the annexation of the Sultanate of Patani by Siam and its consequent marginalization of my people have never formed scabs because they have continued to bleed ever since.
– Attributed to a Local Malay Muslim Senator

There is no document of civilization which is not at the same time a document of barbarism.
– Walter Benjamin

Although Siam/Thailand is the only country in Southeast Asia that was not colonized during the European encounter, or formerly colonized, the physical geo-body of this kingdom was formed through a series of conditional *sia din daen* (territories-ceding) treaties between its benevolent rulers and the French colonial governments of Vietnam and Laos, and the British colonial governments of Burma and Malaya (Loos 2006). "Modern Thai historiography," as Thongchai Winichakul (2002, 263) sarcastically puts it, "is a saga of the unity of Thai people under benevolent rulers, mostly the monarchy, in confronting the threats ... posed by foreign countries, in the course of which the nation survived and prospered. The customary master narrative always begins with the peaceful and independent Thai kingdom facing danger from colonising aliens."

Consequently, under the context of *sia din daen* treaties, most histories that touch on the inclusion of the Sultanate of Patani as a province of Siam tend to focus on the kingdom's fear of ceding more of its southern territories to Britain. Under the 1909 Anglo-Siamese treaty, its southern territories comprising what are now the northern states of Kelantan, Terengganu, Perlis and parts of Kedah of Malaysia were ceded to Britain. In return, the British recognized Siamese authority in the regions situated north of the ceded territories that included Patani (the current provinces of Pattani, Narathiwat, and Yala), Satun, and Trang (Kobkua Suwannathat-Pian 1988; Che Man 1990).

But was it really about ceding some of its territories to Britain in order to formally include others? In other words, prior to the 1909 ceding-territory treaty the Sultanate of Patani was a sovereign state that traditionally sent the *Bunga Emas dan Perak* (Golden and Silver Flowers) triennially to Siam, its powerful northern neighbour, as a token of friendship and alliance. Shortly after the annexation, the Siamese kingdom's decision to establish Islamic courts for the Malay Muslims was one way of displaying the kingdom's purported sensibilities towards the minority's religion and customs (Loos 2006). It was also an effort to showcase the kingdom's form of colonial *modernity* and, I would add, its rationalism and hubris to Britain and Europe.

My work draws on Loos's and Thongchai's work (1994) that talked about the kingdom's split personality as colonizer and colonized, one that tends to re-enact periodically its triumphalist and yet traumatic past as not only the non-colonized but also the most *cooperative* country in Southeast Asia.[1] Yet, I seek to move away from it in order to address an important proposition of the modern nation-state. My move here is predicated on the logic of presuppositions and purposes put forward by Robin G. Collingwood. According to David Scott (1999), reading R.G. Collingwood ([1946] 1993) through the performative language philosophy of John L. Austin (1962), in order to understand a proposition, one has to understand it not merely in its internal logical status but as a "move in an argument." In other words, to grasp why it was put forward in the way that it was in the first place, one has to "recapture the presuppositions and purposes that went into making it" (Scott 1999, 6).

As such, if Western modernity was assumed to be the telos of diverse forms of economic and legal activities in Southeast Asia during the European encounter, did the establishment of Islamic courts in the far south shortly after the region had been annexed reflect Siam's sensibilities towards its Malay Muslims? Or, did they, in fact, provide the pretext for generating narratives of uneasy coexistence, and thus the raison d'être for the state policies – in particular the state's stringent practices, modalities, and projects of assimilation – to institutionally shape the political and economic world of the diverse Malay Muslims in the far south? As David Scott (2004) points out, assimilation has always been a project of conquest, and it cannot be conceived without reference to the project of European colonialism. Following Foucault, Scott emphasizes that "every political order produces an exclusion ... But precisely because this is what politics depends upon, what is important for Foucault (1980) is how, within the context of any such totalization, to pose, as he says, a certain number of question[s] to politics – genealogical questions, in effect, about the edges that such a totalization excludes, the otherness it produces" (1999, 207).

With the Malay Muslims being the majority in Thailand's far south and with their cultural, linguistic, and religious dissimilarity with the modern Buddhist kingdom, an uneasy coexistence can be not only one of the sources that help generate a sense of the fragility of the nation-state but also one that can be used to foster a sense of nationalism, one that can be instructed in patriotism while, paradoxically, creating and maintaining the Other. In other words, it can sometimes be seen by the state on the one hand as performing a correction, rehabilitation, and a strategy of envisaged assimilation, while, on the other hand, as curtailing other ways of being "unThainess."

My move is also predicated upon a critical interrogation of the way in which Siam's alleged modernity inserted itself into and altered the lives of its colonized minorities, namely, in this case, the Malay Muslims in the far south. Here modernity was the principle of its violent hypocrisy. This unleashing of modernity in Thailand, and elsewhere, was enacted around a certain economy: the paradoxical problem of the extension and containment of freedom. Since Siam's formal inclusion of the Sultanate of Patani in 1906, the diverse Malay Muslim societies in the far south have been perceived not only as societies against the state but also as societies under siege by a colonial state abroad (England) and a neocolonial state at home. Implicitly, the relation between the two conditions is one of imbrication rather than opposition. To emphasize it slightly differently, and this is important: Malay Muslims are in fact not at the margins but one of the key problematics for Thai nationalism, one that gives a pretext for continuing to exercise state power and violence. What is important here is a critical investigation of colonialism in the post-colonial present that the diverse Malay Muslims in Thailand's far south inhabit.

If the decision of the kingdom to establish Islamic courts for the Malay Muslims in the far south was a way of displaying its purported sensibilities towards its minority's religion and customs, Bangkok did a remarkable volte-face in 1929 by not only insisting that Islamic family and inheritance laws be codified in Thai but also establishing the Thai language as the language of Islam (Surin Pitsuwan 1985). To be sure, the Malay Muslims in the far south resisted the legitimacy of these legislations. However, in doing so, they provided plenty of pretexts for the state to accuse them of being disloyal subjects. With the military takeover by extreme nationalist General Phibul Songkhram in 1938 and his desire to, on the one hand, accentuate the Western politics of national homogeneity and, on the other, distinguish ethnic Thais from the kingdom's minorities, the kingdom's name was changed from Siam to Thailand.

With it, a series of ultra-nationalist initiatives were implemented that affected not only the Muslims but also other minorities (Surin Pitsuwan1985). As the Second World War was approaching, the Phibul government began mobilizing the population in the name of nation building, enforcing a strident policy of assimilation with no toleration for minority cultures. Under this policy came the invention of Thainess (*khwampen* Thai) and ethnic Thai nationalism. In its origin, "Thainess is an ethno-ideology in that while minority identities can flourish under the adjective, none of them are on equal footing to it" (Connors 2006, 113). Thais of different minorities were expected to privilege national identity over their ethnicities or else be seen as a potential threat to the sovereign (Dorairaijoo 2004), or even be charged with cases of separatism. In other words, Thainess is a form of internal discrimination that relies on this perpetual recognition and disavowal of difference. The key point here is that the recognition of difference serves to discipline difference as much as to recognize it, making demands on the people who are being categorized, a feature that is inherent to discrimination (see, for example, Povinelli 2011, 2012; Hankins 2012). One could also say that recognition of difference is formed both through recognition and through recognition's absences, "and very often through 'false' recognition from others intending to damage, compel submission, or to force other human beings into a distorted and reduced form of existence" (Zemon 2018).

"A modern nation-state," Talal Asad emphasizes, "frames its own patterns of internal discrimination and thus contributes to fears that are distinctive of it" (2012, 284). Asad's discussion on fear as a part of modern European law and on the issues concerning the formulation of "minorities," and thus "majority," deserves to be quoted in full:

> The idea of "minorities" has a long and fascinating history in Europe that then had an enormous impact on the non-European world dominated by Europeans … That history is not simply one in which the liberal nation-state emerges as a beacon of tolerance. It is also and more interestingly a narrative of the emergence of "politics" as an autonomous domain separated from "religion" and yet dominating it through the state. Ernst-Wolfgang Böckenförde has traced this process beyond the treaty of Westphalia to the Investiture Contest in the Middle Ages. In the new secularized space the fear of the church and of life after death is subordinated to a spontaneous fear of the punitive power of the state that Hobbes called "the mortal

God" (Böckenförde 1991, 30). Law becomes authorized by the sovereign and not by the church.

By the time of the French Revolution, the state comes to be imagined as a "social body," an institution for protecting the natural rights and liberties of the individual citizen (40–1). The state's duty is now to use violence to defend the subjective rights of all citizens and not their religious belief. Sovereignty, the right not to be interfered with, the right to govern oneself, becomes invested in a sum of individuals, and it is the fact of their being countable that defines the space of the political ... insisting only on the equality of individuals as countable (and hence substitutable), and on their representation through organized parties.

Although minority rights were to be protected, the state itself belonged in a very special sense to "the majority." A new anxiety now emerged: how to maintain the state's demographic balance so that the majority can be secure in its privilege ... [When the state] classifies its subjects into a legally privileged majority and a legally protected minority, [it is making] a distinction that identifies the former fully with the nation and the latter only indirectly so. (Asad 2012, 284–90)

The distinction between a legally privileged majority and a legally protected minority most certainly applies to Thailand, especially for a modern Buddhist kingdom and its Muslim provinces in the far south. This was especially so following Haji Sulong and his Islamic Awakening movement in the late 1940s when the Malay Muslims were charged under the banner of separatism – *baeng yaek dindaen* (separating the land) – the most heinous political offence against the centralized and allegedly unitary Thai state (Chaiwat 2006). However, as Thanet Aphornsuvan argues, the idea of equating Malay Muslims with charges of separatism is an invented fact of modern Thai political history that assumes "a prior existence of a territorially *geo-body* with its fixed borders and culturally unified Siamese nation-state" (2008, 91). The concept *baeng yaek dindaen* presupposed the notion of a unified territorial kingdom with its dominating Thai Buddhist culture and institutions. In the context of a long-held belief in Thai political history that the Malay Muslims in the far south were untrustworthy subjects, based on their record of resisting Siamese rule since the Ayutthaya kingdoms, charging the Malay Muslims in the far south with separating from Thailand was a logical outcome of the Royal Nationalist historiography (Kachatpai Burupat 1976).

In such a view of historical development and nationalism, there is a myth, in the sense described by Roland Barthes ([1957] 1972): not that it is a lie in the received sense, but that it obscures the reality of modern nation-states, nation-states that grew out of multi-ethnic communities and cultural practices. Furthermore, the discursive language of separatism not only homogenized and cut, metaphorically speaking, the fissiparous Malay Muslims of their diversity, but also encouraged collective discipline and punishment. If nothing else, charges of separatism exonerated Bangkok from its long-standing strident assimilationist policy over the politically active and culturally conscious, diverse Malay Muslim minorities.

As I mentioned earlier, since the late 1940s Thailand's far south has been a hotbed of separatist movements and has added life to the spectre of separatism that the state helped to create. Cases of separatism continued throughout the 1960s as part of the region-wide phenomena in Southeast Asia that included the Moros in the Philippines; the Rakhine, Shans, Karens, Karenis, Chins, Kachins, Kokangs, Mons, Rohingyas, and so on in Myanmar; and the Acehnese, East Timorese, and Papuans in Indonesia. It is important to note that in each of these struggles, the societies were multi-ethnic, yet the circumstances in which the modern nation-states were formed included the promotion of and identification with the majority ethnic community over the minorities (Brown 1988; Christie 1996). These struggles have been prolonged throughout the Cold War in Southeast Asia into the historical present, so much so that, "if there is a single narrative thread that stands out ... which recounts the postwar period [in Southeast Asia, it is] one dominated as much by the question of ethnonationalism as by the ideological conflict between communism and capital" (Morris 2010, 350).

Armed separatism in Thailand's far south subsided when General Prem Tinsulanonda was in power (1980–8). The first thing he did was to end the stringent assimilation policies and make concessions: permission for the members of the minority to register their Muslim names, to wear a niqab in government institutions, to create Muslim prayer rooms at strategic public venues, and to establish Islamic banking. The Southern Border Provinces Administrative Centre (SBPAC) was established in 1981 as a consultative agency between the Malay elites and the government.[2] The Prem administration also started negotiating amnesty deals with separatist organizations and with the Thai communist parties. Compared to what had occurred before the 1980s, the Prem period was, relatively speaking, a semi-spring of freedom for the Malay Muslims in Thailand's far south, albeit one that was only temporary (Joll 2011) – which brings us to the current conflict that has reached a stalemate.

In the year 2023, we are entering the nineteenth year of the latest conflict. The absence of any serious attempt to explain the revival of the violence, together with some explanations for incidents of unnecessary deaths and injustices, remains an important barrier to an understanding between the government and the diverse Malay Muslims of the far south. Of the almost weekly bombings and shootings that have made Thailand's far south one of the security hot spots in Southeast Asia, the Krue Se mosque massacre and the Tak Bai incident, both in 2004, stood out as two of the major sources of contempt among the diverse Malay Muslim populations and as a major political imbroglio for the government. But first, Krue Se.

The Krue Se Massacre

We know more than we can tell.

– Attributed to Karl Polanyi

At pre-dawn on 28 April 2004 more than one hundred Malay Muslim men clashed with the police and the *tahann* at eleven separate sites in the far south. One of the sites was the historic Krue Se mosque. Despite receiving instruction from "higher-ups" to negotiate with the group of Malay Muslim men who were trapped inside the mosque and only armed with machetes, the commanding officer at the scene ordered an attack with rockets and by snipers, leaving all thirty-one "militants" and an innocent civilian dead. To this day, no official explanation has been given as to why the commanding officer gave the order to attack. At the end of that day, 107 Malay Muslim men were killed in the far south.

In his foreword to Sharika Thiranagama's accounts of the civil war in Sri Lanka, Gananath Obeyesekere points out that one of the troubles with some of today's governments is that they feel as if "we are [still] living in the 18th or 19th century [whereby] a nation-state can ride roughshod over minority religions, languages, and cultures (Thiranagama 2011, xiv). Obeyesekere goes on to say: "You can squash dissent, but it is much more difficult to squash the spirit that fosters legitimate dissent" (xiv). His comment aptly applies to the situation in Thailand's far south. Never mind that no official explanation has been offered about who gave the order to the commanding officer at Krue Se to kill; the earlier official announcement was that the incident was non-political, even accusing it of being the work of drug addicts.

The name of who might have given the order to kill was whispered to me on several occasions at Krue Se. However, this is a piece of information I cannot reveal. Not only do I have no means to independently verify the truth, but also because this is a case where I know more than I can tell. This is when the pragmatism in knowing comes with the full knowledge of not saying it. The question of who might have given the order is not really a question but a public secret that magnifies a certain reality; something known, but unspoken and unacknowledged publicly. Thus, *truth* in this case is joined not only with a secret but also with silence: *truth = secret = silence* (Taussig 1999). I might add, *truth* in this case is something that one knows but ought not to talk about because it magnifies a certain legal clause in Thailand. Several interlocutors at Krue Se told me that they could not reveal this legal clause but they "knew" I "knew." They also said that the authority "knew" they "knew." As renown Thai peace scholar Chaiwat Satha-anan pointed out immediately after the horrendous event, perhaps it was something that could not be revealed (2004).

Taussig's extension on Elias Canetti's (1984) pronouncement that secrecy is the very core of power applies to Krue Se: "Knowing it is essential to its power, equal to the denial. Not being to say anything is likewise testimony to its power … it being not that knowledge is power but rather that active not-knowing makes it so" (Taussig 1999, 6–7). Taussig further elaborates on the secrecy of public secret and its concomitant silences in *Palma Africana* also applies to Krue Se: "Everyone knows, nobody knows, not just it is generally unwise to speak but because of what you might call blurred vision or double vision and the magma of fear under the surface of everyday life … Secrecy magnifies reality and public secrecy magnifies it even more, encumbered by a brittle silence" (2018, 15).

What also makes the massacre at Krue Se so difficult to narrate is the lack of Thai historical discourse on the impunity of the state in the killing of its own people (Thongchai Winichakul 2002; Klima 2002). In other words, the recollection of the Krue Se massacre is an anamnesis that calls the present into question, against the meta-script of Thailand's national historiography, that there is more to Thailand than lovely smiles. It deviates sharply – as in the cases of the students massacres of October 1973, October 1976, and May 1992 – from the conventional view of Thailand as a stable paradise for citizens and *farangs* alike. Against this historical background, what happened at Krue Se mosque, especially who gave the order to kill, is politically unspeakable. What Margaret Steedly points out about the self-censorship of the 1965 massacre in Indonesia applies here: "The monument unbuilt the story unspoken, is no more than an invisible inscription along history's silent edge, marking an official limit placed upon the past by the present" (1993, 238).

To be sure, what happened at the Krue Se massacre is recoverable. Despite that, there has been no effort to investigate the incident, and it is hard to trace the blame precisely. First, those who were involved are unlikely to speak out. Second, suppose that sufficient evidence is gathered, the truth could be devastating to certain individuals and institutions, namely the *amaat* – comprising the top echelon of the military, the monarchy, and other officials who control power and command respect in Thailand – and even to the Buddhist monastic order, the *sangha*. What happened at Krue Se is off limits. But it is clear to me that the historical meaning of that day has not been lost on the diverse Malay Muslims in Thailand's far south, and I will elaborate on it in this ethnography.

With such invisible inscription along history's silent edge, Chaiwat Satha-anan and Thanet immediately noted the significance of the date of the clashes (28 April 2004) and its relevance to Haji Sulong Abdulkadir al-Fatani and the Islamic Awakening. Both Chaiwat (2004, 2006, 2007) and Thanet (2004, 2008) point out that it was exactly fifty-six years previously, on 28 April 1948, that the incidents at Dusun Nyior village took place. Although the incidents are often referred to within the Malay Muslim communities in the far south as Kebangkitan Dusun Nyior (Dusun Nyior Awakening), in a convoluted move to obscure the aspirations of minority culture and identity the state preferred to call it Kabot Dusong Yo (Dusong Yo Disturbance). The fact that Chaiwat had three publications and Thanet had two to make the connection of the day and month of the clashes is significant – something that was ignored by the media, the state, and the so-called Malay Muslim leaders.

Haji Sulong and the Dusun Nyior Awakening

There is much to say about the history of the Dusun Nyior Awakening, and this section offers some important points that will serve as background. We might say that Dusun Ngior is the ur-village or the ur-history of the recurring conflict in Thailand's far south. Besides being one of the sites of *ziarah* (an important form of local pilgrimage in the identity-shaping experience of being a Muslim), the Krue Se mosque is also a political site for the Muslim communities (Ockey 2011). As an ancient mosque, it was officially declared a historical site by the Thai government in 1935. However, its geographical, architectural, and temporal aspects are all enigmatic because its round columns and windows are of European gothic-like design, but a Muslim lawyer wrote in a local Muslim newspaper that the design of the mosque was Persian. Even the date on which it was built is controversial: the official data book says it was in the year 1785, but under the section "Religious Site" the same book says it was built around 1578–93 during the reign of King Naresuan the Great. Anant Wattananikorn, the former educational commissioner of Yarang in the province of Pattani suggests that the mosque was built in 1142 (Chaiwat 2004).

Regardless of its enigmatic history, Krue Se mosque, which is located in the subdistrict (*tambon*) Tanyong Lulo of Pattani's Muang district, is also in the hometown of Daub ibn Abd Allah, one of the region's most well-known Muslim scholars (Matheson and Hooker 1988). It was in this subdistrict that young Sulong attended an Islamic boarding school before his father sent him to Mecca. While he was in Mecca, Sulong was greatly influenced by the modernist teaching of Muhammad Abduh. At the same time, the entire Middle East was experiencing tremendous change: the collapse of the Ottoman Empire, a world war, colonialism, and the rise of perhaps the most diverse revivalist movement in the Muslim world. It was a period of expanding pluralism of thought and pluralism of politics and identities, during which Shafi'i, Islamic reformist, fundamentalist, Arabic, and Ottoman identities were all available to the young Sulong and his fellows al-Fatani (Surin Pitsuwan 1985; Ockey 2011).[3]

It should be noted that the centrality of Islamic modernism in the struggle for aspirations and Muslim identities and equality in Thailand's far south did not materialize until Haji Sulong gained prominence in the late 1930s (Ockey 2011; Davisakd Puaksom 2008). Politically, it also marked an aspiration to depart from the traditional struggles against Thai subjugation under the auspices of the rajas of the former Sultanate of Patani. Such aspirations, however, also got Haji Sulong and his movement into trouble. He was a figure trapped, figuratively, in Foucault's panoptical prison. His actions were watched, his remarks reported.

As mentioned earlier, with the Second World War approaching, Prime Minister Phibul began mobilizing the population in the name of nation building, enforcing a strident policy of assimilation with no toleration for minority cultures and aspirations. Under this policy came the idea of Thainess (*khwampen* Thai) and ethnic Thai nationalism. In a cynical effort to smooth regional differences and the tentative forging of new identities and loyalties under the Thai Rathaniyom (Thai Custom Decree), the Phibul government began promoting *desirable* labels for certain minorities. The north, which historically and even today has no love for Bangkok, was labelled as *thin thai ngam* (a region of beautiful people), and the northeast, especially Isan (one of the backwaters of Thailand and one with allegiance to Khmer), was *thin thai dee* (a region of good people). However, there was no desirable label for the Malay Muslims in the far south. On the contrary, the Malay Muslims who were indigenous to the far south were labelled as *khaek* (Thanet 2004). There are several connotations to the label *khaek*. Under the discourse of Thai racism, *khaek* is attributed to someone with a darker skin (read "Malay Muslim"), which can be read by Buddhists as a sign of impurity and inner badness (Keyes 2010; Jerryson 2011). In other words, it was and is such Thai racism and state Buddhism that create identity formation, exclusion, and inequality in Thai society.[4]

Naming Malay Muslims as *khaek* highlighted not only the degree of insult and audacity of the Phibul administration but also the verbal violence of hurtful language that it had towards the Malay Muslims in the far south. One might even say that, quite often, the act of naming minority groups, as in the case of Thailand, with certain labels is crucial to the enterprise of conquest, an act of taking possession and creating a new reality, and thus freezing reality. Taussig puts it well: "When we name, we freeze reality, as with facing the Gorgon. In naming ... we make it protuberant in the vortex that is history. The naming not only petrifies but awakens life, no matter how spectral, in congealed things" (2003, 277).

The labelling of different minorities as such was nothing short of "racism with a distance" (Asad 1993, 111) whereby certain cultural differences could be tolerated or even celebrated, or not tolerated and celebrated, but from a distance. Differences that could be commodified were celebrated, whereas differences that could not were seen as a threat to social cohesion. Symptomatically, the act of naming the Malay Muslims in the far south as *khaek* not only was pejorative but also provided the Phibul administration with a verbal grammar of superiority and exploitation against them. It was also a fundamental part of the semantic battle that annexation (read "colonization") of a contested territory enjoined in the removal of the historiography of the colonized past in Thailand's far south. As verbal nominatives and adjectives, they were terrifyingly impersonal. Besides the violence of naming, the traditional Malay Muslim men's *songkok* (hats) and women's headscarves and sarongs were prohibited, and Muslim courts were abolished. Effectively, what the labelling and the restrictions did was to impose further a binary discourse upon its Malay Muslim subjects, forcing them into choosing either a Thai (Buddhist) or a local (Muslim) identity (Ockey 2011). This was the racist and paranoic atmosphere that Haji Sulong and his reformist movement were facing at the time.

Apart from the state, Haji Sulong's modernist teaching also elicited jealousies and opposition from the conservative Muslim *ulamas* (religious scholars) and *ustazs* (religious leaders). Haji Sulong was an anathema to them, so much so that some of them even inaccurately accused him, in the most absurd way, of spreading Wahhabism. Meanwhile, rivalries among the Malay Muslim elites also affected his political position. For example, when Tunku Mudka from the powerful Abdunlabut family and two other Muslim candidates ran for Parliament in the first direct election in 1937, Haji Sulong supported Charoen, a Thai-Buddhist candidate. For Haji Sulong, it was Charoen's politics that mattered; both Haji Sulong and Charoen were modernists who believed in democracy and equality (Thanet 2004). In short, Haji Sulong found himself, simultaneously, famous and infamous. He was as much admired by many ordinary Malay Muslims as he was vilified. Many conservative *ulamas* and *ustazs*, Malay Muslim elites with allegedly sultanate descendants, and the government hated him. He threatened a sense of the racial order; he appeared as a dangerous deviation to the superstitions of the Malay world; he was, in his refusal to conform to any of the above, destabilizing the status quo.

When news broke that a commission of inquiry from Bangkok was heading to Pattani to listen to local grievances, Haji Sulong and a group of leaders met and produced seven demands concerning the political rights and religious affairs of the Malay Muslims. At the same time, upon Haji Sulong's invitation, a *Straits Times* British correspondent visited Pattani, and she later reported on issues of corruption, blackmailing, and persecution of the Malay Muslims, especially by the police. Bangkok was infuriated that what was happening and contained within the far south had been broadcast by an international newspaper. This negative report by an English correspondent would become one of the chief pieces of evidence used by the court in prosecuting Haji Sulong on sedition charges. It is important to note that these developments were happening when Phibul was in exile. However, there was a coup in November 1947 that returned Phibul to power, a shift that sent shock waves to the far south and explains why Haji Sulong and other Muslim leaders felt that any hopeful dialogue with Bangkok had effectively ended (Suhrke 1975).

Although the seven demands were regarded as the most vital evidence of the alleged separatist plan led by Haji Sulong, the court found no legal ground to prosecute him even though the demand that the highest ruler of the four provinces be a Malay Muslim, or that the Islamic and civil courts coexist, was a particular problem for the prosecution. But the court did find Haji Sulong guilty of making public the letter to Tengku Mahayiddin, who the government believed was the leader of a separatist movement. On 16 January 1948 Haji Sulong and his associates were charged with treason and arrested. Their arrests sparked protests and clashes across the far south, the biggest one being at the village of Dusun Nyior where more than four hundred Malay Muslims and thirty Thai policemen were killed (Che Man 1990).

Following the clashes and suppression, an estimated 250,000 Muslims signed a petition requesting that the United Nations preside over the separating of the four Malay Muslim provinces (Pattani, Yala, Narathiwat, and Satun) and their joining with Malaya, then a Malay Muslim–majority colony of Britain. The issue attracted international attention, including from the Asia Relations Organization and the United Nations. Calls for support were also made to the Arab League, Indonesia, Pakistan, and Malaya. Perhaps it was due to international pressures and spotlights that the first concession made by Phibul upon his return to power was to release Haji Sulong and his associates on bail in 1952. However, on 13 August 1954, Haji Sulong, his eldest son, and a few companions were summoned to the police station in Songkhla. They were then escorted to a mosque in Hat Yai in the province of Songkhla for their *zuhr salat* (obligatory prayer performed around noon). That was the last time they were seen. The police claimed that they mysteriously disappeared along their way home. The most widely believed story is that they were tortured, forced to consume alcohol, and killed, and their bodies stuffed into barrels and dumped in the sea (Chaloemkiat Khunthongphet 1986).

To this day there are many versions of what transpired at Dusun Nyior that question whether it was spontaneous or planned. But one thing remains true: it solidified the deep prejudices and fears of Thai officials about the real motive of the Malay Muslims in the far south (Chaiwat 2004). To sum up, the state needed to justify the suppression of local aspirations, and the so-called Dusun Nyior rebellion allowed it to narrate the nature and causes of separatism at the time. Without doubt, this meta-narrative affects the political relations between the Malay Muslims in the far south and the Thai state to this day. My invocation of the late-1940s Islamic Awakening refers not only to what followed the awakening in Thailand's far south in the long twentieth century but, more broadly, to the meaning of that awakening in the politics of the twenty-first, especially after 11 September 2001 and the Arab Spring.

I bring up Haji Sulong and the Islamic Awakening because my interlocutors talked about it. If the history of Haji Sulong and the Islamic Awakening is treated as an aberration by the Thai State and local elites, including the conservative *ulamas and ustaz*, in order to deny its eventfulness – something I will touch upon in the next section – have the events that transpired during the 1940s been forgotten, erased from the consciousness of ordinary

Malay Muslim civilians? If not, how can we write the dimension of disdain and its messiness back into the fore of their history?

Following Benjamin's critiques of the conflation of history as progress, and in remembering Haji Sulong and the Dusun Nyior, we find ourselves confronted by an archive of violence in such a way that we might be able to perceive the layers upon layers of violent historical debris that have propelled us into the present, which brings us to another event.

The Tak Bai Tragedies

Another one of the most atrocious human rights violations in Thailand occurred a few months after the Krue Se mosque massacre. To this day there are still divisive opinions about what happened at Tai Bai and who should be held accountable – ranging from the prime minister's office to the police and the *tahann* unit involved. But the facts remain as such: on 25 October 2004 a group of Malay Muslims, including women and children, protested in front of the Tak Bai district police station in the province of Narathiwat. They were demanding the release of six youths from their fishing village who had been arrested on the grounds that they were linked to militants. When the police could not, or *would* not, control the crowd, the *tahann* were called in. Witnesses and other reports diverge on what happened next. Videotapes showing clashes between Malay Muslim youths and the security forces, although widely distributed on YouTube, were initially banned.[5] The confrontation between the security forces and the demonstrators quickly escalated into violence, resulting in several deaths among the protesters. When the *tahann* and police finally managed to subdue the crowd, hundreds of young male demonstrators were ordered to strip off their shirts and, with hands tied behind their backs, were forced to lie on the ground on a blistering hot day. This was during Ramadan, their holy month. The demonstrators were then made to crawl to the waiting army trucks. Piled in on top of one another, like livestock, they were driven off to Camp Ingkayuthaborihaan in Pattani province, a five-hours journey. When the trucks arrived at the camp, seventy-eight of the men were dead – apparently from suffocation or being crushed in the trucks (Askew 2010b).

To this day, the *tahann* and the government have rejected all claims of malfeasance. The then prime minister Thaksin even suggested that these victims were weak from fasting during Ramadan, which was thus the reason for their deaths (Scupin 2013). When the court's verdict was given five years after the incident, in 2009, it stated that the army personnel could not be charged because they were performing their duties under a state of emergency. Years later, the leader of the junta government that ousted Thaksin, Prime Minister Surayud Chulanont, travelled to Muang Pattani in the province of Pattani (not to Tak Bai or anywhere within the province of Narathiwat) to issue an apology and reparations to the victims' families, and to drop the charges of ninety-two "riot instigators" who had survived the violence. Since then, there has been no attempt to explain how seventy-eight men died on the way to the army camp and thus to give some kind of closure.

Indeed, one might ask, How can there be closure when Surayud travelled to Muang Pattani (and not to Tak Bai) to apologize? The diverse Malay communities perceived the move as not only blatantly insincere politics of regret but also a mechanism for the express aim of apologia, designed purportedly to overcome an aporia, one that reflected the convergence of a particular stratagem of the nation-state, an epistemology of loss, and a politics of regret. Let me explain. Historically, the word *apologia*, from which the word *apology* derives, refers to a defence against accusation or charge. The word *apology* has come to mean the admission of error or wrongdoing, whether or not punctuated by sincerity. Since the time of Plato's *Apology of Socrates*, state apologies have often brought these conflicting views of the ancient and the modern into a paradoxical resolution. In the courtroom of Socrates's trial for impiety and corruption, he staged a defence of his innocence. What Socrates takes as his defence against corruption, a practice of philosophical engagement that the people of Athens do not want to recognize, is mistranslated as an admission of wrongdoing, as a performative re-enactment of his corrupted position.[6] The *Apology* demonstrates that the institutional knowledge of wisdom can be based on a logical chimera.

In a reversal of Plato's *Apology*, Surayud offered an apology at Muang Pattani in the province of Pattani for something horrible that had taken place at Tak Bai in the province of Narathiwat. His move had the effrontery, not to mention the deficiency of any sense of irony, when he travelled to Muang Pattani and not to Tak Bai to make his apology. As such, even if there was the slightest hint of the admission of wrongs committed by stage agents, Surayud's apology was also mistranslated by the Malay communities as an admission of guilt, albeit his alone, but also one without any true interest in reconciliation and closure. In each case, apologies were constructed for their audience. Nonetheless, Surayud's apology reflected a defence of the state's continued impunity and right to assert its control, especially in a permanent state of emergency. It was a defence of the state as an institution that has the power to decide and mediate the terms of future reconciliation. I am not suggesting that will ever happen. But most important, facing this aporia, the absence of any serious attempt to explain the deaths of some ninety Malay Muslim men on 25 October 2004 remains an important barrier to an understanding between the government and the heterogeneous Malay Muslims in the far south, and especially the communities at Tak Bai. And make no mistakes about it, the shadowy insurgents are using the insincerity of Surayud's apology as a recruiting tool.

Over the course of conducting my field work at Muang Pattani I also made friends and acquaintances with a few professors at a local university. Ajarnn Abdullah and Sumree were two of them. I had even given talks, or what they called "conversation series," to their students on the current conflict. On one occasion, in their office, Ajarnn Abdullah and Sumree both emphasized that what did not escape them was that Surayud's apology was being offered with faux humility wrapped perfidiously in hypocrisy. Ajarnn Abdullah said, "Surayud's apology at Pattani and not at Tak Bai … saying I am sorry or we are sorry is like those uttered by young children. If you really think about it, it is as if *immaturity* has become the virtue of the *truth*." In other words, if such truth is taken to be a virtue, it is also one that sees no need to grow up.

If Surayud's apology was a speech act in the Austinian sense, it was a perlocutionary act instead of an illocutionary act, something that achieved no positive effect on the Malay Muslim communities.[7] Surayud was far from convincing when it came to delivering the sincerity of his apology. One might even say his apology was a performance that yielded a present that was ghostwritten, especially to the communities at Tak Bai. In short, it left unmoved the communities at Tai Bai and elsewhere in the far south. Most of my Malay Muslim interlocutors would have liked to see the day when they could have their doses of Schadenfreude, but that did not happen. There was another coup, in 2014, one that replaced Surayud in power with yet another army general.

Glorious Patani

Sejarah kita bukan yang di-lepas tapi sekarang. Sejarah kita sekarang. Ini lah yang penting, sejarah sekarang. [Our history is not about the past but now. Our history is now. This is important, our history now.]
– Faosee, recently released from prison after serving five years for being charged as a member of the BRN (a separatist organization), which he denies

History is not the past. History is the present. We carry our history with us. To think otherwise is criminal.
– James Baldwin

As this chapter has alluded, if the current shadow insurgency is a revival and a full retelling of the story and memory of the 1948 Dusun Nyior Awakening that has become the symbol of Malay Muslims' struggle against injustices, a position taken by Chiawat, Thanet, and many of my Malay Muslim interlocutors, why was such a reawakening sidestepped not only by the state but also by some local Muslim elites in the historical present?[8] In fact, both state agents and local Malay elites circumvented the issues of a Malay Muslim awakening by broadcasting instead another history, that of a sugar-coated, glorious Patani past and of a harmonious relationship with Siam.[9]

In the summer of 2005, slightly over a year after the Krue Se massacre, I visited the mosque with a local university student whom I shall call Hassan. On that afternoon, standing next to us inside the mosque, an elderly man who had a melancholy look on his face asked if we knew why there were so many holes in the walls. Aware that I was not going to offer any response, he spoke again: "Government needs to explain why the *pembunuhan* [massacre] happened." He let me meditate a little on his words before pointing towards a coffee and tea stall across the street. We walked over to it, and he took his time as we sat down, even turning a few times towards the mosque. After much protraction, he told me he was a *cikgu* (teacher) and used to teach history at the *ponok* school (Muslim religious boarding school) in *tambon* Tanyong Lulo. He also mentioned that he was connected to the sultan of Kelantan's palace.[10] The last point is important and will be elaborated upon in the following pages. Perhaps to conceal his emotion, he once again turned and stared at the historic mosque in silence as if, in a Proustian sense, he was looking at the object in which the traumatic emotion of a recent tragic past was hidden. I could sense, by the look on his face, his grief.

At that moment, by mentioning the date of the Krue Se mosque massacre (28 April) and what happened exactly fifty-six years ago at Dusyn Nyior, I thought that perhaps the memory of trauma might trigger him to talk about 1948. Instead, the *cikgu* turned towards Hassan and asked if he knew much about the Sultanate of Patani. Without waiting for Hassan to respond, he said, in a censorious tone of voice, that Hassan and others of his generation must take pride in the history of Patani, a maritime kingdom that was once a *maso loning* (renaissance) kingdom of the Muslim world. He then sighed and expressed how the recent event had left him with a sense of helplessness, if not hopelessness. This, he said, was why the community at Krue Se felt so powerless, as if the present was acting as a spoiler to the memory of a glorious past.

Once again, he turned and stared at the mosque. With his hands outstretched, he let out a huge sigh and mumbled something to himself.

Hassan and I were silenced by his grief, his hopelessness, his helplessness, and his sense of injustice. My reaction was that the violence or the evil that had descended upon Krue Se did not require one to believe that evil had passed. Evil is, in fact, in the historical present, the never ending *now*. Similarly with regard to the struggles of African Americans, James Baldwin has echoed that their history is not in the past but in the present. As he puts it, to think otherwise is criminal. Or, following Benjamin, the structure of history is "time filled by the presence of the now [*Jetztzeit*]" (1968, 261).[11]

When I once again asked the *cikgu* if the recent clashes had anything to do with Haji Sulong and Dusun Nyior, he looked at me and then at Hassan. And just as he had had words, he now had silence. He shrugged his shoulders, got up, and left. I was perplexed that for him – to borrow from Mary Zurbuchen who speaks in an Indonesian context – the history of glorious Patani "continue[d] to magnetize [his] historical consciousness" (2005, 27) to the point of obliterating events that had more significance to the Krue Se massacre. If memory, to think with Thongchai Winichakul (2002), is always a projection from the present onto the past, but the perspectives in the present are informed by historical discourses, why was a glorious Patani past invoked at the expense of negating the meaning of more significant events – the 1940s Islamic Awakening? Could it be that what is often called memory is not about remembering at all but a certain stipulation that locks the story in our minds? (Sontag 2003).

Or could it be, from a temporal logic, that a glorious Patani past was more narratable than the 1940s Islamic Awakening and its subsequent series of unsuccessful struggles, a series of events that had produced from the outset – to invoke Koselleck (2002, 2004) – not only no future but indeed a discredited past? This is especially so if one were to take the current recurring violence into account, when there is no end in sight, a present that is bracketed from the past and the future. To put it slightly differently, what Thailand's far south lacks is a usable past. What we have instead is a series of past and current struggles that have produced no structural changes for the diverse Malay Muslim communities, a region that remains a patriarchal backwater in Thailand's socio-economic and political landscapes. Perhaps surreptitiously, to narrate about that discredited past can be seen as resuming that old political struggle, one that can be repudiated as a potentially catastrophic effort to go backward. And if the series of past and current struggles have been, by my definition, a recurring if not repetitive violence, it would fit what Taussig wrote when he invoked the passage on the rosary from Benjamin, that "it at least provides the steadiness of ritual in the space of death, which chips of messianic time remain violently silent" (Taussig 2003, 185) in the pages of my ethnography.

As it turned out, the *cikgu*'s stipulation of a glorious Patani past and his silence when it came to Haji Sulong and its reformist Islamic Awakening were not at all atypical. That summer, Hassan and his university friends also invoked Patani on many occasions, a Patani they had learned about during their *ponok* school days. But they always used the same script: Patani was a glorious kingdom. They could not, however, provide detailed information about its gloriousness but repeated, more than once, that the era had ended. "We did not read much about Patani during our *ponok* school years," one of Hassan's friends said apologetically. But then he brightened with another thought: "We learned mostly that that glorious history had ended." It is as if Patani was glorious precisely because its era had ended. In other words, this assumption seals Patani in a glorious past that is then deemed its only authentic temporality. One might even say that the glorious Patani had become a phantom, one that was foremost the illusory Patani whereby the precise chronology, historical actors, and historical debris prior to the Patani sultanate's decline were beside the point. Surely, at the very least, if what they were taught was an artifice of historical memory making, some of them could have mentioned the oft-cited account of Patani from *Hikayat Patani* (Teeuw and Wyatt 1970) or the *History of the Malay Kingdom of Patani* (Syukri 1985). They drew a blank when I asked if any of them had ever heard about these texts. Paradoxically, what they learned during their *ponok* school days were the voices of nostalgia, nostalgia for a past that never was.[12]

I also encountered another glorified description of Patani that summer. Sitting with a company of men and university students at a tea shop outside Prince of Songkhla University campus, a local politician, who was also a lawyer whom I shall call Faosee, reminded his audience that the current conflict had roots in the traumatic *sebahgiyae hok* (annexation) of Patani by Siam. Similarly, all he could say about Patani was its glorious past. Or, more notedly, he repeated like a mantra to his audience information about the kingdom's Zaman Emas (Golden Age) – that Patani was once a thriving maritime kingdom and had at times even defeated the Siamese armies – at which his audience nodded enthusiastically.

Faosee had this habit of insinuating his alleged royal lineage when he talked about glorious Patani. Over tea he took pleasure in regaling us with stories of his frequent visits to the Kelantan palace and would repeat to us that his *ketughunae* (ancestry) was from the sultanates of Patani and Kelantan. His voice, manner, gestures, and attitude became increasingly reminiscent of an accomplished boaster as he was puffed up with conceit. Doubtless, Faosee thought he was promoting his audiences' case that afternoon as he elaborated an image of himself as reflected in the eyes of those who reacted to what he said. He registered my disapproval. I was struggling to hold my composure as I realized then that I was conducting fieldwork in a conflict zone. However, when I pressed him further on his lineage, he prevaricated and could not even reveal the names or genealogies of his ancestries even as he fetishized them. It would seem that a modicum of knowledge would suffice as he refashioned in order to resurrect glorious pasts behind humiliating presents. To alleviate the stress of the historical present, as David Lowenthal cynically remarks, "'The charm of the past is that it is the past,' says Wilde's Henry Wotton, as if to preclude further explanation" (Lowenthal 1985, 49). Furthermore, "collapsing the past into a single frame not only made the past felt distinct from the present but also making it felt familiar" (Lowenthal 1996, 139).

When I asked Faosee if the current insurgency could be interpreted as a reawakening of the Dusun Nyior Islamic Awakening (and I pointed out to him the similar date – the day and month – of the Dusun Nyior and Krue Se incidents), he demurred. He then went on to dismiss my interpretation by saying impertinently that Haji Sulong and his so-called Islamic Awakening movement were nothing but a variant of Wahhabism. He also said that the current insurgents were radical extremists. When I countered Faosee's exclamation on Haji Sulong, by saying that he was not an extremist but a reformist and that the Wahhabi association or accusation was made by his rivals, conservative *ulamas* and *ustazs* whom the prevailing government then happily accepted, he gave me a slight smile. It was an uncomfortable smile. However, unwilling to be deflected from my line of inquiry or counterclaim, he responded, "Haji Sulong was a Wahhabi. Wahhabism is the problem back then and Wahhabism is the problem now." And then he muttered the common mechanical response: "Truth is Allah. Allah is Truth. Allahu Akhbar! Laailaha ilaAllah Muhammad RasulAllah." (God is great! There is no god but the God and Muhammad is the messenger of God.) Clearly, he had become my bête noire.

At his office, Farok, a lawyer, who also laid claim to a Patani aristocratic ancestry, straightaway got into what he called the golden-age story: "Patani was a maritime kingdom, and its sultanate was one of the most powerful and richest in the Malay Archipelago." However, he stressed that Patani was not always at odds with Bangkok. He also said that Patani could never return to what it had been because Wahhabism had replaced that era of Islam. The vital point in his meta-story, as well as the stories of Faosee and the Malay *cikgu*, is that the glorified past can never return. In other words, it is a collective story of loss that is supposedly already inscribed within the larger story of the *orang* Patani (Patani people). The Malay Muslims in Thailand's far south are a people defined by their collective loss of a glorious sultanate, a loss of a certain Islamic religiosity that has been allegedly replaced by Wahhabism, a loss of human dignity, and a loss of territorial sovereignty.

In their retelling of this meta-story there is a certain stability in that it is based on repetition; it is a story that has been told and retold to many a listener, in which a glorified past can be expressed and heard. It is also important to note that it is a story that appears to lack the gaps and silences that usually accompany life stories and personal narratives. It reminds me of the rehearsed and repetitive speeches that government officials gave at the never-ending cycle of "opening ceremonies": opening ceremonies of hospitals, Buddhist *wats*, roads, bridges, and other monuments that immortalized the founding violence of the state. These speeches were so well rehearsed and so repetitive in that there were no gaps and silences in their (un)performative aspects of language.

As mentioned earlier, the appearance of Haji Sulong and his modernist teaching marked a departure from the traditional struggles against the Thai subjugation under the auspices of the *rajas rajas* of the former Sultanate of Patani. As such, I suspect that having an aristocratic background would explain why Farok, Faosee, and the *cikgu* were uneasy with Haji Sulong and his modernist Islam. Like Farok and the other elites I met, many conservative *ulamas* and *ustazs* have also unhelpfully, if not incorrectly, accused Haji Sulong and his modernist Islam of being a form of Wahhabism. It would seem to me that it was this shift since the 1940s, and the consequent accusation of Wahhabism, that lent the elitists and the conservative *ulamas* and *ustazs* an atmosphere of (often acute) anxiety about their established positions, a threat to their historical hegemony, and a threat to the seamless authority they once had.

Accusation of Wahhabism

The term *Wahhabism* has been misappropriated in Southeast Asia since the beginning of the twentieth century by traditional religious teachers, local elites, and government agents. As Farish Noor (2007) points out, at the turn of the twentieth century a group of Kaum Muda (Youth Movement) progressive *ulamas* gathered in the Malaya Straits Settlements (Penang, Malacca, and Singapore) to set up their modern madrasah and to launch their journals. They were deeply influenced by the writings of the Egyptian reformist Muhammad Abduh and of Rashid Rida, who argued that Islam was a religion of the intellect and reason and that the time had come for the Muslim communities to free themselves from the shackles of superstition and chauvinism that were neither Islamic nor rational. One of their modus operandi was to free themselves from the shackles of colonialism. For all that, the group was incorrectly condemned as Wahhabi by the British authorities.

At the same time, the Kaum Muda movement was also growing in Indonesia, led by the Muhamadiyah. Likewise, they were also accused of being Wahhabi (Noor 2007). Haji Sulong and other al-Fatani in Thailand's far south also saw the need to advance Muhammad Abduh's modernization program by reforming Islamic teachings and education, as well as implementing modern political and legal systems within an Islamic context. But their progressive teachings upset some conservative *ulamas* who were responsible for the teachings that these progressives wanted to purify. In fact, these conservative *ulamas* requested that a government investigation be conducted to determine whether Haji Sulong was fomenting rebellion – something the government was all too willing to oblige (Nik Mahmud 1999).

I touch on the long history of the misappropriation of Wahhabism in Southeast Asia because such accusations continue to this day and they are important to the propaganda of the conservative *ulamas and ustazs*, to the elites who claim lineage to the aristocracy, and, obviously, to the government. Such accusations work because the ground has been well prepared. The profuse mythology concerning Wahhabism, or I should say the poverty of this Wahhabi story, dates from long before the current insurgency, and it fell on ears that were finely tuned by the style and imagination with which the so-called elites had long depicted the far south: namely, the glorious past can never return because Wahhabism has replaced that era of Islam. The glorious past was, of course, no less a patronizing and time-honoured frozen mythology as it was fiction masquerading as a fact.

In fact, any Malay Muslims can be accused of being Wahhabi in Thailand's far south. It was a Friday afternoon when I walked into Ajarnn Abdullah's office, like I had on many different occasions. He had just returned from *zuhr salat* (midday prayer). When I asked him at which mosque he usually performed his Friday *salat* (prayers), it triggered this response. He told me he usually performed his *salat* at the mosque inside the university compound, and then he emphasized to me that the current forms of Islam in the far south, at least the kinds he subscribed to, were those that hoped to do away with superstition, alcoholism, and drug addictions among their youth. And for all that, they were labelled as Wahhabism by some conservative *ulamas* and *ustazs* and government agents.[13] He laughed when he told me that those who prayed at the mosque inside the university had been accused of being Wahhabis.

Shaking his head, Ajarnn Abdullah stressed that it was unfortunate that in the midst of all this madness, there was the general tendency among the media to see only one dimension of the current conflict – the Thai government versus the Muslim extremist groups – and to dismiss the competitions, jealousies, and historical rivalries among the diverse Muslim communities that existed not only between the three provinces but also within each province. "Are you aware of the problems between the Islamic councils of Muang Pattani and Sai Buri?" he asked. I noticed his eyes were twitching. I nodded but kept silent. He leaned across his desk and whispered, "Do you know why Sai Buri has become one of the *panas* [hottest] sites in Pattani of late?" I remained silent even though I had heard it from some of my interlocutors, deciding to err on the side of caution for fear that what I might say could be construed as something dangerous, if not seditious. Ajarnn Abdullah looked at me and was waiting for a response. I sensed he was getting impatient. His look was a gaze, an evaluative one. There was a silent dialogue going on between us, even within each of us.[14]

Finally I took the risk and asked if he was insinuating that the escalating numbers of killings and shooting at Sai Buri had something to do with the rivalries between the Islamic councils of Muang Pattani and Sai Buri or, more accurately, between its respective presidents. He smiled. It was a nervous smile. And then, perhaps feeling he might have revealed too much information to me, an outsider, information that might be construed as too sensitive, even dangerous, he begged me somewhat apologetically, "Please forget what I have just said … The presidents at both councils are all right, good Muslims," as if trying to take back his earlier insinuation by now offering a measuredly neutral tone about the two councils' presidents.[15] He left his office and came back with more biscuits.

When I asked if violence and the fear it produced might be one of the reasons that some young Malay men, even teenagers, were attracted to joining the insurgency, he furrowed his brow and thought for a minute before offering his opinion. He said that the far south was ripe for the recruitment of angry young Muslim men and boys, the children of the "culture of terror" as he called them, because of the underlying poverty and neglect that the region had suffered for so long, which had left scars that ran deeper than what was visible. "Among us oppressed people," he continued, "there is always too much division, division that is created by ourselves as well as by our oppressors." (I think he meant the state.) "If anything else, it gave our oppressors a reason to delegitimize our experience, and the militants' violent tactics made it easy for the state to stereotype us." He gave me a long look to see if I agreed with his assessment. I nodded. He continued, "These young men and boys who were recruited by the insurgents were born out of previous men and boys, and potentially waiting to be killed again." He gave a sinister laugh before adding: "Of course, you are not entirely incorrect. It is all about violence; RKK with their guns and bombs might be it, they might be attractive ... Any rebels are clever in manipulating the situations, taking advantage of insecurities, misunderstandings, promising a way out of poverty, stimulating desire, envy, autonomy. In many ways these organizations who see themselves as countering Thai state policy actually mirror it. And just like our *tahann* and their huge budgets for weapons and whatnot that attracted so many Thais, these separatists' weapons and their violent tactics are also attractive. They reinforced hierarchies and, once created, tend to be self-sustaining."

I agree with his assessment about weapons and the creation of hierarchies. One only need to look at the history of violent resistances throughout the world to recognize this. I also agree with his assessment concerning poverty and neglect. Taussig's decades of research on violence echo the same observation that the principal arm of any culture of terror is unemployment, never mind the psychological fear (Taussig 2003, 130). The taxi-van drivers whom I got to know over the years, the ones who were in constant contact with public opinion – which, of course, they also helped create – would flatly state that *keminiskinian* (being poor) was the root of the problem in the region. It is unemployment, one of the principles that generate *keminiskininan*, that enables the Runda Kumpulan Kecil (RKK) to recruit young Muslim men and teenagers.

Chapter Two

Militarized and Islamified

After travelling with Hanisah in the van from Hatyai to Muang Pattani, I went for a walk in the neighbourhood that evening to see if much had changed since my reconnaissance visit in 2005. If counting by the numbers of checkpoints from Hatyai to Muang Pattani, as well as within the area close to my service apartment, was an indicator, it most definitely had. After a few days in Muang Pattani I also noticed the tremendous increase in military and paramilitary presence, even at the soccer field next to my service apartment. I soon developed the habit of counting the number of military and police roadblocks within the township. Within days I was no longer spooked by the sounds and sights of dark, camouflaged military helicopters hovering in the sky at night. I got used to their sights and sounds. Cellphone signals were jammed whenever the military top brass or VVIPs from Bangkok were in town, and I would see one or two helicopters circling above, low enough that I could read the numbers in white on their bellies.[1] Round and round they went for ten to fifteen minutes.

The bars and karaoke joints (they were not that different from each other) that I had seen in 2005, those operated by non-Muslims and serving alcohol along the traffic-jammed road leading to Prince of Songkhla University, had been demolished. Instead, standing in their locations were teashops run by Malay Muslim establishments. In addition, most 7-Eleven outlets had taken beer and other alcohol off their shelves for fear of the store being bombed. When I went to visit a few *ajarnn* at Prince of Songkhla University, I noticed an exponential increase in Malay Muslim students, especially female Malay Muslim students. During my reconnaissance trip the Malay Muslim students, although very active, had been a minority body. They had since become the overwhelming majority, so much so that a few *ajarnn* at the university joked to me, and among themselves, that their university had become a *ponok* (madrasah). Just like the bars and karaoke joints that had disappeared, all university fairs had become alcohol free, much to the complaints of its non-Muslim students.[2]

It also caught my attention that all the motorbikes parked by the roadsides (and there were literally hundreds and hundreds of them) had their seats lifted up. I was told this was to prevent or discourage anyone from placing explosives in the compartment underneath the seat. And most motorists were not wearing their helmets. They had been told by the police and the *tahaan* to stop wearing them, especially the full-faced helmets. With the constant attacks being carried out by the insurgents on their motorbikes, the wearing of helmets was, ironically, disallowed on the pretext that it would make it difficult for law enforcement officers and/or closed-circuit television cameras to identify these assailants, especially those wearing full-faced helmets. As a friend put it, "Welcome to the wild, wild far south, their security over our safety."

Carolyn Nordstrom (1997, 2007) points out that in societies that use terror and security by state agents as a means to control communities, and in which civilians, rather than soldiers, are the tactical targets, violence often becomes cynically normalized and a part of life. Her observation raises at least two relevant questions. In any chaotic and violent atmosphere, can one live on justice alone? Does the state matter to the lives and livelihoods of its civilians? The answer was poignantly given by Farok, a *nasi dagae*[3] food vendor who said, in a tone more of cynicism than of contempt, "Here nobody is afraid of the law. We are only afraid of the police and the *tahann*." He also commented on the worsening drug trade and the corruption it stimulated, by quoting a common rephrase I had also heard from others: "If you are caught with these *dadah* [referring here to the white powder, usually heroin, cocaine, or meth], with money they will turn into flour." What, then, is the law when the concept often takes on an extra-legal definition? To put this in perspective, what, then, is the civilians' understanding of the relationship between violence and the law when the Law is about money, when Law can easily be bought?

I ask these questions because they challenge the preoccupation that some of us within the academy have with the notion of legality and legitimacy, and to overemphasize the significance of the state to ordinary civilians. According to a leading scholar on Thailand's far south, the current conflict in the region stemmed from a crisis of the legitimacy of both the state and the local elites (McCargo 2009). In other words, the thesis is scripted in an ontology whereby the state, and by extension its representatives, remains the entry point of analysis, thereby assuming, a priori, that the state and the local elites had legitimacy with the diverse Malay Muslim subjects in the far south in the past. Not only is such an argument ahistorical, but, following Carl Schmitt (2004), this would be conflating legality with legitimacy, especially when one takes into account, in chronological order, the moments of tenuous tribunal relations during the era of the Patani sultanate with Siam, annexation by Siam in 1909, followed by decades of strident assimilation policies, charges of separatism since the late 1940s, an atmosphere of corrupt peace until the mid-1990s, and the legalization of draconian laws and the declaration of a state of emergency since 2004. In Thailand's far south, as in many parts of the world, Law is not something that ordinary civilians equate with Justice. Quite the contrary. And my interlocutors most certainly did not conflate legality with legitimacy.

As some of my non-Muslim interlocutors commented, Muang Pattani (and the far south) has been not only militarized but also Islamified physically, emotionally, and symbolically. What does it mean then, I asked myself, for a region to be Islamified within a kingdom where Buddhism is hegemonic? Indeed, I was repeatedly told by my non-Muslim interlocutors that more and more mosques were *quietly* being built with funds coming from some Middle East countries. And most of these newly built mosques were located "deep" in the countryside, "deep" into the villages. This is something I cannot verify because I have never visited any location deep in the countryside or deep into the villages. And even if I had, what are the chances that they would reveal to me who had built their mosques? Many non-Muslims whom I have known through the years feel a further marginalization of their status as Thais living in an increasingly Islamified landscapes within a modern Thai Buddhist kingdom. Many Thai Thais and Sino-Thais have since left the far south.

Like my interlocutors, I soon became somewhat familiarized with the militarized presence in my daily routines. I found myself having to deal with their presence each time I passed by certain streets or junctions or had to walk by these armed personnel with their camouflage uniforms, semi-automatic rifles, and other military paraphernalia. It was hard not to stop staring at their reflective sunglasses and their boots that were somewhat menacing, realizing that this was not a joke and that I was actually living in a permanent state of emergency, itself an oxymoronic situation. Time and time again I would see these *tahaan* walking in groups on the streets. You never see them alone. The same applied to the police and the paramilitaries, whether they were walking on the streets, lanes, or sidewalks or riding in their pickup trucks with heavily tinted windows. They were always armed, which made me wonder if these state security agents were charged with "the security of the nation," or had it morphed into an apparatus for "the security of themselves." This is especially so when the state of emergency has been renewed each year since 2004, one that is protected, when the protection is seen here as an alibi not by my interlocutors but for the state, especially the *tahann* to carry out its extrajudiciary activities.

Like my interlocutors, I tried to avoid the security personnel's presence, both physically and mentally. Or when approaching them (either walking or bicycling), I would speed up my pace to pass by them for various reasons, especially for fear that an IED might explode because these military accoutrements were often the target of the insurgents. It is also for this reason that I lacked the data from military interviewees, aside from some I collected in speaking with a few military intelligence agents and local stringers. I was uncomfortable by way of association to risk talking openly to military personnel, not only for my own safety but also for the safety of my interlocutors. And as many of my friends often reminded me, you just never knew who these agents of violence were, lurking invisibly in the shadows. Could they be someone with whom I had spoken, even just in passing? Describing the topography of fear in Northern Ireland, Feldman points out that when terror dominates, violence, fear, and paranoia become the primary forces that spatialize social spaces (1991, 35). It is important to note, as Feldman (1991), Taussig (1987, 1992), Skidmore (2004) and others have emphasized, such topography of fear is not mono-dimensional or uniformly experienced on the ground, serving to remind us of the ambiguity, uncertainty, and unevenness of terror and fear.

Forms of Life

The latest insurgency and counter-insurgency tactics have turned public and domestic spaces into confusing war zones for civilians. There were those who lost or witnessed the persecutions of their loved ones by the insurgents or by the *tahaan*, those who experienced random arrests and intrusive house searches, and those who were tortured in prisons or army detention camps. Children were traumatized when they witnessed their teachers killed by the insurgents; there were a few incidents when their teachers were riddled with bullets from assault rifles. There were execution-style shootings at convenient stores, lethal roadside bombs, or ambushes at rubber orchards. Or the chilling killings of civilians in grotesque ways, like the beheading or burning of victims after they were already dead – images that became one of the most extreme public jolts that there was something profoundly and violently wrong with the latest insurgency.

However, these are not the focus of my research, albeit affected by them. One of the major tasks of my research in working with my interlocutors in Thailand's far south was to comprehend and reflect upon, as much as I could, their forms of life and what the blasé response *biasa* meant as their response to the current recurring conflict. (*Biasa* can mean "used to it," "normal," and much more.) I have plenty of pages to elaborate on this word. At an epistemological level, some of the information I have gathered was gleaned from the shared circumstances of my body inhabiting the same spaces as those of my Malay Muslim interlocutors. My analytic process, as such, is interpretive and inferential. I could only talk with my interlocutors and live for a time with them, and so I must rely on my reading into the dialogic "telling" of their lives and livelihoods and into their words, for traces of meaning, along with other non-verbal actions – bodily gestures, silences, hesitation, pauses, jokes, laughter, tears, paranoia, and so on – all of which are "riddled with cultural assumptions, political tensions, pragmatic moves, rhetorical pitches, and subjective vicissitudes" (Desjarlais 1997, 10). In other words, the ethnographic writing I present here is pregnant with a multifaceted reflexivity in which the voices of my interlocutors have been incorporated into my own, producing what Bakhtin (1981) describes as "a plurilinguistic poetics," an overlapping of voices and exchanging status, of subject and object.

To reiterate, my focus on forms of life also highlights laughter (however cynical it may be) in the realm of precarity, of what it means to live with the omnipresence of actual or potential violence as a feature of daily life, as a feature of one's *dunia* (world), as some would say – in other words, what it means to inhabit a paradoxical historical present in which one appears, in Zygmunt Bauman's vivid phrase (1991, to be "living without an alternative ... [but a] world without alternatives needs self-criticism as a condition of survival and decency" (cited in D. Scott 1999, 134).

Following Robben and others who write about sharing our humanity consciousness with our subjects at numerous violent sites around the world:

[My] anthropological perspective capitalizes on an ethnographic imagination of the everyday realities endured by the [local people] and how they are affected by political forces beyond their reach ... [and, more important,] to show that their lives matter within the larger framework of geopolitical forces, ideological and religious conflicts, ... [and] to emphasize their shared humanity with so many other people whose past has been burdened by violence and suffering, and thus demonstrate that we "are imaginable to each other and that we may conjoin in a shared standard of justice from diverse rationales; in short, that we are equally human beyond our diverse vocabularies." (Hastrup 2002, 40; cited in Robben 2010a, 5)

Here, I follow the tradition in anthropology that has called for a "compassionate turn" in our anthropological enterprises (Sluka and Robben 2007, 22), those that lie somewhat within the tradition of militant anthropology at one extreme, to the anthropology of social suffering, and to the ethnography of everyday life at the other (see Scheper-Hughes 1995; Kleinman, Das, and Lock 1997).

Moreover, one of anthropologists' epistemologies is knowledge situated on groundedness. During fieldwork I was reminded more than once that violence is always local, rooted in the ground, albeit unevenly, and in the quotidian. As such, can the notion of trauma – itself an external, if not a Western, referent – be useful to contextualize and conceptualize the precarious forms of life in Thailand's far south? In the wake of Fanon (1967), trauma for my interlocutors has never been a symptom that can be treated or alleviated by a team of doctors and psychiatrists, because it was never an internalized and unconscious underpinning but, rather, an overtly and consciously open wound, an open sore.[4] Furthermore, my focus on the uncertainty of violence – potential or actual – that is characterized as mundane, in the quotidian rather than in events that befall our subjects, poses a challenge when it comes to conceptualizing pain and suffering, or understanding loss when there is no moment of original violence, when there is no beginning or end. We are talking about a continuing and cyclical violence, the violence continuum that has no end in sight.[5] Like the plights of the Palestinians living under Israeli occupation, "the uncertain character of life may best be described as a 'non-linear permanency'" (Kublitz 2013, 117) – in other words, not "as an interruption of the ordinary, but as an essential part of the ordinary" (Buch Segal 2016, 50). Moreover, it is important to note that the ordinary is not a priori, something taken for granted, but, rather, in the words of Stanley Cavell, it is something that "must be regained every day, in repetition, regained as gone" (1976 172).

The commonly repeated observation by many of my Malay Muslim interlocutors that they were living in an ongoing nightmare was not just a figure of speech; it was an expression of an experience of time that made insurgencies and their attendant violence not at all surprising. They made up the bulk of my interlocutors' existence, that what they hoped to escape was inescapable, and that what they never dreamed of getting, they got. For them to say that they were used to it, *biasa*, or *bosan* (bored) of it, usually accompanied by a shrug of the shoulder, these were verbal and bodily expressions rooted in the quotidian, expressions that were neither given nor abstracted from the structural violence they were enduring and engaging with, repeatedly. It should be noted that to say that violence is an essential part of the ordinary survived daily is already an achievement of some sort (Das 2012). In fact, most of my interlocutors found mundane schedules and conventional habits reassuring, if they were lucky enough to acquire them. With the "compassionate turn" in anthropology, my focus follows the tradition in anthropology that is concern with our subjects' everyday hardships and struggles as they endure and engage with the difficulties of their reality (Robben 2010a).

Like many anthropologists who have commenced fieldwork in sites of terror and precarity and who hope to bring about a more just world, I am aware of the need to write against terror, in elucidating the "complex link" between an anthropologist's analytical tools and the interlocutors' languages and experiences that the anthropologist has witnessed or participated in (albeit never identical), experiences that include laughter, being cynical, sceptical, frightened, confused, disoriented, and at times even angry at their state of despair, as well as my own state.[6] In his splendid and powerful short book that comprises two weeks of notes from his diary (2003), Taussig compares his exasperation in looking for the meanings behind the unnecessary violence in Colombia to that of Jean Genet's memoir *Prisoner of Love*, in which Genet talks about how he failed to understand the Palestinian revolution "because the occupied territories were only a play acted out second by second by occupied and occupier. The reality lay in involvement, fertile in hate and love; in people's daily lives; in silence, like translucency, punctuated by words and phrases" (1992, 3).

Like Taussig, Genet, and others, I too erred on the subjective anthropological accounts of the experiences of my interlocutors, the majority of whom are ordinary Malay Muslims I have come to know quite well. Moreover, what this ethnography tries to illuminate is that what is happening in Thailand's far south is not even a new normal, but a recurring reality, and a difficult reality, to be sure. In many ways my research illuminates the ways in which ordinary civilians are enduring and engaging with, to borrow a phrase from Veena Das (2014b, 2015), the difficulties of reality that have become *biasa* for them.[7] Like in the case of the endless and enduring precarity that the Palestinians have endured while living under an Israeli occupation (Buch Segal 2016), my ethnography is attempting to ask what it means to endure and engage with such a never-ending precarity – not that there are any easy answers – and to offer an acknowledgment that such kinds of living that persist for ordinary Malay Muslims in Thailand's far south and similar zones of protracted conflict across the world are more common than we would think.

Bagzi Dongeng (Fantasy Stories)

Within a week of being back in Thailand's far south in 2009, I decided to meet the local elites I had met in 2005. I wanted to find out what had transpired during my absence, and what this meant. With the conflict in the far south reaching a stalemate, what quickly became apparent to me was that these local elites were no longer interested in talking about Patani and its glorious past. It seemed that the action of that sinister and eminently sardonic character Time had prompted a reconsideration of their stipulation of a glorious past. It was as if, with time, they had fallen victim to their own adoration. Could it be that with the unsettledness in the region dragging on, the weight of the glorious past had become a burden to their present, never mind their future? The southern frontier provinces remained submerged in a sea of troubles – growing unemployment, alcoholism, drug abuse, economic contractions, violent crimes, persistent corruption, and wrongheaded security policies – so much so that the rehearsing of a certain glorious past was now put under tension, a tension that was no longer creative between history and memory. Perhaps the local elites that I had met in 2005, as well as a few self-professed Malay leaders with whom I have become acquainted over the years, were no longer interested in talking about Patani's glorious past because they had become preoccupied with something else, what I would call the economy of fear and terror.

Since the upsurge of violence in 2004 the general portrayal of the conflict has been one of grievances by the Malay Muslim communities against the state's marginalization and disrespect of their religion, culture, and history. Perhaps out of international sympathy and outrage, we have seen the flowing of funds into the region from Europe, the United States, the Middle East, Japan, and the Thai state, funding that materialized into what I call the talking task industry, an industry consisting of international and local NGOs, local and foreign security experts, local elites, think tanks, and job programs, with their endless conferences and workshops under the rubrics of *democracy*, *road maps*, *peace*, *harmony*, *development*, *security*, *reconciliation*, and, the latest, the economic community of the Association of Southeast Asian Nations (ASEAN), that has become the lexicon for talking about the current shadow insurgency. To be sure, these are the new forms of paternalism that come with the notion of security and neoliberalism. And yet all we see are periods of declining violence followed by escalating bombings, shootings, and deaths. Meanwhile peace is nowhere in sight.

In fact, years of a drawn-out and stalled "peace process" have seen the establishment and institutionalization of a gargantuan and far-reaching "peace industry." From Bangkok to Hatyai, and then to Pattani, Yala, and Narathiwat, and back to Bangkok, we have been hampered by agreements, road maps, and conditions that have created a thicket of red tape and limited the researchers' manoeuvrability. Layer upon layer of superficial "process" have obscured the path forward, which is why we are standing quite still. Even some of the participants in the peace process were fakes, those who had absolutely nothing to contribute. Welcome to Thailand's far south where we can choose the players, make up the rules, and set the timetable. As one of the participants put it to me at a conference, without any sense of shamefulness or remorse: "We don't want this game to end … The goal, it seems, is to simply stay in play." Similarly, one of the old guards who was the conference, one who clung to yesterday's narratives for his very legitimacy, put it to me with equal lack of remorse as he laughed and said, "Peace game is a long-term job program."

To be sure, the economy of fear and terror – combined with an explosion of uncoordinated NGO activities – has created new opportunities and the structures for indigenous elite networking. In a series of stereotypical images of timeless and primordialist Patani Malays reclaiming their ancestral land, ethnicity is often reckoned opportunistically by those who stand to benefit from it. In other words, ethnicity has become the politics and the economics of identity when Malay Muslimness is invoked as a form of identity politics and, very often, as a minority in a Buddhist-majority kingdom, as a community that is not only struggling for recognition but also being stigmatized.

Stigma, however can also be an enabling characteristic if one knows how to play with it. As pointed out by Joseph Hankins, on the politics of minorities and multiculturalism in Japan, and using Erving Goffman's (1969) metaphorical analysis, "while stigma can serve to limit the social authority of a stigmatized person, it also opens the possibility that that person might make a career out of their stigma … stigma as an enabling characteristic, a tool through which otherwise marginalized groups might achieve political agency. In forming the basis for a career, argues Goffman, stigma gives a person the means to take what to that point had been liability and 'play golf with it.' However, in order to wield the club, golfers must hold their hands and turn their bodies in particular ways" (Hankins 2012, 9–10). I see this in Thailand's far south among the ethnic entrepreneurs (and there are many of them), including some recent Malay Muslim graduates from the local university who are "playing golf" strategically and essentially with their minoritized and stigmatized status.[8]

Indeed, what we are seeing is a mode of governmental and security thinking that reveals a nihilism at the heart of the neoliberal project: the internal contradictions of the futures they claim to herald. I observed that local elites like Faosee, Farok, and others were busying themselves by attending these conferences and workshops because they seemed to feel licensed by their proximity to the scene in order to address it square on – though they mostly concerned themselves with talking about the conflict rather than about the reasons for it. Besides, part of the reason these local elites were no longer interested to talk about a glorious Patani was that history had found another voice, albeit a rather melodramatic one.

Following the recommendations of the Thai National Reconciliation Commission in 2006 to alleviate the violence, some efforts were made, for the first time, to publicly recognize the ethno-religious and historical distinctiveness of the far south. But there was a caveat: the commission affirmed the Islamic values and culture within the hospitable inclusiveness of an all-embracing Thainess, as belonging to all Thais born under an indivisible *phaendit* (land) and united under the benevolent rule of the monarchy. Under the rhetoric of reconciliation a television series about the Sultanate of Patani was produced, but it revealed its intentions when only a selected version of Patani history was broadcast.

To target what they thought was a pliant (if not a homogenized) Malay Muslim community that could be seduced by fantasy, the Ministry of Social Development and Human Security engaged a celebrity Thai romance novelist, popularly known by her pen name Thommayanti, to produce a particular history of Patani that symbolized its inalienability to Siam.[9] The melodramatic television series (this genre is called *lakhon* in Thai) was named *Raja Kuning*. Focusing on the female ruler ship by that name as an allegorical historical figure linking the past and the present, the series produced a peace-making history that depicted a respectful and benevolent minority-majority configuration. Indeed, as Askew (2009) points out, Thommayanti made it clear that the purpose of the series, though historically grounded, was to invent historical scenes and characters – albeit with contradictions and chronological inconsistency, even substituting fantasy for reality – in the hope of conveying a moral message to the Muslim communities in the historical present: namely, that Patani had a glorious past, a distinctive culture, and, more important, a harmonious relationship with Siam. Above all, the television series was about the lives, personal tragedies, and sacrifices of Raja Kuning of Patani and King Prasat Thong of the Ayutthaya (Siamese) kingdom, and their dedication to the welfare of their respective subjects. The word *sangop* (calmness, tranquility), invoked throughout the series to characterize both Raja Kuning and King Prasat, was a leitmotif to project a moralistic concern that hoped to restore some sense of reconciliation to the far south. Ignoring the possibility of public opprobrium, the melodramatic series began its screening in June 2008 and had a total of twenty episodes.

I asked Zul and Dolah at the service apartment in 2010 if they recalled watching the *Raja Kuning* series. After all, both of them, and all the staff members at the service apartments, watched a lot of television on a daily and nightly basis. The television in the lobby was never off. But both of them gave me a blank and puzzled look as they were drinking the three-in-one instant coffee. Dolah started to laugh as if he thought I was teasing him. He said, "Apa-lah ajarnn Kee, itu cerita tipu. Itu bukan Sejarah ... Ajarnn Kee, awak main main dengan kita, ke apa? Raja Kuning tu bukan sejarah kita, it bagzi dongeng." (Come on, Ajarnn Kee, the series was fake stories. There was nothing about it that was historical ... Ajarnn Kee, are you trying to tease us or what? *Raja Kuning* series was pure fantasies.) Dolah said that any Malay Muslims who had come of age since the 1940s would have recognized with contempt that the *Raja Kuning* series was an attempt to feed fantasies of a harmonious past relationship between Patani and Siam. Zul said that no one (meaning the Malay Muslims) was paying attention to it. Furthermore, it was a public secret that the series was nothing but state propaganda. Besides, his village chief had reminded everyone not to watch it unless they wanted to be insulted. As Zul put it, "As you know, Ajarnn Kee, we only watch the oft-repeated American action movies every other night and our regular weekend Thai boxing, as you so often remind us." They were both laughing, somewhat apologetically.

One of my field sites was at the three open-air markets in Muang Pattani where I had worked with the *mak pasar* food vendors. I will devote many pages in the next few chapters to talk about my engagement with these women. But for now, when talking to them about the *Raja Kuning* television series, I received the same response: that it was nothing short of *bagzi dongeng* (fantasy stories) that underestimated their discerning capabilities of not allowing their consciousness to be shaped by the impersonal forces of history, especially a history full of fantasy and manipulation. To put it slightly differently, if they were still stuck in fantasies and easily manipulated, then *Raja Kuning* did not achieve the deliverance that was intended by the Ministry of Social Development and Human Security. Not only was the series superficial in the sense that it made banal the mutilations of the Sultanate of Patani and the losses it had inflicted upon those who had suffered them, but it was also propaganda: *Raja Kuning* was produced for an older, simpler world that never actually existed.

Zainab, the one with her head always wrapped tightly with a blue headscarf, confessed to me that she had watched a few episodes and felt embarrassed for it. As she put it, "I laughed but also cried when I watched some of it. But I also knew it was not our history." She also said that it was melodramatic and addictive. Many *mak pasar* told me that *Raja Kuning* was nothing but *sensiwara* (stage play). Pla said she would probably have watched some of it if the series had been advertised in the first place as *bagzi dongeng*, as fiction. As she put it, "I have a small black-and-white television in my room. We [Pla and two other *mak pasar* who share the room] normally watched some television after we perform our prayers and while we are having dinner, say until nine, sometimes nine-thirty at night. What is there to do when you are stuck in a room? We would probably watch some just to pass time, but my husband heard from his friends that the series was *tipu* [lies], the usual propaganda. He asked me not to watch any of it."

At that moment, Mariyei, who was probably the eldest *mak pasar* at the market and who always cautioned me to be careful in my line of work, sarcastically said to me: "It was probably because the government made the mistake of airing it during our Waktu Maghrib. Surely, as Muslims we cannot forgo our prayers." That was not the first time Mariyei and others had alluded to me that the state was, once again, insensitive to their religion and their indignations. The melodramatic series was shown without a genuine concern for its susceptibility and, as such, it simply merited laughter. As Askew (2009) remarks, although the state had engaged a top film company and a celebrity romance novelist, they were the ones, in the end, who were addicted to these *bagzi dongeng*, and the agent chiefly responsible for that paralysis was the Ministry of Social Development and Human Security. To be sure, such attempts by state agents to manufacture a certain consciousness for what they thought was a pliant Muslim community were nothing new. What is striking for me and indeed hard to understand was the theatrical, even childish, nature of the deceit. More of a public secret, it seems to me that *Raja Kuning* was intended as a charade; hence it was all the more difficult for the Malay Muslims in the region to swallow. As such, my attempt to search for a mode of truth telling by my interlocutors led to unmasking not only the secrets behind the production and broadcasting of the *Raja Kuning* television series but also, following Walter Benjamin, a revelation that did justice to it (1977, 31).

By Way of Concluding

When the local elites cared to share their thoughts on the conflict when I met them in 2005, some of them stipulated the glorious history of Patani, a glorious Patani that was once considered one of the renaissances of the Muslim world. To be sure, there were tensions and contradictions within the constituted field of remembering Patani – one that forbids recourse to the notion of a singular culture of shared meanings or beliefs. For some local elites, their sense of history, equally fragmentary, if not out of synch, was concentrated in the stipulation of a certain gloriousness that favoured the semiotic value asserted by ancestral mandate in order for them to reassert their imagined social relations, traditions, and morality. Yet, others reprimanded me, saying that Patani was also inhabited by a logic and rhetoric in which the efficacy of religiosity had been displaced by its signifying capacity. Hence, the only terms within which they could assert their primacy were those of a generic pastness, which is why some of them tended to emphasize their *keturunan* (ancestry) based upon a generic Patani alleged glorious past rather than the relationships between particular ancestors and particular sites in the narrated landscape.

The point, of course, is not whether religiosity has descended from the past, but how Patani is being refigured according to the value accorded to pastness and religion – a value that is, I would argue, better understood as individual practices with singular histories. It seems likely that the value of such generic pastness is inherently a belated effect of modernity and not its displaced antecedent. Indeed, could remembering be treated as a form of agency that makes invidious and ideological use of the past in foundational ways in order to make sense of the current conflict? If so, what part does the past play in securing the alleged cohesiveness of the Malay communities, and, paradoxically, how do the ways in which a certain past is summoned up illuminate the shifting, restless character of their current political culture, in essence their Muslimness?

To those who claimed ancestry with the Patani aristocracy, in its inalienability the past could be seen as an affirmation of hierarchy, even as a heritage, as if their selves were enlarged and enhanced by the powers of the past even as these ideal memories of the past were an exaggeration or could be construed as a fiction. But with prolonged conflict these men were no longer interested in talking about a glorious

Patani. Indeed, they might have said that the glorious history of Patani survived because it had become an indescribable "loss" that could not return because the present had disqualified the past. Perhaps they realized that the past could never be recovered, not even by a Proust. Perhaps their reluctance to talk about an allegedly glorious past was their squalid attempt to save themselves from further moral embarrassment. Humility can be gratifying. Perhaps there was a confusion between remembering – or, I should say, celebrating a certain remembering – and forgetting. Lowenthal puts it eloquently: "Forgetting what displeases us is not only normal but necessary; … [it] demands concealing the unspeakable, the unpalatable, and the outdated. To sanitize a seamy past may aid understanding more than laying it bare … Those who knowingly tamper with the past, as in Orwell's doublethink, must then forget they have done so (1996, 161–2).[10]

Besides, the stipulation of a glorious (and harmonious) past has found a new voice, albeit one with just as little susceptibility. To the *mak pasar* and other Malay Muslims with whom I spoke, the melodramatic television series was, in their view, portraying their sultanate past as a squalid prank, a deliberate mockery of moral society perpetrated by a Thai celebrity romance novelist and the Ministry of Social Development and Human Security for their own twisted amusement. In other words, the difficulties of reality in the region far outstripped any indulgence in fantasy for these *mak pasar* and other Malay Muslims.

As long as the state chooses to broadcast sugar-coated *bangzi dongeng* of Patani's past, then the very difficult history that deals with the violent historical debris following the defeat of the Sultanate of Patani, followed by decades of assimilationist politics and practices, the charges of separatism and its aftermath, and the Dusun Nyior Islamic Awakening and its Reawakening, will not be broadcast but will remain silent. However, as long as the state continues to sidestep the historical political grievances of the Malay Muslims in the far south, the internal problem of managed democracy and inequality, and the politics of despair that the state has so successfully fostered, equally propagandistic alternative histories will be produced in furtive spaces, some by agents of the shadow insurgency and some by ordinary civilians.

Chapter Three

The *Mak Pasar*

Pictures of women eking out a living at open-air markets in conflict zones are often used worldwide to elicit sympathy and outrage. Their chillies – synecdoche here for the commodities they sell – constitutes another stereotypical image of these women living on the margins of the economy. What remains missing in most analyses, however, is the focus on the lives and livelihoods of these women who bear the hardships of maintaining family life in precarious circumstances.[1] Indeed, there has been far too much attention spent on the headline-grabbing drama of the state versus the so-called insurgents in the latest conflict, so much so that it has sidelined and obscured the more sordid everyday issues of poverty, street crime, drug abuses, and the nightmare life of kids. These are the fundamental issues that have become a profound enigma for parents.

This chapter touches on the lives and livelihoods of the *mak pasar* food vendors at three open-air markets in the township of Pattani.[2] It deals with aspects of how the current conflict shaped these *mak pasar*: how families were divided and how they coped with indefinite proximate displacement and separation; and how these conditions also gave structure to their lives, as if they needed the security of dogma in order to negotiate their way through the less-travelled corridors of living away from the familiarity of their homes and villages. Working with these *mak pasar*, I have come to understand that struggles do not always have to be confrontational. Indeed, "How are we to struggle?" is a more interesting question, a question of how they struggle with the current conflict in a non-confrontational manner.

Foremost, my engagement with the *mak pasar* allowed me to uncover life at violent sites by seeking to find out not who was killing whom and why, but violence's descent into the ordinary (Das 2007). Following Das, we need to think of the mutual absorption of violence "as always attached to the ordinary as if there were tentacles that reach out from the everyday and anchor the event to it in some specific ways" (2007, 7). In other words, the battlefields in Thailand's far south are fought not only between state agents and the so-called insurgents but also, to invoke Thiranagama's work (2011, 2–3) on post–civil war in Sri Lanka, "as mundane existence, and on the life cycles of individuals, families, and communities that are generated and generate the social life of protracted war." My research touches on the violence that these *mak pasar* habitually experience, which is intertwined with the other forms of violence that have held sway in Thailand's far south and in other contexts in which the manifold forms of oppression against women arise from multiple institutional and structural patriarchy – violence that is multiple and mundane in the quotidian aspects of life, out of which identities are shaped, and experiences are coerced and engendered.

When I first visited the three open-air markets at Muang Pattani in 2009 and approached the *mak pasar*, they were puzzled as to why I would be interested in their lives and livelihoods. It took a while for them to stop asking me, and asking among themselves, why I chose to spend so much time at their open-air markets where it was always blazingly hot and humid, ridden with flies and mosquitoes, and not forgetting the heavy smell of fat from the chicken and beef, as well as the entrails, internal organs, brains, and even a half skull of a cow or a goat smashed open with bulging eyes. In fact, the *mak pasar* always felt uncomfortable on my behalf because there was no chair for me to sit on and the grounds were always wet and fetid with trees (or weeds) growing out of the walls and with drains surrounding the market. This was far from the veranda anthropology that our ancestors used to call their field sites. It took me a while to get used to the environment, and after that I did not even find myself shrinking from the large, bristly rats that hurried along the open drains by the side of the market, and especially by the garbage dumps.

I can still recall their curious, puzzled, and inquisitorial looks when I told them, as best as I could, that I was a sociocultural anthropologist, someone who wanted to know how they were coping with the latest conflict. To be honest, I am still not entirely sure that they understood, even to this day, the reasons, motives, or concerns of my research. However, beneath the measured tone of their curiosity, most of them struck me as welcoming and jovial. Through what I took to be our mutual enjoyment in talking with one another, I was learning about their lives and livelihoods while they raised their frustrations about the endless conflict, the state, and other issues, in particular their concerns for their children, especially their sons and grandsons.

In every aspect these open-air markets were gendered public spaces in that most, if not all, of the vendors and their customers were women, in particular Malay Muslim women. Apart from the vendors selling eggs, chickens, beef, seafood, vegetables, spices, chillies, and so on, there were many other women vendors, some of them quite elderly, who set up their goods outside the open-air market boundaries proper, sitting on the ground with large plastic sheets laid out before them displaying their seasonal tropical fruits. There were some occasional male vendors at the market, and they also set up beyond the open-air market boundaries, selling aphrodisiacs prepared traditionally and packaged as the best sexual, magical, mystical pill, or selling the usual traditional medicinal plant Tongkat Ali (*Eurycoma longifolia*) that purportedly could help one not only sustain happiness in marriage but also have multiple wives. These power pills were ten times better than modern Western Viagra, I would imagine. But I often wondered why these men were selling such merchandise near the open-air market when most, if not all, of the vendors and their customers were women. The *mak pasar* would laugh, as if they were embarrassed, when I jokingly asked them about the potency of these traditional aphrodisiacs. They would say, "*Entah*" (Don't know), if they ever responded. They knew I was teasing them.

It was at these open-air markets that I saw what resembled Bakhtin's ([1965] 1984) description of the carnivalesque marketplace in Rabelais's time, a place that had the reputation of shaping and inducing lively conversations with the qualities of frankness and teasing, and the modulation of laughter about each other, about the government, and about the anthropologist. However, similar to Deborah Kapchan's analysis of a Moroccan open-air market, "the liberating forces of the carnivalesque" need to be relativized here, for "the laugher [did] not drown out the real sufferings" (1996, 35–6) that these *mak pasar* had to endure as they worked tirelessly to support their families in precarious circumstances. As this chapter shows, doubts and insecurity were rampant about the uncertainty of the violence, generating anxiety about becoming unwitting subjects of violent action or retribution (Abraham and Nakaya 2007).

Most of my conversations with the *mak pasar* centred on small details of their daily business transactions and on just about anything they wanted to ask me about Canada. They were very frank with me as to why I should have a religion (hopefully Islam), and they would question my marital status, saying that I should remarry so that I would have a companion when I got older. In fact, two of their favourite questions they never failed to ask me each time I went back for more fieldwork were: "Have you adopted a religion yet?" "Have you remarried yet?"

However, behind their frankness, teasing, and laughter, there were also silences, especially when it came to the current shadow insurgency. For the most part, these *mak pasar* would claim uncertainty or being *kurang faham* (not sure) regarding the political situation in the revival of the latest recurring conflict, and especially who were these shadow insurgents. As and when they were willing to share their views of the current conflict, they were ones who did not claim authoritative certainty of the origins of the violence or, for that matter, its ultimate goals. Thus, their usual responses were: *"tak tahu"* (don't know), *"tak berani nak cakap"* (not brave enough to talk), *"takut"* (scared or feared), or *"susah nak cerita"* (difficult to talk about it).

As in Myanmar and other sites of political conflict, "such wilful ignorance of the political situation is as much a response to repression as armed insurgency" (Skidmore 2004, 8). In essence their silences or lack of knowledge should be read not in the sense of absence but, rather, as that of numbness (as silence and inactivity). They can also be read as a common response to questions about fear, as part of the process of ensuring that fear remains suppressed, buried inside. In other words, their silences can be seen as everyday tactics to keep fear in the back of their minds so as to allow them to focus on the immediacy of their everyday lives and livelihoods.

This was similar to Skidmore's description of Burmese living under the junta government: "it is not easy for people conditioned by violence to free themselves from the enervating miasma of fear even as they don't like to talk about it. In fact, not talking about fear is a crucial strategy to navigate successfully through the topography of 'terror as usual'" (2004, 41). If fear is revealed at all, it is usually not through speech but through the gaps and omissions in speech or, at times, through a bodily gesture, a shrug of the shoulder, that is a speech act in and of itself. This fear is not normally revealed, except through its absence. Like pain, Skidmore adds, fear is primarily felt and defies the ability of language to hold its experiential weight, on Burmese living under the junta government. But, more important, "[f]ear itself is finely nuanced" (2004, 46)

Besides their silences and unsureness, the *mak pasar* would also invoke the blasé response *biasa* when I asked them what they felt about the latest conflict. Their perplexities gave me pause. I found myself caught in this tension: where I was hoping to hear the descriptive words that would describe the conflict, fear, and paranoia, if not pain or death, what I got instead was *"Biasa."* As I briefly mentioned earlier, the Malay word *biasa* can mean "getting used to it; nothing unusual or special; plain, ordinary; boring," and the list of meanings and usages of the word can be endless. What then, contextually, indexically, or referentially, does *biasa* really mean for those living and having to engage with the difficulties of reality in Thailand's far south? This is not just a philosophical or linguistic question but also a philosophically and psychologically engaged anthropological question.

What were some of the referents for their blasé response *biasa*? Surely, they were indexical; they evoked many other emotions, experiences, and troubles that were not stated. Is this blasé response a protective shield from something hidden underneath it, some kind of indexicality or meaning? I like to think so. Or was it that, by offering this blasé response, they were trying to tell me that they refused to be awed by the violence – as distinct from not being "scared any more." This would resonate with the Palestinians' utterance of *ta'wwudna* (we've gotten used to it). *Ta'wwudna*, as Lori Allen emphasizes, "was the constant refrain I would get from Palestinians, a kind of everyday practices whereby they manage, get by, and adapt by simply 'getting used to it'" (2008, 457). Or, as Buch Segal echoes, "enduring suffering in Palestine has become as ordinary as the occupation itself. It is *'adi'* [normal]" (2016, 175). But there was more than just "getting used to it." In my interlocutors' utterance of *biasa*, there was an entire experience – of fear and unease, proximate displacement, the loss of liveliness, the loss of embodiment and emplacement, and an insecure existence – that was felt unevenly. These are the kinds of experiences that are harder to tabulate and quantify. These are the kinds of experiences that are less visible compared to the direct violence of deaths and casualties reported by the Thai media. Like the utterances of the Palestinians and other internally displaced communities who are enduring difficulties of reality within their own respective contexts, my interlocutors' utterance of *biasa* can also be seen as a source of psychological strength, a source of performative speech act to cope with the madness, the hell that repeats itself.

Furthermore, those who uttered the word *biasa* in reference to the reality they lived in had as its object the elimination of the triumph of the adversaries (both state agents and shadowy insurgents). If I am to suggest that *biasa* is also their way to be humorous, I am not suggesting this is a joke in bad taste. I am fully aware that what I am touching upon is a reality of unimaginable precarity and pain; at the same time I am appealing to those inner and mental resources that have often saved humans from total annihilation, one of them being a sense of humour; throughout history humour has served as a vehicle of strength, a vehicle for ideas and strategies that would otherwise seem like madness or delirium (Cortazar 1994, 175).

Getting back to the word *biasa*, and considering Wittgenstein's comments that "every word has a meaning" and that, in a somewhat circular fashion, "this meaning correlated with the word. It is the object for which the word stands" ([1953] 2009, 2), I ask: What then does the blasé response to the current conflict, *biasa*, really mean? As Crapanzano cynically points out, "we know, as Wittgenstein knows, that language – words, meaning – is more complicated, as Wittgenstein himself does remark that embedded in every language is an entire psychology [and a whole mythology]. To be sure, words do more. Like names, they affirmed, indexicalized a certain reality, if not ideology, referentialized or fantasized – and the historical and contemporary assumptions that underlie that reality and ideology: innerness, outerness, permanence, substance, specificity, referentiality itself" (1993, 91–2). Indeed, Taussig similarly points out, "as Wittgenstein noted, a whole mythology is deposited in our language, including, we might note, the mythology of the real and of language as transparent" (2003, 35).

Contextually, the word *biasa* might refer to this entire psychology embedded in another of Wittgenstein's concepts, namely "forms of life." Buch Segal (2016) who studied contemporary Palestine, cites philosopher Stanley Cavell's idea of forms of life:

> We learn and teach words in certain contexts, and then we are expected, and expect others, to be able to project them into further contexts. Nothing ensures that this projection will take place (in particular, not the grasping of universals nor the grasping of books of rules), just as nothing ensures that we will make, and understand, the same projections. That on the whole we do is a matter of sharing routes of interest and feeling, modes of response, sense of humor and significance and of fulfillment, of what is outrageous, of what is similar to what else, what a rebuke, what forgiveness, of when an utterance is an assertion, when an appeal, when an explanation – all the whirl of organism Wittgenstein calls "forms of life." Human speech and activity, sanity and community, rests on nothing more, but nothing less than this. (Cavell 1976, 52)

In my attempt to elucidate the meaning of the blasé response *biasa*, I am also reminded of something Evans-Pritchard once wrote that was posted as an epigraph on the web page of *HAU: Journal of Ethnographic Theory*: "As every experienced fieldworker knows, the most difficult task in social anthropological fieldwork is to determine the meaning of a few key words, upon an understanding of which the success of the whole investigation depends." To emphasize, along with Evans-Pritchard, Wittgenstein, Cavell, and Crapanzano, what then does *biasa* really mean for those living in Thailand's far south, for those who grew up there, who live there and have nowhere to go, no way out?

This set of related questions has been haunting as well as guarding my ethnographic enterprise on Thailand's far south all those years as I try to see and feel through the epistemic murk of the entire psychology and mythology surrounding the word *biasa*. How can I elucidate the difficulties of their response *biasa*, by tracing every possible overlap between the blasé words they used in describing how they felt about the current reviving violence, and the anonymous reality that clearly reflected upon why they were tired of explaining to themselves, not to mention to an outsider, about their ongoing difficulties of reality? I often find myself asking: How can I write about their situation, their existence, in a locally meaningful way for people that have become my friends and acquaintances?

Choiceless Decision

Zainab, who is from Narathiwat province, was fifty-three years old when I came to know her in 2009. As the second wife, she was living with her husband (who was from Pattani province), his first wife, and their children in a village on the outskirts of Muang Pattani. She herself had three sons and a daughter from her first marriage. When I went back the following year, I found out that she was no longer living in her husband's village. Towards the end of 2009 Zainab had decided to share a room with two other *mak pasar* close to their open-air market. With the conflict reaching a stalemate – meaning "not peace, not war" – many *mak pasar* had arranged to live either with their relatives or in shared rented rooms in Muang Pattani.[3] For them, it was not so much out of convenience as out of safety. As I will elaborate shortly, it was a choiceless decision.[4]

Aishah, a *mak pasar* who sells beef, the one who always had her head wrapped tightly with a blue headscarf, explained: "The roads on the outskirts are not safe any more in the early morning and evening hours ... these are the *waktu geriya* (hours of the guerrillas). Travelling from our villages to work and back at these hours has become an endurance test, *penat* [psychologically tiring]." She further emphasized: "We normally get here before five in the morning. We leave our house a half-hour before five when it is still dark. In the evening we used to pack up around eight but not any more. Even now if we start packing up and head home around seven, seven o'clock is already getting dark. It is already the *waktu geriya*."

I was intrigued by what she called *waktu geriya*, the temporal topography of fear associated with guerrillas. Pla, a plump woman who sold vegetables, complained to me that even though her village was only a forty-minute motorbike ride, there had been too many roadside explosions in recent years, especially during the *waktu geriya*, making it unsafe for her to commute back and forth from her village to the market. She said: "Day and night is a different world around here. One is *waktu tahann* [hours of the army], the other is *waktu geriya*. Now that I don't have to be on the road during the *waktu geriya*, I close at seven. I had to pack up at six-thirty when I was living in my village. That's half an hour of business lost."

The owner of a tea shop on the outskirt of Muang Pattani also raised the same concern. "Day and night are different worlds around here. One is *waktu tahann*, the other is *waktu geriya*." He then laughed, saying, "When you travel at night you won't see the *tahann* at the checkpoints ... they would be like sitting ducks. The checkpoints, and there are many of them, are always empty during the night." When I told him I came across checkpoints manned by the *tahann* during the nights I was travelling from Sungai Kolok or Tak Bai in the province of Narathiwat to Muang Pattani, he pointed out that those were trunk roads, the roads between the different townships in the three provinces. "Not on the quiet roads connecting the villages within each province," he emphasised, before daring me: "Why don't you come visit me at night, here at my shop and see if there are any *tahaan* at the checkpoints along the way. *Kosong!* [Empty!]" He was laughing. I do not think I would want to risk my life travelling on a remote road during the *waktu geriya* in a spatial and temporal, as well as psychological, sense.

There was another reason it was unsafe for the *mak pasar* to commute during the *waktu* geriya. Pla asked, "Have you heard of the Chor Ror Bor?" She was referring to the Village Development and Self-Defence Volunteers and other civilian-based defence forces. "Many men in my village belong to them ... Having our men volunteer also makes our village unsafe. It makes us seen as collaborators, collaborators with the *tahann*. It makes us seem as if we are openly against the insurgency. It thus makes us vulnerable to use the road during the *waktu geriya*."

The word *insurgency* in Thailand's far south today beckons to a range of aspiration, from separatist to terrorist, from an aspiration of respect to one of murder, as carried out – and this is crucial – by relatively young men. And the obvious fact is that none of my Malay Muslim interlocutors had openly told me if they supported or condemned the insurgency. This has to be acknowledged. For those living outside of Thailand's far south it is easy to take sides, but, as Taussig reflects on the decision that his interlocutors had to make, "such 'support' may turn out to be a shifting sort of thing, supporting 'the lesser evil.' Moreover, support implies choice. But how much choice does a person have? If you are not supporting us, you are dead – or worse, someone in your family is" (Taussig 2003, 15).

By the end of 2008 the *tahann* had trained and armed more than thirty thousand civilians, operating under an integrated scheme of civilian-based self-defence forces. These forces consist of the following groups in Thailand's far south: Village Protection Volunteers (Or Ror Bor); Village Development and Self-Defence Volunteers (Chor Ror Bor); Volunteer Defence Corps (Or Sor); National Defence Volunteers (Tor Sor Por Chor); Civil Defence Volunteers (Or Por Phor Chor); and Village Scouts (Luk Sua Chaoban). In addition, through three channels the government also supplied arms to Buddhists (including monks) and officials perceived as main soft targets: the dissemination of small arms to civilian forces; the ease of firearms regulations; and the subsidization of gun purchases. Consequently, such policies led to a huge increase in the number of guns circulating in the far south (Askew 2009). The strategies of recruiting civilians to combat the insurgency have had some controversial impacts on the ground, particularly for the Malay Muslim population, as witnessed by the number of assassinations carried out by insurgents of Muslims who belonged to any of the civilian-based self-defence forces.[5] Besides, the privatization of security and state support for civilian armament only substantiates the fact that the Thai state is struggling to fulfil its fundamental task of providing security for its citizens in Thailand's far south (Askew 2009).

Many *mak pasar* complained that their villages had little or no choice to volunteer or not for these defence forces when they were approached by security agents. Mariyei explained the conundrum they faced: "To the government, we [the Malays] are all suspects, sympathetic towards the insurgency. You tell me, what can we do when they come to our villages for volunteers? Can we just say no?" Their decision was that of a choiceless decision.

A Malay senator whom I shall call Faizal once told me that the consequences of enlisting Malay Muslims into these civilian-based defence forces have made them one of the soft targets, not only for the village chiefs and their deputies but also for any villagers who have enlisted into the program. To volunteer or not is not much of a choice for them. Either way it makes them "suspected." On the notion of "being suspected," Catherine Smith (2015) writes that during the thirty years of conflict in Aceh, not only those under suspicion, but also their family, friends, and the entire village, carried with them a sense of threat to their livelihoods. Faizal pointed out to me that the way the *tahann* had been fighting the latest insurgency, just as they had in the past, was a war among the Malay Muslims. Malay Muslims were the targets both to be won and to oppose. In other words, the Malay Muslims in the far south were homogenized as one.

To be sure, Western scholars are also guilty of homogenizing the Malay Muslims. To counter McCargo's anecdote that "if you scratch a Malay Muslim you would find a separatist underneath" (2009, 4), Askew points out that "it is just as common to scratch a Malay Muslim and you would hear him/her uttering the expression *Rak Chart* or *Rak Thai* (love the country / love Thailand)" (2010a, 144). Askew goes on to note that McCargo's essentializing anecdote has the tendency to reduce a host of messy and often contradictory views and positions, including their orientations towards the different Islamic movements that compete in the region (144). As I have briefly noted thus far, what are rarely distinguished in political commentary and polemic are the heterogeneous class origins and varying ideological commitments and religious adherents among the diverse Malay Muslims in Thailand's far south; not only are they not all potential insurgents or sympathetic to the insurgency, but they are also not all businessmen or democrats, and their views on politics are not always the same.

Going back to my conversation with Faizal: he asked, rhetorically, "Do you think the *tahann* were making mistakes after mistakes or were they purposely made to further infuriate the Malay communities? In fact, the insurgents are only too glad to see the government making mistakes after mistakes. Those *mak pasar* are correct. Chor Ror Bor makes their villages vulnerable, makes them suspects." He went on to say that tapping rubber latex has also become a dangerous livelihood activity of late. Indeed, many *mak pasar* told me their husbands had stopped tapping latex in their rubber gardens. As Pla put it, "*Mana tak takut?* [How not to be scared?] Sometimes both husband and wife were killed execution style in their rubber garden. It is on the news all the time. Husband and wife killed in the wee hours of the morning when they were tapping latex ... They were never given any chance to live." What was once a vital source of livelihood had become a potential graveyard.

Once again, Mariyei let out a heavy sigh and raised her voice: "The thing that really makes me sick to my stomach is when I hear of cases where both husband and wife were killed. You read about these tragic stories in the newspapers, something that happened here in Pattani, in Yala or Narathiwat. Who is going to look after these poor children when their parents were killed, without their grandparents around? At my village in Yala [province] I know some children are now staying at orphanages. It is sad to know that many more will end up the same unless these senseless brutal killings stop. This is Muslims killing Muslims ... Can *they* know we really do not have any choices when it comes to volunteering for these civilian defence forces? We are trapped. Either way, we are struck." Mariyei was infuriated with such brutal madness, madness that was creating the supply of orphans, not to mention widows, in the region.[6]

Tapping rubber trees for latex has always been one of the major economic activities in the region. However, it has become not only a dangerous activity of late but also uneconomical. With the falling price of latex in recent years, it was common to hear my interlocutors complaining, "What's the point when three kilos of latex only fetched 100 baht [US$2.80]? It's a waste of time, not to mention the risk."[7] As such, without the source of income from rubber latex, the *mak pasar*'s earnings became even more important to their households. Although this was supposed to reflect their centrality in household economic production, it did not translate into reality. With more and more *mak pasar* making the choiceless decision to share rooms near their open-air markets, their absences from their villages only heightened their insecurity, insecurity about their children, especially their sons, but also about their husbands. Such is the task facing these *mak pasar*: not of escaping but of engaging with the difficulties of reality that constitute the geography of living in these conditions of "not peace, not war" in Thailand's far south.

In many ways the *mak pasar* decision to make the choiceless decision to live with their relatives within the township of Pattani or to share rooms can be interpreted as one way of engaging in all the forms and tactics of precarity in order to be safer, or at least to feel so. As Anna Tsing reminds us, "One way of keeping precarity in mind is that it makes us remember that changing with circumstances is the stuff of survival" (2015, 27). Tsing further points out that "survival in a precarious environment also forces us to acknowledge our vulnerability to others, the help or the services of others, with or without intent" (29), a set of sensibilities I observed among the *mak pasar*. However, such choiceless living arrangements were not without its sacrifices as it posed an existential and emotional dilemma for the *mak pasar*, cutting them off not only from village festivities but also from its daily affairs, which meant the familiarity of daily life, the simplicity of gestures, the unaffected expression of feelings, and the rupture of their domestic lives. Emotionally charged, some *mak pasar* would emphasize: "We are mothers, we are the ones providing the *sayang* [loving parental care] to our children, while their fathers represent authority. And now with us no longer living at home, should we expect our husbands to be both fathers and mothers in the families?"[8] Following Elizabeth Dunn's ethnography on the internally displaced persons (IDPs) in Georgia, the *mak pasar*'s choiceless decision can also been interpreted as a "'burdened agency,' of people acting under strong constraint" (2018, 61).

Proximate Displacement

It was frequent to hear these *mak pasar*, who worked seven days a week at the open-air markets, complaining to each other, and to me, about how they missed – in temporal, spatial, and affective senses – their *kampung* (villages), their *rumah* (homes), their *keluarga* (families), caring for their parents, and attending to the welfare of their children, grandchildren, or younger brothers. Even though the open-air markets were always lively, they often lamented that it did not have the same quality of liveliness as that of their *keluarga* (families) and the bucolic settings of their villages. They missed performing the Waktu Isha (dusk prayer) in the evenings with their family and the Waktu Subuh (dawn prayer) within the quietude of their house; preparing and serving breakfast; the smell of spices permeating the house; the evening meals after getting home from the market; the giving and receiving of food with neighbours; the tone of conversation and sociality around the village; the sound of children; grooming their cats; and so on.

Zainab once told me that cooking breakfast for her family, as ordinary a task as it might sound, was how her day started. She would cook breakfast, get her children ready for school, and make sure her husband and in-laws had their first cup of sweet coffee to start their days. Occasionally she would prepare some special dishes in the evening so that her family could have them the next morning. She smiled when saying that. In short, she missed the liveliness of her family from which and into which sounds, smoke, smells, and taste permeated. Her laughter registered, ironically, the absence of familiarity that had been taken away from her by the current conflict that once again afflicted the region.

Aishah described what was lost so emotionally, so beautifully, in the intensity of her exclamations about being territorially anchored in her home and village: "Our home in the *kampong* is not only a physical but also an intimate existence. We took in everything – rain on the trees and on our roofs, mice above the ceiling, the smell of *belacan*,[9] the mangoes, especially those that we would pluck before they are fully ripe and stuff them inside the rice jar, ahhh! … such fragrance each time we took the lid off the jar when we needed to cook our rice, and the smell of the mango permeating the entire kitchen, the entire house, and what about our cats ... sometimes playing with each other, chasing each other. At night and in the morning we would hear the sound of birds, sounds of adult conversation from the kitchen. The ways we were preoccupied, our homes were more or less emotionally proofed against what was happening outside ... Together as adults we were there to insulate our children and other young ones from the outside."

Missing, and worried sick about the safety of their children, especially their sons, some *mak pasar* decided to take the risk of moving back to their villages. That did not last, however, as eventually they once again decided to share rented rooms within Muang Pattani and into the liminal time and space of another bout of proximate displacement. Cliché along the lines of "You just can't go back to living in the villages" does not even begin to apply to the mix of distress, fear, and disgust that overtook these *mak pasar* when they moved back to their villages and later had to return to Muang Pattani. Their decisions to move back to their villages felt like a momentary layover, always followed by fresh departures, reaffirming the proximate displacement that they must endure and engaged with. Severed from the daily social, psychological, and psychical relationships with their homes and villages, from their attachments to places and the structures and practices they used to create meaning, these *mak pasar* often complained that they felt "out of place" with their current living arrangement, the emotional labour they had to endure, lacking their familiar landscape and soundscape. This lack led to a certain loss of embodiment and emplacement, the fusion of which were fundamental to their efficacious embodiment of self, space, and time.

Following Merleau-Ponty (1962), Edward Casey (2009) reminds us of the intimate relationship between embodiment and emplacement, of place and home. He examines how to be *in place* is to know and to become aware of one's very consciousness and sensuous presence in the world. Casey argues that the experience of place and home is the most fundamental form of embodied experience – the site of a powerful fusion of self, space, and time.

Thiranagama writes about proximate displacement as a ground of sociality, of inhabiting a world transformed by the conflict during the civil war in Sri Lanka. As she puts it, "Proximate displacement ... creates very different ways of inhabiting loss from that of external displacement ... For those who have left the country, 'home' can remain in a static time left at the point of departure, with tantalizing scents, memories, sounds of another landscape markedly different from the one they inhabit. In contrast, [proximate displacement] meant that their past landscape has not disappeared from sensory experience ...

whenever they could, in ceasefires, they visited their homes" (2011 147). Regardless, both proximate and external displacement are critical measurements of belonging and indices of loss, of an existential and material dilemma for those who are experiencing the loss.

In a beautifully written ethnography of the Manggarai people of West Flores in Indonesia, Catherine Allerton describes how liveliness is what Manggarai people value most about their houses: "Sharing a room and a hearth is a source of much pleasure in Manggarai life" (2013, 20). Liveliness, we are told, not only makes her interlocutors feel at ease, but it is "said to make life 'feel delicious,' [and] it also has important protective qualities. The sounds of talk, the crying of children, the noise of machete sharpening or a weaving sword banging on a loom – these are all part of what makes a house alive, 'lively,' and therefore protective" (54).

This kind of liveliness was what the *mak pasar* valued and missed. Indeed, proximate displacement was no less the source of powerful attachments to their homes and villages, their subjectivities and textures. Their comments and laments were biographical commentaries on the production of selves and spaces in time of conflict. Or, to put it differently, these were their senses of normality that had been severed by their new living arrangement. As Navaro-Yashin (2002, 42) describes, the normal situation is what creates place, as material things and spaces are linked in complex relations with one another. Their proximate displacement is predicated on the existence of, love for, and bond with, their home and village; this does not mean that their homes and love for homes are lost, but that loss is inherent in the very existence of both.

What anguished the *mak pasar* most was that they could not be physically present in their homes and villages to make sure that their sons, grandsons, or younger brothers did not get into trouble. They strove to prevent their children and other family members from having any contact with state agents as well as with agents of the shadow insurgency. They were the mothers who made life safe for their children and grandchildren amid the chaos, counselling their children of the dangers of informants, whether these were state agents or the insurgents, the latter being anybody who was ubiquitously Muslim. In short, they taught them the importance of self-censorship.

Once again Mariyei let out a heavy sigh: "And here we are in the year 2557 [2014 in the Common Era), entering the tenth year of the current violence. Do you see any end in sight?" Her questions were rhetorical, indicating the collective political fatigue, if not political impotence and resigned acceptance that there was nothing that could be done but to endure and engage with the difficulties of reality. This reminds me of Elizabeth Dunn's ethnographic question on the permanent notion of transition for IDPs in Georgia who are turned into refugees in their own country: "How do displaced people work against being stuck in prolonged liminality?" (2019, 8). Like the IDPs in Georgia, these *mak pasar* were stuck in a prolonged, if not permanent, liminality, and it was the indefinite nature of these separations that presented the most anguish in their lives – in which the celebrations, rituals, and rhythm of village life were interrupted. In many cases, marriages were broken and homes disintegrated.

Indefinite proximate displacement, however, also teaches displaced persons humility. It has a very strong metaphysical dimension, and for them to ignore it is to cheat themselves of the meaning of what has happened to them, to ossify themselves into uncomprehending victims. It is in the high thin air of proximate displacement that this chapter touches on how one learns to see multiple significances in even the smallest sensation. A private moment of remembering a favourite site in one's home or village, for example, can resonate in political, historical, and psychological chambers. Last, but not least, this chapter also acknowledges the resourcefulness these *mak pasar* drew upon – both physical and mental – as "bodily techniques" (Mauss 1973) in order to live sanely in an insane world.

Fear and Troubles

The *mak pasar* were always happy to see me each time I went back for more ethnographic fieldwork. That was no different in 2013. In fact, it had become a yearly ritual that each time they saw me back, they would call out my name in full – "Kee Howe Yong, Kee Howe Yong" – as they welcomed me back into their fold, into their open-air markets. And each time they would ask how long I was planning to stay, or say that I had gained or lost weight, or that I looked older or younger. And, of course, they never failed to ask if I had taken their advice to remarry or adopt a religion, hopefully their religion. They were alarmed when I once playfully told them I had not adopted any religion because I knew too much about religion. I also told them that I believed in evolution and then tried my best to explain what I meant by evolution. They looked at me bug-eyed. "Do you really believe we came from apes, that chimpanzees are our close cousins?" They thought I was crazy.

Regardless, everyone at the market was cheerful that morning in 2013; they were happy to see me once again – everyone except Suraiya. Suraiya, who always wore a colourful, and usually bright red, headscarf and loved to sing, was not her usual, cheerful self that morning. She was by herself at her stall and tried to look away when I looked in her direction. I sensed that something was different but thought it best to be less intrusive, especially on my very first day back. I left her alone and continued to chat with the other *mak pasar* as I handed out my yearly duty-free chocolates. Later that day several *mak pasar* quietly confided to me that Suraiya had just came back from her village. I sensed there was something odd but did not know what. It was only when I went through and expanded on my notes that evening that I realized something was different. I realized that whenever any of these *mak pasar* went back or came back from their villages, whether to attend a wedding, funeral, or other urgent matters, they or their fellow *mak pasar* would always mention the name of the village they came back from. But that morning they only mentioned to me that Suraiya had just come back from her village, instead of the name of her village. And unlike most of the other *mak pasar*, Suraiya had never revealed to me where she came from.

Several days later Mariyei confided to me that Suraiya was under a lot of stress because her seventeen-year-old son had disappeared and her twelve-year-old son's *ponok* had been shut down by the authority for accusation of being "a jihad factory."[10] This was one of the biggest *ponok* in the far south, something I will touch upon in chapter 7. I could tell that Mariyei was clearly uncomfortable in divulging such private information, judging from a few twitches in her eyes. But that was not the end of it. Through time, from snippets here and there, I found out that Suraiya's younger brother had been in and out of prisons on insurgency-related suspicion. The *mak pasar* with whom I spoke all seemed to know and to empathize. What had happened to Suraiya's sons and brother appeared familiar to them, and it was through such snippets of information that I also heard about the fear and troubles of other *mak pasar*. But the fact that Mariyei and others were not explicitly engaged in telling me in detail about Suraiya's sons and brother, but rather they narrated here and there upon my probing, only goes to show how their reluctance to talk about events that might link them to the insurgency was an important part of what was said. And there were always some elements of guilt, even betrayal, when the snippets were revealed to me. They went like this: "Her husband, or brother, or son was … enough, I have said too much." Mariyei once asked me why anyone would reveal that someone in their family had been charged with allegedly insurgency-related misfortunes. "*Tidak mungkin* [Highly improbable]," she said emphatically. She reiterated a point that many had voiced, "Here in the three provinces, any one of us Malays is a suspect."

I wanted to ask Suraiya about her sons and younger brother but could not muster the courage, especially in front of the other *mak pasar* as that might also make them uncomfortable. Working with these *mak pasar* who always preferred to talk about their livelihood issues rather than the current conflict, and who always found ways to laugh about this or that issue, I found it incredibly difficult, if not awkward, to probe each time I learned about their families' misfortunes – whether it was when a family member had been questioned or arrested by the authorities, or had gone missing, or their sons' or grandsons' *ponok* had been shut down by the authority; or worse still, if one of their kin had become another statistic. The tight spatial arrangement of the open-air markets also made it very rare for me to talk to any *mak pasar* individually about sensitive issues.

My opportunity came one day when I saw Suraiya at the Kentucky Fried Chicken outlet inside the department store across from the market. She smiled awkwardly and, to justify why she was eating at KFC, where the chicken was far more expensive than the local fried chickens by the roadside, Suraiya showed me the discount coupons she had accumulated. She also said she could use some air conditioning as the weather had been extremely hot the past several days, if not weeks. "Hanyat lah," she emphasized.[11] These *mak pasar* had been complaining about the extreme weather, a sullen heat averaging thirty-four degrees Celsius. As they put it to me in the mornings, "Sekarang baru sepuluh pagi. Masih panjang lagi sebelum matahari turun. Hangat lah." (It is now only ten in the morning. It is a long way before sunset. Really humid.)

Sitting across from me, Suraiya offered me a piece of the chicken, which I politely declined because I had already had my lunch. I felt this was my opportunity while she was eating a piece of drumstick and sipping ice-cold Coca-Cola. I started by asking what I thought was the least sensitive question, about her youngest son's *ponok*. She forced a smile but kept quiet. She was uncomfortable. Finally, she said, "Don't know yet. We have not decided whether to enrol him at a government school or …" She did not finish the sentence. I waited for her to continue. Then sounding somewhat optimistic, she said, "Perhaps I should wait for his *ponok* to reopen or I can enrol him at another *ponok* even though they are not as famous. Getting an education is very important. Who knows, *Alhamdulillah!* [Praise be to Allah!], someday he might get a scholarship to pursue his studies in the Middle East."[12] She and I smiled.

Apparently Surayai was aware that Mariyei had divulged to me about her eldest son and her brother. "My eldest son is now in Kuala Lumpur. He works at a *tum yum* restaurant. He is safe. *Alhamdulillah!* Perhaps the restaurant is close to where your sister lives," she laughed. I laughed as well.[13] She paused before continuing: "As for my brother, he cannot go to Kuala Lumpur. He cannot leave Thailand. The government has spoken to my parents about a certain scheme, the Bawah Rakyat Balik (Bring People Home). They say if my brother is willing to confess … he would then go for rehabilitation."[14] I felt relief that it was Suraiya who had said something about her eldest son and younger brother instead of me asking about them. She then hurried to eat her KFC chicken as raindrops were beginning to hit the windowpane. Across the street the *mak pasar* were putting up their umbrellas. Judging from the raindrops, it was going to be a very wet day at the market, but at least the rain would finally get rid of the humidity, or some of it.

I should elaborate on why it was always Mariyei who revealed to me snippets of information regarding some of her fellow *mak pasar* dispositions. For that I have to talk about a new market in Pattani. In 2013 the township council decided to build a new market, one with a proper roof and equipped with a centralized refrigerator. That was a big deal for the *mak pasar*. They explained: "Unlike in our markets, the vendors at the new market can store their chicken, beef, seafoods, and vegetables in the centralized refrigerator," to which they juxtaposed: "See those [Styrofoam] boxes underneath our tables? We fill them up with ice to store our meat. The vendors at the new market will be saving quite a bit of money on ice. And they don't have to deal with the extreme heat or heavy rain each time it rains." Many *mak pasar* had applied for a vendor's permit at the new market while it was still under construction but only a handful were successful. As it turned out, the rest of the *mak pasar* were not really that disappointed after all. For reasons that were beyond their comprehension, the new market was only open for business every Monday, Thursday, and Saturday and only from six in the morning until twelve noon. Perhaps having sour grapes, they said they would not have bothered to apply in the first place. Even the vendors at the new market were equally at a loss as to why they were only allowed to open for three days a week and only in the morning.

Mariyei was the only one at her open-air market to obtain the permit at this new market. However, she was given a lot that was situated not inside (and thus cooler) but on the outer wall of the new market. But she did not complain. As she put it, "At least I can store my beef in the refrigerator. I don't need to spend money on ice." Mariyei was hoping that the management might allocate her a proper lot inside the market once there was a spot, even though she was not that optimistic. As such, on every Monday, Thursday, and Saturday she would start off in the morning at the new market and then hurry back on her motorbike to her open-air market after twelve noon. I mention this because it was mostly at the new market that she revealed snippets of information regarding her fellow *mak pasar*. It is also worth mentioning that not once have I heard or sensed any jealousies from the other *mak pasar* regarding Mariyei's good fortune. In fact, Hanisah and Zainab, whose stalls were adjacent to Mariyei's, would attend to any customer who wanted to buy beef from Mariyei when she was at the new market. They would cut up the beef the customers wanted and put the earnings inside a separate plastic bag for Mariyei. Although there were other stalls selling beef, Hanisah told me that each of them had their own regular customers who had been cultivated over the years, if not decades.

Over time I realized that I would only hear snippets of stories of misfortunes afflicted upon any of these *mak pasar* family members not from the particular *mak pasar* herself but always from her fellow *mak pasar*. One of the key insights I gleaned from this is that violence does not necessarily lead to a shared subjectivity or political position among those it affects unevenly. As Mariyei once explained, "That could only imply, directly or indirectly, their own family members' alleged complicity with the shadow insurgency." Mariyei was not alone in making these pensive comments and assertions. To reiterate, not once have any of my Malay Muslim interlocutors informed me that someone in their family has been arrested or charged by the authorities. Not once have any of them told me they knew that someone was an agent of the shadow insurgency.

Once again Mariyei sighed, and she tended to sigh a lot – and could you blame her? – before speaking in a more pensive tone a comment she had made several times: "Here in the three provinces any one of us [Muslims] is potentially a suspect ... Ajarnn Kee, I have never heard from any of my *sisters* they have family members as being part of ... You know who I am talking to."[15] She let out another sigh before repeating another constant refrain of hers: "Do you see any end in sight? Here we are, nine years, ten years, and counting. Apa nak buat? Apa bolih buat? [What can we do? What should we do?] We are stuck."[16] The latest conflict is for the duration.

Reparation

I should mention that it took me more than three years after I first met Aishah to learn that she came from the very village that is directly related to the Tak Bai incident. That was the day in 2012 when the then Yingluck government finally agreed, eight years after the infamous incident, to hand out reparations to family members of the Tak Bai victims. Mariyei's granddaughter and her fiancé were at the market that morning, and everyone was cheerful and happy for them. It was a bright shining morning, and the temperature had cool down from the rain the night before. The couple was at the market to fetch their grandmother to look for a pair of wedding rings at the goldsmith down the road. The *mak pasar* were offering their *tahniah* (congratulations) to Mariyei and the young couple, but especially to the soon-to-be bridegroom. They were teasing him that he did not deserve to be marrying such a beautiful girl. He was blushing, and the *mak pasar* and I were thoroughly enjoying it. We were all laughing, giggling.

However, our joyful mood was suddenly shattered when, just as Mariyei and the young couple were about to leave, Aishah slammed the newspaper at her stall before throwing it to the floor. Even at a distance I could sense she was crying. Two regular customers of hers whom everyone called Kak Pla (a Malay Muslim) and Pi Song (a Thai Buddhist) were consoling her.[17] Fatimah walked over and picked up the newspaper. "Have anyone read this?" Fatimah raised her voice, slapping the front page with the back of her fingers, "And only now, after all these years? What are they [the government] thinking? That we are forgetful? That we easily forget?" Mariyei knew why Aishah and Fatimah were so enraged. She whispered to me something about the then Yingluck government.

As I walked over to Aishah's stall, she did her utmost to avoid any eye contact. She lifted one hand to the side of her face as if to shield it from the tears in her eyes. But she could not hold them back as her tears were flowing down her chin. She then shut her eyes in anguish before looking away. She was choking when she asked: "Can reparations bring back dozens of loved ones? Mothers who have been widowed, children who lost their fathers, and mothers left childless?" She once again looked away. We were all silent. At that moment I felt like a stranger to her, which I was not. Aishah has always been warm and friendly towards me. We all stood there in silence, feeling immensely uncomfortable and sad. And then Aishah's cell phone rang. After a very short conversation she asked Fatimah and Mariyei to pack up her stall as she hurried off. The call was from her uncle. The Tak Bai communities had read about the news.

There was a sense of uneasiness in the space between us as our earlier laughter and giggling were drowned by grief and despair. Grief and despair had no religion and ethnicity at that moment. The faces of the *mak pasar*, including Kak Pla and Pi Song, displayed suppressed emotions of anger and, in a sense, also relief. Perhaps I was the only one that morning who thought about relief, relief that reparations would finally be paid, but also anger that it had taken eight long years before the administration finally came to a decision. Pla then took the newspaper from Fatimah and asked repeatedly, as Aisha had asked earlier, if reparations could bring back dozens of loved ones, women who had been widowed, children who had been orphaned, and mothers left childless. She said emphatically, "Ini tidak patuh. Ini salah" (This is not right. This is wrong). Suraiya echoed her anger and despair, "Berapa yang mati hari itu" (How many had died that day), to which Pla interjected, "Bukan berapa yang mati tapi kenapa mereka perlu mati? Macam mana mereka mati!" (It is not how many had died that day but why they needed to die? The way they died!)

Their feelings towards the tragedy at Tak Bai were not only of tragic hopelessless but also of frustration with helplessness. Theirs were not a tragic pain but a sorrowful one. Suraiya said it was a *malu* (shame) they had not fully comprehended (*memahami*) or realized (*sedar*) the magnitude of the loss until the decision of the Yingluck administration on reparation. The *mak pasar* were infuriated that morning. The awareness of the magnitude of the loss and the sense of guilt for not having done more (not that there was much they could have done) finally caught up with them that morning. As human beings, no more, no less, they realized their share of responsibilities for the indescribable loss of those who could not return, to those who had perished on that infamous day while protesting in front of a police station and on their forceful and inhuman journey to the army camp. As far as the *mak pasar* were concerned, justice had not arrived. They did not see reparation as any form of justice. The indescribable loss was a debt that would never be paid off.

Veena Das (2007, 62) once wrote that at such difficult and uncomfortable moments, as we stood there in silence with Aishah and later seeing her rush off, our eyes were not organs that saw but organs that wept with her grief. We were all quiet, speechless, lost for words, which urged me to think closely about the relationship between pain and language, that certain forms of pain defy language, as a sense of despair and emotion "that clings to the body" (Desjarlais 1992, 90; see also Scarry 1985; Asad 2011). As I now recall that day when we stood there with Aishah as she grieved, it reminds me of what Wittgenstein writes on the relationship between pain and words: "So are you saying that the word 'pain' really means crying? On the contrary: the verbal expression of pain replaces crying, it does not describe it" (2009: 244). It also begs the question: As in most stories of reparations and exercises of attempted closure, is it possible to lessen a horrific past that continues to yield and haunt a present that was not ghostwritten, a past that is always here through the present?

Ironically, if it were not for Aishah sudden outburst of rage that morning, I might never have found out that she came from the same fishing village that was directly related to the Tai Bai incident. But it makes perfect sense that Aishah did not reveal to me where she came from. And even if she had, I doubt I would have had the stomach to ask. In my engagement with these *mak pasar* over the years, I learned not to open up more windows of misery unless the *mak pasar* themselves were the ones who talked to me about it. And even then, we would feel uncomfortable talking about other *mak pasar*. Mariyei once told me that she and the rest of the *mak pasar* shared the same ethical concern whereby silence was their usual appropriate response each time any of their *mak pasar* family or relatives were afflicted with tragedies, something that I later learned is the culturally appropriate behaviour especially when insurgency-related deaths are lived, felt, and endured.

Aishah was back at the market two days later. She had with her a wooden netting needle and was showing it to Fatimah. I was not within hearing distance to hear what they were talking about, but I suspected it must have been something about this object. A few *mak pasar* went over. Mariyei grabbed my hand and made eye contact as if telling me to stay put. I hung around for a little bit longer before heading off for an appointment with an *ajarnn* at the university. Aishah was not there when I went back to the market in the afternoon. The atmosphere remained solemn, and there were the sounds of occasional sighs from various *mak pasar*, including Mariyei. Mariyei told me that the wooden netting needle belonged to Aishah's brother. It was something that used to structure his daily livelihood, an instrument routinely used by him, like any other fisherman, to mend his fishing net. The needle had since become an instrumental object of loss and mourning. It had become a *lieu de mémoire* (realm of memory) through which memories of a recent past are perpetuated – the tragic memories of the Tak Bai incident.[18] As a matter of fact, these *mak pasar* were shocked and horrified to find out that Aishah's brother had been one of the horrific victims; all along they had thought that the victims at Tak Bai were Aishah's fellow villagers but never her immediate family members, let alone her brother. It is difficult to imagine how Aishah could have kept it a secret from them for all those long eight years. And they were angry (if not shocked) that it was the Yingluck administration's decision to make reparation to family members of the Tak Bai victims that had provoked Aishah into finally revealing to them that her younger brother was one of the statistics.

Feeling sad for Aishah (indeed what anguish it must have been for her), Suraiya raised her voice to reiterate: "It is not only how many of them died but how they died. One on top of one another, crushed! Imagine … and on a blistering hot day. And it was on Ramadan. Now I understand why Aishah had refused to watch [that infamous incident that were circulating on] the YouTube. It was too much for her. It hurts." There was an awkward feeling of guilt as soon as she said that, as if she and her fellow *mak pasar* had watched it. Mariyei and other *mak pasar* were clearly uncomfortable with what Suraiya had just said. Mariyei wanted to say something but refrained. She did not want to talk about the horrific images that had been circulating for weeks on YouTube immediately after the tragedy. Instead, she uttered, "May Allah grant them *Jannah* [Paradise], *inshallah!*" The blessing was repeated by the other *mak pasar*.

Perhaps because the event had been so tragic, the deaths so brutal, it prompted them to comment, rather sarcastically, that even though the Yingluck administration's reparation decision could have violent consequences – as in the escalation of violence by the insurgents – they were between the government and the insurgents. In a sense, the *mak pasar* seemed to be seeking some distance between them as ordinarily civilians and the agents of the violent conflict from either side of the equation. As for the agents of the violent conflict from the Malay Muslims side, some of these *mak pasar* confided to me, reluctantly as well as embarrassingly, that since it was Muslims killing Muslims, they had not the slightly clue as to who these agents of the shadow insurgency were. They were just as clueless about it, because the whole thing made no sense to them, as they were about exactly what this shadow insurgency hoped to achieve. Mariyei remarked in the most poignant way to describe the impossibility of the realities that they much endured and engaged-with: "What is happening to us, around us? These days you can be killed for just surviving. And we are not for the insurgency." And she looked at me seriously. "Nor are we pleased with the ways we have been treated by the government. Either way, we are suspects. What more can we do? We are living in this *dunia* [world] of total uncertainty. Either way, can you tell us, Ajarnn Kee, how can we escape from this?" She raised her hands in desperation, even affording at that moment a tentative smile that hung upon her mouth. I wished I had answers to her dispositions, her desperate pleas, their precarity. But I had none to offer. How could they emerge from the Sisyphean impulse? I was and am equally desperate. I do not have any answers. I can only plod along, as in … the next paragraph, next chapter, so pathetically. I have learned that their hopes and grievances were woven together, so tightly, so inextricably.

Once again it was Mariyei who confided to me a few days later at the new market that Zainab's brother-in-law had been shot in the head when he was tapping rubber back in June 2003. He was a civil defence volunteer at his village. However, since his death happened before

January 2004, the arbitrary date set by the government for insurgency-related deaths to qualify for reparation, Zainab's sister and her in-laws were denied any right to file for legal compensation. It was while working with these *mak pasar* that I learned about stories of the unresolved nature of other violent incidents, of male relatives who had *disappeared*, including those who were alleged victims of torture and inhumane treatment while being held in custody.

As Helbardt (2015) notes, even though the shadow insurgency in Thailand's far south is quite similar to the Liberation Tigers of Tamil Eelam (LTTE) in Sri Lanka, the Kachin Independence Organisation (KIO) of Myanmar, or the Sinn Féin in Northern Ireland, similar in that they link political demands with acts of violence, not once has any group, be it the RKK or BRN-C, taken the credit for the outbreak of violence in the latest conflict. And even if it was carried out by the RKK, as alleged by the authorities, not once has this group taken any credit for violence, and it has made nearly zero public statement. Indeed, there has been a near-total absence of identifiable actors on the Malay Muslim side of the insurgency. In fact, few rebel groups have been so successful in shrouding themselves in darkness from the outside world. However, just like the LTTE, KIO, Sinn Féin, and other rebel groups, unfortunately the problem lies with the fact that potential killings and bombings have taken place within public spaces, and therein lies the danger and inconvenience to the lives and livelihoods of ordinary civilians, especially the Malay Muslims in the far south.

The *mak pasar* were not the only ones who predicted that there would be troubles following the decision for reparation. Many of my Malay Muslim interlocutors had the same prediction – including myself. We were right. A week after I had returned to Canada, there was a surge of violence in all three provinces, the most of which took place on 31 August 2012. There were 103 attacks across the three provinces on that day. Over an email, an *ajarnn* told me that there was something significant about the number of attacks as well as the date. This *ajarnn* had read in a local report (in Rumi) that the number of attacks (103) symbolized the number of years Patani had been oppressed under Siam's rule. And 31 August was also the Malaysian Independence Day. On that day in 2012 several Malaysian flags were raised and tied to trees and lamp poles across the three provinces to represent the insurgents' expressed intention of aligning itself with Malaysia, or at least to bring Malaysia into taking a serious role in helping to solve the problem between them and the Thai government. The message was political and symbolic. However, the *ajarnn* also mentioned that the number of attacks on that day or its symbolic association with Malaysia's independence would be treated by the Thai government as just another event so long as the conflict was confined to the far south. "*Biasa lah*" (As usual), as this *ajarnn* put it.

The Staging of the Krue Se Anniversary: Another State-Manufactured Blunder

Similar to Aishah who came from the village related to the Tak Bai incident, Fatimah also did not tell me that she came from the village at *tambon* Tanyoong Luyo or ever talked about the Krue Se mosque massacre. She even once mentioned she was not familiar with the Krue Se massacre when I asked. It was only when I found out that she came from *tambon* Tanyong Lulo that she responded, but with this sad refrain "What's the point to dwell on it," which made it impossible for me to probe any further. As with my previous engagement working with several communities that had been displaced and dispossessed in Borneo (Yong 2006), my interlocutors in Thailand's far south who had family members directly afflicted by the current conflict were often the ones who would vociferously claim to be unfamiliar with this or that episode of violence. In essence, their unfamiliarity are indeed the narratives about just how, or how less often, one remembers, or, in the case of Thailand's far south, about the willingness to remember a certain tragic recent past when there has been such a disquietude towards a government that has repeatedly shown little understanding or empathy towards their feelings.

Sometimes stories need time, however, or a certain event for *lieux de mémoire* to emerge. Prior to my returning for more ethnographic fieldwork in June of 2011, I read in the *Bangkok Post* about an event held at Krue Se mosque to mark the seventh anniversary of the massacre. I thought that the event was not only insensitive but also disconcerting to the Malay Muslims, especially to the Krue Se communities. How can one stage an anniversary of the massacre when no investigation or explanation has been given as to who gave the order to kill. This is roughly what the *Bangkok Post* reported: On 28 April 2011, to mark the seventh anniversary of the Krue Se massacre, around five hundred Malay Muslim children from various districts of the far south were invited to the mosque. Organized by the state, the intent was for these children to learn about the glorious and multicultural Patani that had been in harmony with Siam in the past so as to make them less susceptible to misinformation spread by the insurgents.

The narrative fed to these children was childish, making up a past for itself; it was deliberate, constructed, direct, and totally fabricated, just like the *Raja Kuning* television episodes – and there are a few more I will talk about in the pages of this ethnography. The ambition of the narrative for the seventh anniversary of the Krue Se massacre was to rob its subjects (these children) of the meaning of the Krue Se tragedy by distorting and falsifying it according to actual political requirements. These children were told that Krue Se was a place where unnecessary divisions and hatred in the region against the government and its multiculturalism had unfortunately led to violence. The mainstream media coverage of the event highlighted, needless to say, the amount of compensation the state had given to families of the victims. Meanwhile, nothing was mentioned about the loss of hopes and dreams, and the grief these families had to endure especially when, to this day, no attempt has been made to explain why thirty-two Malay Muslim men were killed or, to state the impossible, who might have given the order to kill. It was not even a case of *sub judice*.

When I went back in June 2012, I asked Fatimah what she thought about the staging of the event to commemorate the seventh anniversary of the Krue Se mosque massacre. She gave me a cold stare before telling Pla she was heading for lunch. That was an incredibly unwarranted question and insensitivity on my part. After that incident, I stopped asking Fatimah about the Krue Se massacre. Several weeks later I made another visit to Krue Se mosque, and by that time the walls that had once been riddled with bullet holes were plastered over. I then headed back to Muang Pattani with two plastic bags of *goreng pisang*, those plantain-looking, crispy, crunchy banana fritters that these *mak pasar* love. Standing at Mariyei's stall, I told her and Pla about my visit to Krue Se and that the holes in the walls had been plastered over, which they already knew. I also told them about my first visit back in June 2005 when the walls had been riddled with hundreds of bullet holes. Pla's face brightened up. She said she too had seen those bullet holes. She had taken half a day off in the week after the horrific incident just to see for herself the material evidence of the carnage. Mariyei also said she went to the mosque when peoples started talking about the bullet holes. It attracted a lot of visitors, both Muslims and non-Muslims, to Krue Se after the massacre. I was one of those visitors, and twice I went there in 2005 with my Thai and Sino-Thai friends. "A lot of people wanted to see for themselves the degree of violence, not just us Muslims, that had descended upon Krue Se when they heard about the hundreds of bullet holes in the walls," Pla said emphatically.

As Taussig once wrote, "When the human body, a nation's flag, money, or a public statue is *defaced*, a strange surplus of negative energy is likely to be aroused from within the defaced thing itself" (1999, 1;

emphasis in the original). A certain illuminating power was unleashed at the moment thirty-two helpless men were massacred, and the hundreds of bullet holes were the material evidence of the carnage. Ironically so, violence does titillatingly have its attraction.[19] I would also add that what descended upon Krue Se on 28 April 2004 – against the backdrop of the customary master narrative of an independent Thai nation-state and its benevolent rulers that protect its own people – is a counter-history, one which can no longer be written out of the biography of the nation-state. Perhaps this counter-history is where the attraction was for those of us who went to Krue Se to see for ourselves the hundreds of bullet holes in its wall. In other words, the attraction was achieved by the cooperation – that is, the hostility – of history.

Both Mariyei and Pla looked in the direction of Fatimah as I was conversing with them about the bullet holes. I sensed they were hoping Fatimah might say something since she must have been listening to our conversation. They were hoping that our mentioning of the hundreds of bullet holes might trigger her into saying something. And yet, at the same time I also felt it might trigger something too painful for her to recall. And just as I wanted to switch the topic, a regular customer whom everyone called Kak Yah and who must have overheard our conversation, asked Fatimah what she thought about those bullet holes. Fatimah was clearly uncomfortable and remained silent for what must have been a long minute or two before finally gathering the courage to say: "Those bullet holes, they were left there for almost a year. They were left there as a reminder of the *pembunuhan* [massacre]. The government offered to plaster up the holes but we refused. [Pause] I do not know why *they* [the mosque committee and the elders at *tambon* Tanyong Lulo] later agreed to let the government plaster up the bullet holes. Perhaps they were pressured. But we do not need the bullet holes to remind us of that day."

Kah Yah felt compelled and extended her arms to console Fatimah. Once again Fatimah summoned enough courage to continue as her eyes were welling up: "As long as the government cannot tell us why and who gave the order ... those men who were only armed with *parang* [machettes] ..." There was a long pause, and in a choking voice she said: "We shall always remember that day, that date. We will not forgive what they did to those helpless men. We heard who gave the order but ... [again long pause] this is Thailand, I cannot say. And the seventh anniversary you were mentioning the other day, it only goes to show how ... [pause] I don't even know how to describe the way I feel about our government. Do they sincerely believe we would look at the event as some kind of goodwill? Some kind of excursion? Do you know how many children around Krue Se lost their fathers that day? And here they brought these children from all over the three *wilayah* [provinces] to Krue Se. What kind of a joke is this? There is no need for the government to apologize. In fact, we don't want them to apologize. What's the point? We shall never forget, we shall never forgive."

Mariyei and Pla echoed the same sentiment, that they would never forget, never forgive. Fatimah was choking with tears when she heard Mariyei and Pla making the same declaration. Mariyei and Pla went over and hugged Fatimah, feeling sorry that our conversations had provoked her into recalling the horrific event. I could see the anguish on their faces. Kak Ya was clearly uncomfortable as well. Fatimah's declaration and her anguish resonated with the other *mak pasar* who felt that the government had not only, once again, failed them (which was nothing new for them), but also disrespected and insulted their dignities and pride, their humanities.

I wondered: Had the government known that its decision to stage the seventh anniversary of the Krue Se massacre and to bring in these children from all over the three provinces would be met by contempt, especially by those at Krue Se? If so, it might have given the government pause. But then again, I realized how naïve I was to even have such a thought. The authority's aim of plastering over the bullet holes was an attempt to annihilate a certain violent past so that Krue Se and the tomb of a Chinese saint, Lim Kun Yew, that lies adjacent to the mosque could, once again, be commoditized and subject to tourism, as they had been prior to the eruption of the latest conflict. However, its attempt to annihilate a certain past was also, paradoxically, a restoration of memory for the Muslim populations in the far south, especially those at Krue Se. As Fatimah declared, "We shall never forget, we shall never forgive." As a counter-history, the silences surrounding Krue Se are also history, history produced and always sustained by silencing (Trouillot 1995).

To be sure, the staging of the seventh anniversary of the Krue Se mosque massacre featured allegations and assertions with little regard to the truth. For me, one of the most disconcerting aspects of the staging of the anniversary has been the leading role assigned to fear, insinuation, and rumour. The government founded its arguments not on the values and virtues of multiculturalism and coexistence that existed among many Malay Muslims, Thais, and Sino-Thais in the region but on what might conceivably go wrong if these values and virtues were to cease. It was as if multiculturalism in Thailand's far south was in crisis because there were parallel communities (these shadow insurgents) threatening the fragile social cohesion of the region, *enemies within* cultivated by irresponsible cultural relativism, medieval practices subverting the Thai national "ways of life" and universal values.

The diverse populations in Thailand's far south, and I am referring here not only to the Malay Muslims but also to the Thais and Sino-Thais, it seems to me, have been poorly and meanly served by these assertions and allegations that have been aired on their behalf by the government, not to mention by agents of the shadow insurgency as well. And whichever side could claim victory on any given day, week, month, or year will not have done much to deserve it. It is not too far-fetched to suggest that what we are witnessing in Thailand's far south (as well as in many other crisis sites) is not so much a rejection of multiculturalism but a projection of neoliberal anxieties onto the socio-political reality of lived multicultures. In short, it is the transnational crisis that travels and is made to travel, and where rejecting multiculturalism is central to laundering this increasingly acceptable form of racism.

Chapter Four

Households and Marital Unions, the Subject of Insecure Existence

As mentioned earlier, the violence these *mak pasar* had habitually experienced since the start of the latest conflict is intertwined with myriad forms of oppression that arise from prevailing inequalities and structural patriarchy. Before I elaborate further, let me just note here that, as an outsider to their culture and society, I hesitate to claim knowledge about the married life of these *mak pasar* as well as other Malay Muslim women. But I do want, however hesitantly, to take the kinds of marriages and divorces among the conditions of their conjugal relationships as a prism through which we can understand how conflict and patriarchal hierarchy work themselves into the most intimate of relationships. In the context of the latest insurgency, the marital unions of some of these *mak pasar* who had made the choiceless decision to share rented rooms in Muang Pattani were adversely affected by the concrete rearrangements of their notion of homes and domesticity. Allow me to elaborate.

Besides being haunted by the memories of the Krue Se massacre, Fatimah had an insecure existence. She was in her mid-thirties when I met her. She had a fifteen-year-old daughter from her first marriage and was currently married to an older man as his third wife. In less than two years after she had shared a rented room in Muang Pattani, there was gossip at the market that her husband was constantly away from home. After all, he had gone *hilang* (missing) in the past, sometimes for as long as three months, and each time the story was the same, that he was having another adulterous affair. Consequently, Fatimah was not entirely sure about her marriage and her future.

She confided to me one day, albeit reluctantly, when she thought none of her fellow *mak pasar* was listening: "Ajarnn Kee, saya tidak tau macam mana masa hadapan … dimana abea pun tak tau" (Ajarnn Kee, I don't know what future to expect any more … I don't even know where my husband is). *Abea*, which literally means "elder brother," is an affectionate register for addressing not only one's husband but also the patriarchal hierarchy, and thus inequality. Feeling embarrassed that she might be insinuating to me that her husband was once again having an affair, she immediately offered a somewhat apologetic remark, as if blaming herself for her husband's absence from their household due to the rearrangement of her domesticity: "Lagi-pun, saya sekarang tidak di rumah. Sewa bilik dengan Siti dan Hamsiah, yang kami panggil wanita Melayu modern." (Besides, I am not home any more. Sharing a room with Siti and Hamsiah, the "modern" Malay women.) She laughed. "Ibu-bapa menantu kisah keadaan saya. Mereka orang baik. Mereka sayang anak saya. Mereka jaga dia." (My in-laws are equally concerned. They are good people. They love my daughter. They are taking care of her.)"[1]

"What about his other wives? Are they equally concerned that your husband is seldom home?" I asked, to which she immediately responded: "We get along just fine. I think *mak pertama dan kedua* (first and second wives) are equally concerned about his absence. Mak kedua sayang anak saya seperti anak sendiri. Dia mandul" (The second wife loves my daughter as her own. She is barren). She immediately offered somewhat of a guilty smile. Here we see how polygamy and patriarchy were simultaneously evoked and sidestepped, in part out of her in-laws' concern about her well-being as well as that of her daughter. Accordingly, Fatimah both understood and rationalized the practice of polygamy even though it did leave her with a sense of insecure existence.

In her study on the 1947 partition between India and Pakistan, Das included in her analysis that women who had been abducted during that violent period would rather not talk about it. As Das puts it, "rather than bearing witness to the disorder they had been subjected to, the metaphor that they used was of a woman drinking the poison and keeping it within her" (2007, 54). Although there is no exact similarity between the experiences of the women that Das describes and those of the *mak pasar* with whom I worked, I do find the metaphor "poisonous knowledge" somewhat evocative when Fatimah had felt guilty for revealing to me something that could invite gossip and shame to her conjugal relationship, something that was by no means unique to her.

The great care taken by Fatimah not to mention the potential rift in her conjugal life was made palpable to me when I was given a friendly lecture by none other than Mariyei: "I am surprised she told you about her *abea*. To you, both as a man and an outsider. These are very private

Households and Marital Unions 91

matters that are usually discussed only among women. But then again, Fatimah has always been somewhat outspoken. She has never been afraid of gossips ... Of course, she would tell you everything is fine. You are an outsider ... *Cukup*! (Enough!) I have said too much, *cukup, cukup*! [enough, enough!]"

When I saw Fatimah the following year, she told me rather nonchalantly that she had divorced her *suami* (husband). What she did not tell me was that she might be getting married again. It was Pla and Mariyei who revealed to me that there had already been two suitors, albeit both were older men and had families of their own. If Fatimah were to consent to any of the two, she would once again be the third wife. As if trying to justify Fatimah's decision to marry again, Pla offered an explanation: "Ajarnn Kee, dia masih muda. Belum sampai empat puluh. Baru tiga puluh lapan." (Ajarnn Kee, she is still young. Not even forty years old. Only thirty-eight.) This prompted Mariyei to rebuke Pla's remarks that Fatimah should perhaps wait. "After all," Mariyei emphasized, "Fatimah is not even forty yet and both suitors are already in their sixties, and one of them in his late sixties. Besides, she would be the third wife if she married any one of the two suitors." Mariyei also emphasized that Fatimah had only one daughter, to which Pla quipped, with a chuckle, "And a modern one as well, Ajarnn Kee." Once again Mariyei offered her usual sigh as if showing her disapproval. I did not react. I kept my silence even though I felt a little sad for Fatimah and their remark and somewhat condescending disapproval of her daughter for being a *modern* Muslim girl.

Of the *mak pasar* that figure in this ethnography, unfettered by old obligation and unswayed by cultural assumption (at least for a moment), Fatimah was not the only one to file for a divorce. Her emotionally charged lament about her previous marriage and insecure existence was echoed by other *mak pasar*, especially those who were in their second or third marriages and those who were the second or third wives in their current conjugal relationships. Her lament was especially shared by those whose husbands seemed to have the knack of going *missing* from their households and, if they were not, as these *mak pasar* were prone to say, would *lepak* (lounge around) at home, when their tradition called for husbands to be the responsible breadwinners of the family.

With all the above contexts and contents, it is important to note linguistically the shift in how they addressed their divorced husbands. Notice how Fatimah substituted the word *suami* (husband) after she got a divorce, for the word *abea* when she was still married. Looking over my fieldnotes, I saw that the *mak pasar* who were still married when I met them would address their husbands with the word *abea* (or some of them would say *abang* if they chose to speak to me in Malaysian Malay). However, those who were divorced would always refer to their former husbands as *suami dulu* (former husband) instead of *abea dulu*. *Suami*, which is the formal word for "husband," was used here to substitute for the more affectionate and respectful (albeit unequal) register, *abea*. This was especially the case for those who had been divorced by their husbands for not bearing them any children. However, as Mariyei and others would quip, it never occurred to these men that they might have been responsible for their childlessness, especially for those *mak pasar* who had had children from previous marriages. It is also important to note that in cases where their husbands had passed away, they would speak of their late husband as *abea yang meninggal* (he who had left this world).

Following the work of Buch Segal on the wives of martyrs and political detainees in contemporary Palestine, I find her plea of paying attention to the juxtaposition of hesitancy and argument to be not only compelling but also crucial with regard to my engagements with "contexts suffused with myriad forms of violence" (2016, 124). For these *mak pasar*, the ideal self was not a bounded, unique individual but rather a relational person, configured to patriarchy and with permeable borders between self and other (Joseph 1999). In a somewhat paradoxical way, when their relationships with their husbands were severed through divorce, it was quite natural that these divorcees would become integrated tightly among each other. Beyond their nonchalant tone regarding divorces, their overall feelings towards failed marriages reflected the unsettling situation that was a predicament for these women who were married to men who could, by virtue of their religion, practise polygamy and, by virtue of patriarchy, assume a sense of hierarchy and thus inequality.

However, this is not to suggest these women were not without recourse. Sometimes they were the ones who initiated the divorce. Nurul, one of the youngest *mak pasar* and who operated a beverage stall, had no qualms in talking about her husband who went missing a few times over the course of the three years they were married. Tired of supporting a husband who liked to *lepak* at home and play with his songbirds, she finally gathered enough courage to petition a *khula* (the right of a woman to seek a divorce) from her husband's village *imam* after he had once again gone missing.[2] I was at the market on the day Nurul got her divorce. She confided to me that their childless marriage was another reason for a divorce. When I saw her the following year, Nurul had remarried and she was quick to tell me that her *current abea* was an honest and hardworking man. "Otherwise," she said, while laughing,

"I will kick him out ... and I will never marry again. But my *abea* also has a few songbirds, much like all the men in this region. *Biasa lah* [Normal lah]." Immediately Nurul did a face palm when she realized, or she must have felt, what she had said was a little bit unabashed for a moral Muslim woman. That got all of us laughing, but I could sense there was the feeling of both envy and disapproval – envy of Nurul for divorcing her lazy and adulterous husband, and disapproval because she had not made any effort at reconciliation.

For the *mak pasar* who experienced marriage insecurity or divorces, the normal rationale they would offer was that of their society's acceptance of polygyny. As ironic as it may sound, some of those who experienced divorce attributed their marriage insecurity to their current indefinite proximate displacement from their households. It was as if they were saying that because their religion and polygyny were beyond critique, they could only search for faults in themselves. What we see here is not only the ethical considerations from an Islamic perspective but also the daily ruminations, conversations, and difficulties these women encountered in their ethical journey as pious Muslim women.[3]

Some of them even blamed themselves for not being able to give their husbands any children, even though, as some of them were quick to point out, who was infertile remained unknown. Within the constraints of their habitus, such is part of the conundrum facing some of these *mak pasar* regarding the ideas about household and marriages. Rather than being the pre-existent and stable foundation of "cultural life," ideas about household and marriage were in fact the very subject of precarity, part of the struggle for these *mak pasar* as they strived to remain as moral Muslim women, not to mention, for most of them, as the main breadwinners or to become the main breadwinners of their households.

I hope what I have written thus far is not construed as stereotyping the consequences of Islam and patriarchy (and thus inequality). Rather, what I am longing for is not quite about marriage stability or instability but an active escape from the quicksand of relativism, a way of crediting their realities (and their realism, if you must) without anxiety or apology. Here I am following the advice of Samuli Schielke (2010) on the anthropology of Islam that even though Islam and Islamic practices are braided into the everyday life of these *mak pasar*, I had to follow their cues not to make Islamic practices stand out. As they would say, their daily prayers, their caring, and so on were small acts, and so long as they did their best, these were their *ibadah*, an opportunity to contribute to the betterment of their life and their society. In other words, these were not the grand schemes of Islam but rather the way in which the practices were lived on a day-to-day basis.[4]

Similar to Cecilia Menjívar's description of how the ladina women in Guatemala endured violence, this was the veiled or "misrecognized violence that [these *mak pasar*] routinely experience in familiar, commonplace spaces ... violence that is difficult to see and to measure (and therefore often difficult to define as violence) because it is not confined to individual acts or horrific crimes that can be reported or tabulated (2011, 4). Like Menjívar, I also focus on what Kleinman, Das, and Lock describe as "the effect of the *social violence* that social orders – local, national, global – bring to bear on people (1997, 226; emphasis in the original)." In other words, this is the kind of "veiled violence in forms of social control of women that result in devaluation, humiliation, a lowered gaze, the kind of violence that does not shock the observer because it is part of the everyday" (Menjívar 2011 4). However, Menjívar and others have equally and importantly pointed out that this is not to suggest that these kinds of veiled or misrecognized violence and the attending problem of gender inequality can be laid at the feet of religion alone.[5] But rather, poverty and authoritarianism – conditions not unique to the Islamic world and produced out of global interconnections that implicate the West – are often more decisive.

What's There to *Cerita* (Dwell On)?

Unlike the Holocaust, the Cambodian genocide, and other traumatic incidents whereby thousands of survivors have made their personal memories public, the horrific events at Tak Bai and Krue Se mosque had scared the Malay Muslim communities so much at both areas that there had been a silence about them. Perhaps, given that the number of people who were personally involved was relatively small, the traumatic events can be compared to the 1968 massacre in Mexico City, the 28 February 1947 incident in Taiwan, and, closer to Thailand, even the 1965 purge in Indonesia that cost the lives of half a million to one and a half million (depending on which sources you choose to believe), whereby not only did it take decades for the silence to be broken, but the full accounts of the incidents have never been compiled to this day.

To invoke Derrida's provocative reflections on the spectrality of the nation-state – *on living in dying* – the genesis of the nation-state in the post-colony (although the kingdom of Thailand had never been colonized) is characterized not so much as a stillbirth but as the monstrous birth of a pathological chauvinism, one whose violent outcome is predictable (1994, 25–6). Indeed, as I have earlier asked, is the formulation of the category of the Thai Malay Muslim minority in juxtaposition to a Buddhist Thai majority in Thailand influenced by a homogeneous notion of culture that is essentially modern (i.e., Western), if not national, in origin? In other words, it is an outcome of the politics of European cartographic imperialism and conscription that has become a characteristic feature across post-colonial Asia and elsewhere, whereby the relationship between the state and the people (nation) has always been a tenuous one, especially when we set the bearings and experiences of the minorities in motion against a backdrop of the politics of colonization, neocolonization, assimilation policy, Cold War military economy, the rhetoric of development's progress, and capitalist imperialism.

As David Scott emphasized, the "belief that majoritarianism is always democracy has been one of the major fallacies of [any nation-state's] political thinking and one of the major causes of ethnic conflict ... [and] to use such procedures to resolve the issues of minority is actually antidemocratic because it inevitably spells the tyranny of the majority. [This paradoxical] connection between political legitimacy and the rationality of number – the seeming ideological neutrality of pure number ... [is, after all] a tactic of colonial governmental calculus" (1999, 162). In this scheme a minority population is often coterminous with a threat to national security, allowing for the rapid securitization (read: militarization) of the threatened region whenever political circumstances call for it (Abraham and Nakaya 2007, 2306). It is with such reading of the state policy that the court's verdict of the Tak Bai incidents and the total official silence about what had happened at Krue Se did not surprise the local communities at all. Perhaps this is the reason why – despite the enormity of the violence at Tak Bai and Krue Se mosque – many *mak pasar* and other Malay Muslim interlocutors would tell me it was pointless to *cerita* (dwell upon) them as their lack of resolution only implied an allegory for the impunity that defined in so many ways what Thailand's far south had become, not just recently but for decades.

A regular customer at one of the open-air markets whom everyone called Kak Ha said something that echoed the sentiment of the *mak pasar*: "Why should we be surprised with the court verdict? Everyone knows the *tahann* are powerful in Thailand. Why do you think so many Thais become *tahann*, especially those who have to think through their *perut* [stomachs]? The *tahann* is where the power is, especially when we have a *tahann* government. You get paid for being a *tahann*." At this point Pla said something that I thought was spot on in describing the power dynamics of Thailand: "The *tahann* is one of the most powerful components in Thailand, and not only after a *rampasan* [coup], and a *rampasan*, and a *rampasan*." That got all of us laughing, but not too loudly. Pla continued, "Even when we have an elected government, when any political parties ... the Democrats, Pueh Thai or whatever are the government of the day, it has always been profitable to be a *tahann* in Thailand. The *tahann* is tight with the monarchy or the other way round." Several *mak pasar* asked Pla to lower her voice. They asked if she was aware of what had just been announced regarding a certain order.

On 30 March 2016, despite criticisms from human rights organizations, the junta-installed Prime Minister Prayut officially issued an order under Section 44 of the interim constitution to give military personnel from the rank of sub lieutenant and above the powers to summon, arrest, and detain suspects in a wide range of crimes including Article 112 (lese-majesty crime), extortion, labour abuse, and human trafficking, and the power to search any property without a warrant. There had been a surge in the number of lese-majesty cases since the current junta regime came into power. *Lèse-majesté* is archaic French term meaning "to do wrong to majesty." In the case of Thailand, it is an offence against the dignity of the king and the monarchy. As a local senator told me, the latest official decree obscures the current regime's push for total power as disingenuous because it is dangerously undemocratic by invoking the lese-majesty when it suits it. It would keep civil rights lawyers and civil servants in employment for decades to come.

Futures Past

Our standard Western vocabulary of oppression, choice, and freedom, and thus the trajectory of the future, is too blunt to describe the lives of these *mak* pasar as well as the other Malay Muslim interlocutors with whom I worked. As such, I am not entirely sure I can talk about their futures, or the notion that they have any visions of the future, from immediate to the long term. More than once when I asked them what kind of future (or "future horizons," which has become so catchy within our Western academy) they were hoping for, they would give this blank look on their faces, as if saying, "Uh-huh!" If probed further, their standard responses were usually about how much they hoped to earn that day, the next day, and so on. They also hoped that the day would not be too hot and humid, or raining too heavily. They would not mind a little rain to get rid of the heat and humidity, but not raining cats and dogs.

Speaking about future(s), these *mak pasar* would not even go beyond *tomorrows*. More than anything else, they hoped that it would be another peaceful day for themselves, their families, and their villages. Mariyei, who always cautioned me to be careful, would also hope that it would be a peaceful day for the anthropologist. I bring this up to note that they were preoccupied with many quotidian things instead of dwelling on the possibility of a future, whether imaginative or otherwise. In fact, more than once Fatimah, Zainab, and many other *mak pasar* would quip, as they became tired of my question: "What future? Each day we think about how much we could sell at the end of the day. At most we think about tomorrow or the following day's earnings. If the earnings are adequate, we are happy. We never think about the future. We will go mad if we start thinking about the future."

I take the blunt and sarcastic responses of these *mak pasar*, these subaltern subjects if you may, to align with the convincing arguments made by David Scott (2006) that post-colonial subjects (including post-colonial scholars) have unevenly experienced and thus, in the aftermath, have become jaded when it comes to talking about futures (or future horizons). It is as if most of my interlocutors have abandoned all hope before they have even entered Dante's Inferno. And can you blame them (or us)? Scott asks. Scott poses this as an invitation that challenges the progressive temporal relationship between past, present, and future that has seduced most of our analysis for way too long – that seductive purr of the gospel-like commanding roar of a hoped-for future that is carelessly invoked for everything to everyone. In asking whether the Romantic genre still has its saliency in our historical present, Scott writes:

> A good deal of contemporary moral, social, political, and cultural criticism ... is driven by an appeal to an agent who, with conscious intention, and by resisting or overcoming the constraints of habitus, makes history ... In the best formulations ... this humanism is articulated in the outline of a subaltern subject who, in however small and barely visible ways, contributes to remaking her or his own world from below ... In the mythos of the West, the story-form of this drama of being human is Romance. But this story-form derives its point in large measure from the assumption of an imagined horizon of emancipation toward which the subaltern subject strives ... It seems to me, however, that ours is a time in which such an imagined horizon is harder and harder to sustain; the hoped-for futures that inspired and gave shape to the expectation of emancipation are now themselves in ruin; in Reinhard Koselleck's grim but still felicitous phrase, they are now futures past. (D. Scott 2004,152)

By talking about the miscellany of my interlocutors' everyday actions, instead of dwelling on the future that might drive them insane, we see among these *mak pasar* and others, these post-colonial subjects, both their actions that came about from their understanding of a certain shared and uneven history, and their reactions to their ongoing predicaments and precariousness. To reiterate once again, rather than reify and valorize agency that is quite frankly obsolete or dated as if we still had televisions with antennas, with the latest recurring conflict reaching a stalemate and in a perpetual state of uncertainty, it would be not only naïve on my part but also idealistic and epistemologically bankrupt to indulge in any kind of romantic script towards their temporalities or hoped-for futures.

On the notion of an imagined future, more than once these *mak pasar* and others would tell me, and here I am paraphrasing: "We don't indulge ourselves on any *masa depan* [futures] … we don't even want to think about the madness, the inconvenience we have endured for so long in our lives. We turn our eyes aside and try to see things pleasantly, with whatever is useful and comforting to our circumstances: friends, enough daily revenues, freedom from politics, *especially freedom from Thai and local politics*" (this they would underscore and emphasize). Ajarnn Abdullah and Sumree similarly emphasized: "If we were to suffer some painful calamity, we must summon the peace of spirit by drawing upon the good still left within us, using our own resources to smooth out the roughness of what comes from within and outside ourselves. *Inshallah!*"

Most certainly, the *mak pasar* and other interlocutors with whom I worked did not partake of the sort of belief in historical necessity and progress that some of us have learned to be deeply embarrassed by of late. Or, for that matter, my interlocutors were not seduced by the belief that the world's problems, or their own, could be solved if we could, somehow, transcend the current onslaught of neoliberal capitalism, to the end of capitalism, to post-capitalism, whatever that means. To reiterate, when these *mak pasar* talked about what they hoped for, their indexed conversations were suffused with the dilemmas surrounding what they hoped for, such as their daily earnings, the safety of their families and themselves, the passage of years, the process of becoming a Muslim woman, their marital unions, and so on in the recurring conflict-ridden far south of Thailand. In other words, instead of talking about any futures, they seemed to be talking about the concept of "horizon of expectation." I am here alluding to Reinhart Koselleck's insistence that concepts are not just derivations but "have a semantic function and performance" in social and political life (2004, 86). As he puts it, a concept is "not simply indicative of the relations which it covers; it is also a factor within them. Each concept establishes a particular horizon for potential experience and conceivable theory and in this way sets a limit" (85). For Koselleck, words such as *democracy*, *revolution*, and here I would add *household* and *family*, are such concepts because "the entirety of meaning and experience within a socio-political context within which and for which a word is used can be condensed into one word" (85), or one concept.

Important to this discussion is Koselleck's notion of the two general historical categories: the "space of experience" and the "horizon of expectation." Experience, both direct and alien (conveyed across generations and institutions), is the "present past." Expectation is the "not yet," the non-experienced, the "future made present." These are not, for Koselleck, symmetrical: one is collected (experienced), while the other can never be experienced and can always be revised (expectation); "the presence of the past is distinct from the presence of the future" (2004, 260). However, Koselleck suggests that while events may have happened, experience of them alters over time. This structure is made possible by the temporal structure of "retroactive expectation"; new expectations, new futures, that were not always anticipated continually become possible. New imaginations of possible futures continually alter our experience of the past (168).

Expectations are also temporally structured and can be "temporally exceeded"; new experiences transform and exceed the limit of our possible futures, for instance the end of the war or, in the case of Thailand's far south, the end of the recurring conflict, which seems like an aporia. However, Koselleck argues that "'past futures' that have been exceeded do not by any means disappeared or neutralized; sometimes they can continue to 'emit impulses' reformulated here more strongly as ghostly warnings. Past futures may have not happened, but they can continue to have a life that exceeds their actualization, the hidden surplus of new imagined futures" (2004, 169). I sincerely hope this is the case for Thailand's far south even as I remain pessimistic and cynical. The empirical evidence on the ground strongly suggests otherwise.

The Phayta Tani Cannon

I want to elaborate on why I remain pessimistic and cynical. Here is another incident of how insensitive the Thai government can be when it commits itself time and time again to making mistake after mistake, mistakes that infuriate the diverse Malay Muslim communities in the far south. But then again I am instantly reminded by this rhetorical question: "Do you think they were making mistake after mistake, or were they making them intentionally?" I am referring here to the making of a replica of the legendary cannon that carries a lot of symbolic meaning to the diverse Malay Muslim communities in the far south.

One day at the market in 2013 Fatimah asked if I had already heard about what had happened at Krue Se mosque of late. I was surprised by her question because I thought she would never want to bring up Krue Se again, not since the day she could not control the tears flowing from her eyes. But this day in 2013 she was laughing, albeit cynically. Again she asked, "Have you heard about the cannon they placed at Krue Se?" to which Mariyei interjected, "Yes," while also laughing and then saying, "Ajarnn Kee, have you not heard about the cannon they recently placed at Krue Se?" That got the other *mak pasar* interested. They began to gather around Fatimah's stall and were laughing and shaking their heads at how sillily, stupidly, and insensitively the government had once again been acting, something that had become so *biasa* for them.

The cannon they were referring to is the Phayta Tani cannon, one of the heritage objects from the Sultanate of Patani. This historic cannon, which is a monument to the battles between the Sultanate of Patani and Siam, was seized by Siamese troops two hundred years ago and is now installed in front of the Defence Ministry in Bangkok. I do not have to remind my readers how insensitive this installation in front of the ministry must have been for the diverse Malay Muslim subjects in the far south. Over the past few decades there have been repeated calls by the Muslim communities in the far south to have it repatriated, but their requests were never entertained. As if to add insult to injury, on 2 June 2013, without any consultation with the Malay Muslim communities in the far south, a replica cannon, which was rumoured to have been built by some undergraduate students at a certain university in Bangkok as part of their art project, was installed at the historic Krue Se mosque, amid the chagrin and anger of the local communities at *tambon* Tanyong Lulo. Some residents questioned the motive of installing the replica cannon at Krue Se, and others wanted to know why it was pointing south towards Malaysia instead of Bangkok. Others insisted on having the original cannon back and installed at Krue Se and not pointing towards Malaysia. Nine days after the replica cannon had been installed, an IED shattered it into two halves.

As far as the *tambon* Tanyong Lulo communities were concerned, including the *mak pasar* and others with whom I worked, the installation of the replica cannon at the historic Krue Se mosque was never an attempt to promote reconciliation and healing, just like the staging of the Krue Se anniversary and other manufactured blunders by the state. On the contrary, it was another disrespectful and shameful act, an act to provoke anger further. But I want to underscore, and this is important, that these blunders did not mean that the anger provoked by being disrespected and shamed would produce sympathies towards the shadow insurgency. Like the government, the other side of the violence equation also provoked anger, if not fear and violence. Speaking softly and rather seriously at the new market, Mariyei offered lengthy and elaborate remarks that captured the opaqueness, if not the overall ambivalence, she and others felt towards the latest insurgency, as well as the insurgencies in the past:

> We are trapped in this mess ... us Muslims and non-Muslims. But it's worse for us Muslims ... especially our youths, including some women.[6] The government thinks we are sympathetic towards the insurgency ... At the same time the insurgents ... expect us to be on their side ... Quite frankly, most of us are simply bystanders and mostly terrified. We are not choosing a side, but it has been chosen for us. This was true in the past ... But after you were constantly harassed, especially our men and youths, sometimes slapped and kicked by the soldiers, you tend to hate the government. And as you know, Ajarnn Kee, the government kept making mistake after mistake, and they seem to be mistakes made on purpose.
>
> My relative once vowed he would never leave Pattani to find work in Malaysia, but finally left after receiving two bullet wounds while tapping rubber one day. He was not even a volunteer with the civil defence. His crime was that of being the brother of someone who is a volunteer. He now taps rubber for others in Malaysia. Why do you think a lot of Muslim men, our young men, even teenagers, have left the three provinces for low-paying jobs in Malaysia? Everybody knows or prefer not to know they are being taken advantage of by our so-called fellow Malaysian Muslim brothers and sisters. Our men and teenagers are paid half the amount at *tom yum* restaurants, at construction sites, or tapping rubber, in just about any kind of work they can find in Malaysia. They are treated no different from the Bangladeshi, the Nepalese, the Indonesians, even the Rohingyas. Imagine the Rohingyas, they are paid so lowly in southern Thailand. Now our own are paid on the same level as the Rohingyas in Malaysia. They are there because they are fed up. They are trapped, we are trapped.

Mariyei looked resigned. She then asked, "Why do you think so many of our men, our youths, are into all sorts of *barang* [drugs]? Kratom, cocktail drinks, ganja, and what have you." Her questions and concerns were something everybody knew and preferred not to know or to ask. Mariyei's long-standing remarks reminded me of what James Scott (1985) once said: in any war or conflict, hostilities are conducted over a shifting terrain where there are many neutrals and reluctant combatants. However, expanding on Achille Mbembe's (2019) concept of necropolitics, which refers to the sovereign power of the state to dictate who may live and who may die, along the frontier provinces in Thailand's far south civilians who are caught in the crossfire of the latest recurring conflict very much live in the shadow of the state's necropolitical and sovereign power. Moreover, these *mak pasar* and other Muslim interlocutors were subjects ensnared in a paradox, in the sense that their allegiances were not their own to give but, instead, presumed by both sides of the violence equation – not just by the state but also by the shadowy insurgents. Either way they were caught in "being suspected."

Doing Things with Words

In September 2012, as it had happened in the past, I received several emails from several *ajarnn* that word had spread that the RKK would once again attack Muslim businesses that opened on Fridays. According to the RKK, Friday is supposed to be the traditional day of rest and prayer for Muslims. When I went back to Pattani in June 2013, several *mak pasar* confided to me that they took the risk of opening on Fridays but were very concerned because leaflets forbidding them to open for business on Fridays had been found at several open-air markets throughout the far south, including their own. "Takut-lah," they confessed, "separuh tiga minggu terdapat risalah di pasar. Mungkin di waktu malam … Takut nak buka hari Jumaat tapi apa bolih buat. Nak cari wang, cari makan." (We were worried, for three weeks there were these warning leaflets. Perhaps they were left here at night … We were worried to open on Fridays, but what choice do we have. We need to earn a living.)

Mariyei said that as many as fifteen vendors at her market did not open on Fridays for a month. "That's four business days of lost *untung* [profit]," she emphasized, before continuing, "But they eventually took the risk like the rest of us." At that point Hanisah laughed, and I laughed at her nervous laugh, before she turned towards Mariyeh: "Tunggu-lah, mana tau … nanti beri amaran lagi." (Just wait, who knows … *they* will be issuing threats again.) Mariyeh and Hanisah shrugged their shoulders at the hopelessness of their situation before uttering the rhetorical question, "Apa bolih buat, apa bolih lagi kita buat?" (What can we do, what else can we do?)

Instead of the *mak pasar* treating these warning leaflets from the RKK as statements of truth or falsity, their decision to open or not to open on Fridays could be seen as actions and expressions of a challenge or counterchallenge. Using McDowell's analysis of the Austinian performative analysis of language, I consider that those warning leaflets were most definitely a public speech act: "Speech acts are publications of intentions [that they might be harmed if they opened for business on Fridays]: the primary aim of a speech act is to produce an object – the speech act itself – that is perceptible publicly and in particular to the audience [those who opened for business on Fridays], embodying an intention whose content is precisely a recognizable performance of that very speech act. In other words, recognition by an audience that such an intention has been made public in this way leaves nothing further needing to happen for the intention to be fulfilled" (McDowell 1998, 4, cited in Das 2014a, 294). The last sentence is key here for the warning leaflets by the RKK, in the apt title of Austin's (1962) book *How to Do Things with Words*, public speech acts that *do things with words* and with a certain ghostly force: that these *mak pasar* and other Muslim businesses might be harmed if they opened for business on Fridays.

A fundamental aspect of Austin's theory of performative language is that action and speech are aspects of each other, that action does not follow or precede speech but rather is the speech act itself. As Das (2014a, 294) points out, "we might say McDowell's analysis would separate the aspect of performance from the aspect of action. Performative utterances would be completely on the side of expression, albeit expression in the public sphere. This theoretical move knits together the inside and outside, intention and action, primarily through the communicative acts in public between one who has expressed an intention and another who has received it." The *mak pasar* were the recipients of this communicative act in public, at their open-air markets.

Moreover, there is an affective temporal dimension to these warning leaflets. In Brian Massumi's discussion of the temporal dimension of threat, threat "emerges from the future and is always rising, just over the horizon, projecting itself backward in time to cause an affect but never actually arriving, or at least never arriving at any finality – there will always be a future threat" (2010, 53). This is crucial because it gives threat its affective power. Massumi further elaborates: "Threat is not real in spite of its nonexistence. It is superlatively real, because of it" (53). It is real because, even though it is always emerging but never fully emerged, it produces fear felt in the present, fear that has a real affective power. In other words, "the affective power of fear is not dependent on the reality of the threat or the likelihood of its emergence, but rather fear can become self-causing, fear begetting fear, with fear of fear itself as the most powerful affect of it all" (53). In Massumi's words, "fear is the anticipatory reality in the present of a threatening future" (54). This kind of threat is real because it produces fear felt in the present, fear that has a real affective power to interrupt many kinds of everyday activities, including livelihood activities.

Although Mariyei did not tell me why those *mak pasar* who had closed on Fridays eventually decided to take the risk of opening for business,

I suspect there were several reasons that affected their decision. First, those who took the risk of opening on Fridays were not attacked. Second, and this is obvious, there were the lost revenues incurred by those who had chosen to close on four Fridays. I might even suggest that those who closed on Fridays were jealous of those who did not. On top of all these, the warning was not a *fatwa* (legal pronouncements in Islam), something these *mak pasar* were quick to point out. The threatening leaflets were not issued by the respective Islamic council in the three provinces of Yala, Narathawit, and Pattani.

But one thing is also certain. None of these *mak pasar* and the few *ajarnn* with whom I spoke could confirm that these leaflets were issued by the RKK. When I pressed them on numerous occasions if they were not sure these leaflets were issued by the RKK, they demurred. Mariyei and the other *mak pasar* would always gesture, with their fingers to their lips, each time I asked them about the RKK. They would respond, "Shh! One does not talk about them or who and what they are," which prompted me to make a mental note: What if their silences have to do with the fact that they might have been silenced? And silenced by what? Ghosts, shadows, because you just never know who is listening or always listening. After all, the latest insurgency is appropriately called the *shadow* insurgency.

They must have been tired of my occasional asking about the RKK when finally Zainab explained: "Ajarnn Kee, we do not know who they are but they are everywhere and nowhere. To the authority, they are just Muslims. So I guess any Muslim can be RKK." And Mariyei commented, as others have, that if there was no RKK, there would be another organization taking advantage of the cycle of fear that had afflicted the region for decades. As they put it, the far south has had too many sides that were wrong, not just the government. As such, the RKK seems like the latest actualization of long-standing fear and paranoia, taking advantage of that fear and paranoia to hijack the region, using violence to stop violence, fear to stop fear, violence and fear that have preoccupied people in the back of their minds for as long as they can remember.

Indeed, what is happening in Thailand's far south has strong echoes with the conflict in Aceh, Northern Ireland, and numerous other conflict sites. These were all protracted-conflict sites involving insurgents and counter-insurgents, and there were mostly ethnic and religious components to them. In each of these conflict zones the so-called enemy fell within the language of the divisive "we" and "them," depending on which side one was on. However, unlike the situation in Northern Ireland where repressive tactics by British troops and local police had bred some community support for the insurgents (Feldman 1991), the RKK has not achieved the moral high ground as far as I am aware. Ambiguity remains especially when the insurgents attack "soft" targets, Malay Muslims, or threaten Muslim businesses that open for business on Fridays. Moreover, even though there are "we" versus "them" divisions in Thailand's far south – Malay Muslims versus Thai Buddhists – the "we" is not a pure "we." This was or is also true in other conflicts that were or are couched in Manichaean terms, as in Pol Pot's Cambodia, Suharto's Indonesia, Argentina's Dirty War, and especially after 9/11 when the first-person plural *we* and possessive plural pronoun *our* were constantly invoked to amplify this alleged sense of national community under the rhetoric of the fragility of the nation-state (Hinton 2010, 31).

As with these other protracted-conflict sites, while the Muslim moralist in Thailand's far south was impelled to deplore the atrocious nature of the RKK's campaign of bombings and killings, and especially the killings of Muslims, at the same time one's mere Muslimness was appalled by the disrespectfulness of the government – not just the *tahann* and the police but also the state and its other agents. In other words, the perception of the minority citizen who had grown up conscious that his or her group was distrusted and discriminated against in all kinds of official and unofficial ways, was at one with the poetic truth of the situation in recognizing that if life in Thailand's far south were ever really to flourish, change had to happen. But that perception was also at one with the truth in recognizing that the very brutality of the means by which the RKK was pursuing change was destructive of the trust upon which new possibilities would have to be based. In other words, rather than strengthening, the terrifying violence of the RKK, especially the ways in which it killed its victims, had the effect of weakening the autonomous aspirations of the heterogenous Malay Muslims and the possible political avenues they hoped to achieve. Thus, this contradiction or uneasiness of hope has proven to be impossible, to me, for consolidating their realism upon what we call change. It is with this impossible situation in mind that we should think about the temporality of violence and our subjects' endurance as repetitious, as habitual in the quotidian sense. Captives of the immediate present, they have been enduring and engaging with the difficulties of reality whereby time does not seem to pass, whereby they remain as subjects ensnared in a permanent temporality of what Deleuze calls "the paradox of contemporaneity" (1994, 81).

Besides the warning leaflets that the *mak pasar* believed were issued by the RKK but could not confirm, a certain Minu Makaue, a self-proclaimed leading Malay Muslim scholar from the province of Yala, even went as far as demanding that Fridays be declared public holidays because this had been practised in other parts of Southeast Asia. As far as I know, this is true for Muslim majorities in the state of Johor in Malaysia. However, there is a caveat. After the Johor sultan gave his consent for government institutions and government schools in the state to be closed on Fridays, they would then have to be open on Sundays. Outside of the state of Johor, Saudi Arabia, the United Arab Emirates, and Bangladesh do consider Friday a non-work day, and Pakistan counts it as a half-day of rest, after the noon prayer. This so-called leading Malay Muslim scholar from Yala went on to say that with the declaration of Fridays as holidays in Thailand's far south, the threat from insurgents would become mute. What this person was not aware of, or chose not to be, is that nowhere in the Quran does it state that Friday is a holiday.

When I emailed an *ajarnn* about Minu Makaue, I received an immediate response:

> Your *mak pasar* are absolutely right. Islam been hijacked again and again by the West, by their so-called leaders, intellectuals, in their films and recently, even in their cartoons. But my faith has also been hijacked by our own local morons, these *munafiks*. Who is this Minu Makaue from Yala? I have never heard of him. I just wish there are louder voices here in the three provinces that could give a clear declaration that "Fridays holidays" have got nothing to do with Islam. Actually, it is crystal clear in the Quran that when you hear the call for Friday prayer, you go to the congregation and pray, and when you finished your prayer, you GO BACK TO CONTINUE YOUR BUSINESS [emphasis in the original] (please refer to the Al-Quran, Chapter 62, Verses 9–10). It is important to note that these two verses must be read together, or simultaneously. It is degrading when people resort to using one Quranic verse taken completely out of context and in isolation of other verses in order to bury the issue.

This *ajarnn* went on to write in a subsequent email:

> I think those who claim Fridays as holidays must have got the idea from the Jewish Sabbath tradition because for them Saturdays are holidays, and Jews are not allowed to work on Saturday because it is supposed to be the day that their God takes a rest! But there is no such tradition in Islam. Allah needs no rest and fatigue can never penetrate Him. Allah's attributes are beyond humans' realm of imagination, and He does work in every existence. That's why in Islam we consider every step of our life as an *ibadah* or an opportunity to contribute to the betterment of our life and our society. Regardless of how trivial your act is, it does not matter as long as you do the best you can. Actually, there is no such thing or an idea

called holiday or "holy days" in Islam; every of our act is a meaningful act, an act to serve God and humanity. I wish our "Muslim scholars" would make this point clear. Loud and clear!

Moreover, and this is strictly hypothetical, if Friday is to be declared a holiday in Thailand's far south, would there also be other fatwas, however ridiculous they might be, that the RKK and some so-called Islamic scholars would issue in the future? Perhaps even suggesting banning Muslims from selling (and not eating) food before the opening of fasting (*buka puasa*) during Ramadan? This is precisely what has been suggested in Aceh of late, after the Gerakan Aceh Merdeka (GAM, Free Aceh Movement) had achieved its autonomy, and after most, if not all, of the international NGO conflict workers and so-called terror experts had packed up their bags to go in search of other violent sites.[7] And just because some *ulamas* and *ustazs* had issued a fatwa, some Malay Muslim women in Aceh were caned in public when they were caught selling food before the opening of fasting hour (*buka puasa*) during Ramadan.

It seems to me that these *ulamas* and *ustazs* have forgotten that, besides being a holy month of fasting and religious activities, Ramadan is also a month of festivities. The selling of food at the markets in the afternoon is part of the festivities. In fact, special dishes, sweets, and so on are only served during Ramadan to mark the festivities of the holy month; it is part of the tradition in the Muslim world. For these *ulamas* and *ustazs* to issue a fatwa forbidding Muslims to sell food in the afternoon at the markets during Ramadan is equal to erasing the festivities of the holy month. If such a ridiculous fatwa were imposed in Thailand's far south, most, if not all, of the *mak pasar* with whom I worked would be publicly caned.

Another Massive Explosion

A few months after the warning leaflets were issued in September 2012, a massive bomb exploded inside a department store across the road from one of the open-air markets in Muang Pattani. At about the same time, an IED hidden inside a motorcycle was detonated right by the township's clock tower. These explosions happened in the middle of the night. When I met the *mak pasar* in the summer of 2013 and asked about the incidents, they shook their heads in disbelief. The department store was located less than ten metres from their market. Zainab gave a huge sigh before saying: "We were lucky, very lucky, the bomb exploded at three in the morning. Imagine if it went off at five in the morning. We would have been right here. Imagine that. That was a 50 kilogram, a huge bomb. The same size as the one you experienced at the hotel, a 50 kilogram. The interior [of the department store] was completely destroyed. *Habis* [Finished]. Kita nasib baik, sangat nasib baik [We were lucky, very, very lucky]. *Inshallah!*" It was common to hear my interlocutors talking about the enormity of each explosion by denoting the size or weight of each IED.

Almost in unison, Mariyei and Pla repeated what Zainab had said, "Nasib baik, nasib baik" [We were lucky, very lucky]. Zainab continued to emphasize, "Imagine if we were all here when the bomb exploded" [pointing to the department store across the street]. Pla chipped in, "Or worse, imagine if it went off much later that morning, or in the afternoon when all of us and our customers were here." This prompted Fatimah to add: "And what about their staff and customers [at the department store]? As you know, many of our relatives and friends work there, … and our customers also shop there … The whole thing was crazy. It made no sense at all. Imagine how many people would be killed or injured if the bomb exploded during the day. Whoever was behind the bombings must be mad. What if it happened at our open-air markets?"[8] Hanisah immediately interrupted Zainab by saying: "Shhh … Stop saying that! What open-air markets? Are you not *pantang* [superstitious]?" That got them all laughing as they shook their heads in disbelief – or rather, relief.

Were the explosions at the department store and the clock tower connected? Were they done by the RKK or whoever were the insurgents? The newspaper reports were inconclusive. Zainab reasoned that since the bomb had exploded at three in the morning, it must have been only a warning and might not even be insurgent related. Instead, it might be a business-rivalry issue because the department store was one of the busiest stores in Pattani. Mariyei concurred with Zainab. Perhaps it was economics all along, a business rivalry that was taking advantage of the atmosphere of unrest.

Anti-Hobbesian Spaces

I do not want to suggest that all that these *mak pasar* did each and every day was to lament over their livelihoods or the government and the insurgency. In fact, it was at these gendered public spaces that I saw a lot of social cohesion and trust. In an anti-Hobbesian take on the function of society without the state, Ernest Gellner makes an interesting comment: "The Hobbesian problem arises from the assumption that anarchy, absence of enforcement, leads to distrust and social disintegration … but there is a certain amount of interesting empirical evidence which points the other way. The paradox is: it is precisely anarchy which engenders trust or, if you want to use another name, which engenders social cohesion" (1988, 147).

Empiricism was never so alive! It was at these open-air markets that I saw the shaping of sisterhoods, of feelings of consensus and trust, of sensations and sensibilities solicited amid their teasing and laughter, as well as the unease of having to engage with the difficulties of reality. It was also at these open-air markets that I would hear gossip about which *mak pasar*'s husband had a new mistress or a new songbird or songbirds. Some of these *mak pasar* even joked that their men felt they had licence to practise polygamy because their prophet Nabi Muhammad started the precedent, as delegated power is delegated yet again. This was a recurring joke that I would often hear also from many other Malay Muslim women, not just from the *mak pasar*. But this is not a joke in bad taste, because I know full well that they are also touching upon an area of open wounds and unimaginable pain.

Taking a *longue durée* perspective, these *mak pasar* viewed the current conflict as cyclical. Hence, what is more important than discreet outbreaks of violence are their economic underpinnings, which have shown themselves, repeatedly, to be one of the continuing sources of unsettlement for them. As mentioned earlier, what truly matters to them are bread-and-butter issues, how things are getting more expensive, and the longing for the liveliness of their homes and their villages. Some would even go into detail without my asking: the amount of capital they needed each day to operate their stalls, and the average revenue they needed to make each day. These *mak pasar* worked from sunrise to sundown, seven days a week, and they would take a day off when it was absolutely necessary – like attending a family wedding or funeral. And despite the threat from the RKK, most of them refused to close on Fridays. Let me recount an episode to illustrate just how much and how hard they worked to support their families.

Much like in many Muslim countries and societies, the celebration of Eid ul-Fitr (Festivity of breaking the fast) in Thailand's far south – also called Hari Rayo or Malay Muslims' New Year – is premised upon the sighting of a crescent new moon. Eid ul-Fitr is also a celebration of having endured thirty days of fasting during Ramadan. As mentioned earlier, since there are no refrigerators at the open-air markets, those who sell chicken, beef, and other perishable items need to determine how much merchandise to order for the last few days of Ramadan before they take a day off to celebrate Eid ul-Fitr. As in any Muslim countries, the last few days of Ramadan are the busiest festive shopping days. Any wrong prediction of when Eid ul-Fitr would take place would translate into a missed opportunity to earn more income for these *mak pasar*. Unfortunately this was what happened in 2012.

On that year, the *mak pasar* of all three open-air markets adhered to the prediction by the local religious council that the eve of Eid ul-Fitr would be 17 August, a Friday, and, as such, they ordered their perishable merchandise accordingly. When I tried to tell them that the Malaysian and Indonesian religious authorities had announced otherwise, that the eve of Eid ul-Fitr would be 18 August instead, the *mak pasar* countered by telling me that in Thailand's far south they still adhered to the ritual of the sighting of a crescent new moon, and their local religious authority had predicted that it would be on the evening of 17 August. They also said it was not only more religious that way but also their *tradisi* (tradition).

The three open-air markets I visited that Friday, on their predicted eve of Eid ul-Fitr, were packed with the highest density of bodies, and the *mak pasar* looked overtaxed and exhausted but happy. It was also an incredibly hot and humid day, more than usual. Unabashedly, some of them confided to me how they wished Hari Rayo that year would fall on 19 August instead of 18 August, thereby giving them an extra busy business day. However, upon saying that, they also realized they would have nothing to sell because their suppliers would also be closed on 18 August. As it turned out, no crescent new moon was sighted that Friday evening, and they wished they had listened to me. When I visited the markets the next morning, only a handful of *mak pasar* were there to sell whatever remaining chillies, sugar, and cooking oil they had, all non-perishable items. However, the rest of the *mak pasar* were back in business on Monday, and sure enough, they complained to me, and to themselves, how they could have had another busy business day if their local religious council had made the correct prediction. When I playfully reminded them what I had told them about the Malaysian and Indonesian governments' announcements, they reiterated that was not how they did things in Thailand's far south, not their *tradisi*.

I bring up this episode to illuminate not only the entrepreneurial spirit of these women but also how tirelessly and diligently they worked to support their families within tumultuous circumstances. They were the most enterprising entrepreneurs who were doing business every day by occupying little space. Indeed, why wouldn't one interpret their labour as one of the economic engines in a poverty-infested region instead of it being alienated to the margins of the economy? This question becomes even more acute if one considers the violence of the economy with its unemployment; miserable pay at most, if not all, the retail outlets within the urban areas of the three provinces; and the falling prices of rubber latex in recent years. We could even conclude that, thinking of the tireless labour of the *mak pasar* as one of the economic engines in the region, it has also made it possible to identify alienation as a puzzling and extraordinary feature of capitalism. Indeed, it is precisely because this kind of value upsets economic common sense that makes it useful for us to think about its alternatives in value creation. What is more, these *mak pasar* provide an example of women who have created their own public culture that is inextricable from their working class and ethnicity.

By stepping into the public sphere at the market because of economic necessity, they exemplify self-sufficient women who are nonetheless alienated by economic analysts. Instead, to quote Tsing, here one sees "the rift between what experts tell us about economic growth, on the one hand, and stories about live and livelihood, on the other … livelihoods that are simultaneously inside and outside of capitalism" (2015, 132–4). Carolyn Nordstrom (2004) echoes the same sentiment in her analysis of profiteering and power in parts of Africa when she asks: Is it because what is deemed as development is to be found in places in which economic analysts are not looking, because they would then have to reassess the ideas about the morality of economics and development?

In my work with the *mak pasar* all these years, what really caught my attention was the nonchalant manner in which they looked after each other, how they attended to their fellow *mak pasar*'s stalls when they took turns to perform two of their five obligatory salat (daily prayers) – *dhuhr* (around noon) and *asr* (in the afternoon and before sunset) at a *surau* by their markets – or when they had to run some errand. As mentioned earlier, when Mariyei, who sold beef, and Zainab, who sold chicken, went to perform their daily prayers, any *mak pasar* next to their stalls – who were also selling beef or chicken – would attend to Mariyei's and Zainab's stalls when their regular customers were there to buy chicken or beef. They would chop up the meat, charge and change the money accordingly, and then put the cash in a plastic bag to be handed to Mariyei and Zainab. It was amazing each time I observed these nonchalant economic transactions unfolding in front of me. I almost wanted to say they were … I do not even have the vocabulary to describe them. They were as if free from the level of competition and rivalries, if not greed, found in our modern and violent economies.

To be sure, there were village communities, families, and ethnic and linguistic ties between them that might have engendered such a level of trust, cooperation, and cohesion. But I think it is not inaccurate to say that the determining factors behind the formation of these cliques, these trustworthy and nonchalant alliances, were their reactions towards events that were most immediate to them, such as the imminent danger to the lives of their sons and grandsons, as well as to their own, and the emotional underpinnings of having severed their connections to their villages and the liveliness of their homes that they so missed. In many ways their struggles and their difficulties unite them. They understand themselves as belonging to a family, simultaneously creating and being created by it. Where they pray, what they eat, where they eat, when they eat, how they eat, can only be part of who they are. They are unique but not exceptional. They are most definitely not our so-called economic experts, which is why we have much to learn from them.

Chapter Five

Hiding the Clouds with the Palms of Your Hands

I consider the *mak pasar*'s open-air markets as local sites of struggle as well as islands of peace formed in a region officially in conflict. These were sites in which I found representation of lived experience, not only a culture of disbelief but also a culture of laughter and cynicism that contradicted the grand modernist narratives of nation, progress, and development. As surrealist Alfred Jarry puts it, this is laughter that is "born out of the discovery of the contradictory" (cited in Shattuck 1965, 25) – in other words, the emerging forms of relation derived and organized by forms of sceptical and cynical knowledge.

They say that sunlight is the best disinfectant, that despite attempts at cover-up and concealment some light will still shine through the cracks. If there were a particular phrase that captured the spirit of the preceding sentence and one that best described my interlocutors' cynicism towards how they felt the state had been dealing with the conflict, I first heard it in 2010. A few *mak pasar* stunned me with this phrase: *katok langik denga tapok tangae* (hiding the clouds with the palms of your hands). Zainab pointed to the clouds above, with a distant look in her eyes before covering her eyes with the palms of both hands. Then she pointed to the spaces between each finger even when they were pressed tightly together. She emphasized: "See, you can still see through them, you can still see the clouds, you can still see lights shining through between my fingers. You can see the government's *kejahiran* [ignorance] and *kebodohan* [stupidity] on display." These *mak pasar* could not have said it more pointedly than my translation hoped to convey.

I said to myself: *These are words that must be said, be written*. For these ordinary civilians, the consolidation of their cynicism became in itself an act of defiance or, at least, a gesture of defiance. *Katok langik denga tapok tangae* was their way to express metaphorically that regardless of how much money the government had spent to address the conflict – in terms of stationing more *tahann* and military equipment in the region, the (un)delivery of developmental projects, the funding by local NGOs, the constant staging of cultural festivities to purportedly unite the different ethnic groups in the region, the endless organizing of conferences and workshops on the conflict, and so on – they all amounted to nothing more than theatrics and, worse, scandalous performances that could not obscure the truth, the truth that the government was not entirely serious about resolving the conflict. In other words, the government thought that it could pull the wool over the eyes of the heterogeneous Malay Muslims in the far south. I read *katok langik denga tapok tangae* as expressing not so much disappointment as scepticism and cynicism towards the state that they no longer trust (not that they ever did) – a feature that constitutes the very texture of everyday life as lived by these *mak pasar* and other Malay Muslims with whom I worked. Why then, they would ask me, do they even want to *cerita* (dwell upon) other smaller, unresolved incidents of impunity, incidents that have become so *biasa* for them?

A Malay Muslim senator and former professor was beaming with pride when I told him what the *mak pasar* had said. "These *mak pasar*, these ordinary folks, could not have said it any better," he declared, before adding: "We Thais, or I should say the Malays, in the regions are used to window dressing. If politicians say the right things, some people might be impressed. But they are rarely followed by action. What we are seeing now is nothing new, how the government is addressing the conflict. They never change, just like in the past." He paused and nodded his head before continuing: "As a linguist, even I could not have come up with such a phrase. *Katok langik denga tapok tangae*. So accurate, so discerning. For us the truth, if not the hypocrisy of it all, is as clear as the sun." He continued to smile before turning serious to give an educated and sombre analysis of what was happening not only in Thailand's far south but in Thailand as a whole:

> Let me offer you a perspective which I hope you will consider. In my view, what is happening here in the three provinces is merely a symptom of a much larger problem that Thailand has been facing for decades. The present situation is a culmination of decades of practising a culture of double standard for us Malays and non-Malays. Decades of brainwashing, racist supremacist statements by those who called themselves leaders, and a system that condones and encourages racial polarization have brought us today into a mess we can't get out off. Even ordinary folks could see through and through it, like those *mak pasar* ... No disrespect but these *mak pasar* are ordinary people, and if they could say such a discerning phrase

to describe the situation, what does that tell you about our consciousness of the blatantly racist regime after regime that have governed this country? As an educator, I am alarmed at where we are, given that this is the twenty-first century we are talking about, and we are by no mean a young nation any more. The systematic creation of a narrow and bigoted thought process may help in a political agenda, but it does nothing for the recipients of such tutelage. What our leaders, if we can even call them leaders, regardless of their political parties, never mind the juntas, have done is to stunt the potential of our youth of all ethnicities and religions in Thailand, both in their hearts and in their minds, making it difficult for them to compete globally ... Even the *farangs* (western foreigners) are beating us in Thai boxing of late.

He viewed the current recurring conflict as an inevitable result of a system that has been in place for years, if not decades, and one that is sanctioned by those in power. He asked if I knew the system he was talking about and who was in fact prolonging the conflict. I wanted him to explain, but he did not give me a straight answer. Instead he offered more questions: "Why do you think the government, its agents and institutions, kept making mistake after mistake, ... one blunder after another? The way the *tahann* are fighting the latest insurgency, just as they were in the past, is a war among the Malay Muslims. In other words, we are both the targets to be won as well as opposed.[1] Do you seriously think the *tahann* were making mistake after mistake, or that they were purposely made to further infuriate the Malay communities? In fact, the insurgents are only too glad to see the government making mistake after mistake."

The senator continued: "You have to give us some credit. We have endured this recurring conflict. [Give] us some credit for our endurances, our talent for survival. And credit those *mak pasar* ... Katok langik denga tapok tangae," he smiled. I get it. Keeping the region in conflict is a justification for the presence of the *tahann*, as well as its expanding yearly military budget for the acquisitions of hardware that keep the international weapons contractors happy.[2] So long as the top brass within the *tahann* and the international weapons contractors were happy, it did not matter if these hardware acquisitions had any value at all in combating an insurgency or whether the majority of the hardware would even be deployed in the far south (Abuza 2011). War is about business, about trade. Trade, business, is about war.[3]

Concerning the possibility of peace, the senator did not see how that could be achieved unless the government were willing to offer some political concessions to the insurgents, and that would be a thorny issue for any Thai government. Not only the *amaat* but most Thais would resist such concessions. Besides, as his sources had informed him, the insurgents were reluctant to negotiate and were adamant about achieving full independence or at least some form of autonomy. This has been a thorny issue because some Malay Muslim nationalists would welcome some concession, even if it were limited. Some *tahann* top brass would go as far as granting full amnesty to the insurgents, but, at the same time, some would insist on some rehabilitation. There is a lot of division and uncertainty on all sides, to say nothing of the ailing eighty-three-year-old King Bhumibol's well-being at that juncture.[4]

Meanwhile the insurgency had killed not only many security forces (including civil defence volunteers) but also Thai Buddhists, including monks and more than a hundred schoolteachers. It is widely believed that the government schools that taught exclusively in the Thai language were seen as state acculturative implements for "Thai-icizing" the Malays. Hence, more than three hundred government schools have been burnt down since the start of the current conflict. This has had an impact on access to education as not only were these schools frequently shut because of arson attacks, but also, to avoid further attacks, class times were shortened, taking place from 10:00 a.m. to 2:00 p.m. Soldiers have been escorting teachers to schools, and monks during their morning alms. Some monks have even armed themselves with guns (Jerryson 2011). It was common to see monks, more like boy monks, escorted by soldiers and one or two Humvees when they went around in the morning collecting alms.

A large number of government schoolteachers have requested to be transferred from the regions, leaving a short supply of qualified teachers. Some non-Muslim villagers have even stopped sending their children to school due to fears of attacks on the way to or while at school. Meanwhile Muslim parents are feeling uneasy about enrolling their children in government schools.[5] As mentioned earlier, there were cases where these children were traumatized in watching their teachers being shot execution style inside their classrooms. With such brutality, the senator said he doubted that the insurgency had the support of the overall Muslim population in the region. As he put it, it was the indiscriminate, if not the spectral, nature of the killings – shootings, bombings, and sometimes beheadings of victims, or pouring kerosene on the victims and then lighting it – that had reinforced the perception that everyone could be a statistic, and this had fed the sense of fear and unease among the population at large. Consequently, many non-Malay Muslims had fled the region (Abuza 2009). For those who stayed, the conditions have forced them to adapt their lifestyles and create coping mechanisms to deal with the difficulties of reality. Those who tapped rubber as early as two o'clock in the morning have since deferred their work until sunrise. The *mak pasar* had to make the choiceless decision of living away from their villages. Many restaurants operating in neighbourhoods with Malay residents (even when they were located in non-Malay-majority neighbourhoods) have stopped serving pork. More and more bars and karaoke joints have closed. All 7-Eleven outlets have stopped selling beer and hard liquor.

As far as I know, the only business enterprise, and one that was immensely popular, that refused to compromise was Kentucky Fried Chicken. Unlike Malaysia and Indonesia (both Muslim-majority countries), KFC food is non-halal in Thailand. Apparently there was a rumour that a fatwa had been issued in Thailand's far south forbidding Muslims from eating at KFC. As far as I know, not a single religious council in the far south has issued such a fatwa. Regardless of whether or not such a fatwa had been issued by a religious council, this is a case where rumour was also a carrier of fear. As Michel de Certeau notes, rumour "is always injunctive, … the creator of mass motions that shore up an order by adding make-believe to make-do … rumour totalize" (1985, 143).

Some of my interlocutors said that they had not heard of such fatwa but, at the same time, they were not sure if it was safe to eat at KFC. Here their acquiescence is not "explained," so that it can be "explained away," as in the forlorn attempts of social science. To cross-check the truth of such fatwa was necessarily Sisyphean. As always, there were rumours and counter-rumours. There were rumours that might have been true, and truths that ought to have been just rumours. Alternatively, we can say that whether or not a fatwa against eating non-halal food at KFC had been issued is a non-issue, and we can interpret it neither as rumour nor as disguised signs of truth, but as something real and scary. As always, everybody believed what they wanted to believe.

Much to the disappointment of the Malay Muslims in the region, instead of making the necessary changes to operate as a halal-food establishment, as in other Muslim countries, the Bangkok-based franchise holder for KFC decided to close all its outlets in the far south. However, immediately after the KFC closures, many KFC imitations started popping up all over the far south. They certainly knew how to fill this hugely profitable gap, and these imitation KFC outlets operated by Malay Muslims looked like KFCs, with red and white colours but they always had big "halal" signs written across their shop windows and entrances. But some of my Malay Muslim interlocutors confessed to me that *these* were not exactly KFCs.

Speed of Normalcy

As far as specifying heuristically the situation of my being with my interlocutors in general, nothing was more real than one late afternoon when an IED exploded at the luxury C.S. Pattani Hotel. It was 1 August 2012, around 6:30, and I had just returned to my apartment from one of the open-air markets. It was another blistering hot and humid afternoon. I had my air conditioning switched to the maximum turbo mode when, all of a sudden, *bang*! It was immensely loud, and I also felt the pressure of the blast all over my skin. Even though the sliding glass door of my veranda and the windows were shut and I was inside the concrete-walled bathroom with the door slightly shut, I felt this sudden gush of wind rushing across my body. It was so intense that my keys flew off the hook. Immediately there was a blackout. Gathering my keys, I rushed to the hotel, which was less than a hundred metres away.

There I saw the debris-covered clothes and faces of the hotel's employees and guests as they were being evacuated. They were clearly in shock. I stood there, watching their blank looks and really felt the meaning of violence, of violence-related materiality. Within minutes the entire area was swamped with police, *tahann*, military intelligence officers, ambulances, and fire engines. The fire from the blast had quickly spread to the upper floors, and all the windows were shattered, right up to the eighth floor of the hotel. The few vehicles parked at the back of the hotel had been destroyed. There was smoke everywhere and a certain smell that the police later confirmed as benzene. I tried calling several hotel employees on their cell phones but there was no signal. A military intelligence officer was talking to a few police officers. When he saw me, he walked towards me and started a conversation, rather nonchalantly as if what had just transpired was not something out of the ordinary. He told me that the authorities had already jammed all mobile phone signals in the area in case there were more attempts to detonate more explosives. I was amazed by the speed of the assessment of the situation when he told me it was a fifty-kilogram IED that had been planted inside a stolen Isuzu pickup truck parked next to a concrete wall behind the hotel.

Luckily there were no fatalities, unlike the first time when the hotel was bombed in 2008. But the kitchen located on the other side of the concrete wall facing the blast site was seriously damaged. It was a miracle that none of the kitchen staff was seriously injured or killed. One hotel guest sustained a minor hand injury, and at least three hotel employees were injured by shattering glass. The military intelligence officer told me that the pickup truck had been parked strategically next to a concrete wall behind the hotel to cause minimal damage. As he put it, "It was meant to be a warning." What warning? That was a fifty-kilogram bomb. Two power transformer stations were also bombed in downtown Muang Pattani half an hour later, causing blackouts across many locations in the township.

That evening all the restaurants near the hotel remained opened as soon as the electricity was back on. At the restaurant across from my service apartment, the regulars were having dinner at their usual pace as if what had just transpired appeared to be *biasa* for them. Upon seeing me, one of them pushed a chair for me. Rumour had already started to spread about the motive of the explosions and whether the three explosions were connected. And just like the blasts at the department store and the clock tower that I mentioned earlier, they believed that the bomb was related not to the insurgency but to business rivalries. In other words, the insurgents were paid to do the jobs because they had become so darned good in planting and detonating IEDs. Some said that it was a way to create panic so that money could be made in future conferences and workshops related to the insurgency that would be held at other venues. I kept wondering if the people who were telling me these tales knew them for themselves or they had come to them second-, third-, or fourth-hand. This part of public allegations and rumour is, undoubtedly, not verifiable; perhaps it was even a fantasy that had come out of their own jealousies at the amount of revenue generated by the luxury C.S. Pattani Hotel since the escalation of the conflict in 2004, a collective fantasy that resisted truth and made its own reality. But I will not deny the power of rumour; it produced its version of truth and reality about the latest conflict. As Das points out, "the power of rumor lies in how experiences can come to life through the act of telling" (2007, 208).

After an hour of listening to their speculations of what or who were behind the bombing or bombings, I got on my bicycle and headed to the busy road leading to the local university. The road was eerily quiet with very heavy military presence, and checkpoints had been installed at both ends of the road. Just like the restaurants close to the luxury hotel, the teahouses along the road had opened as soon as the streetlights and electricity had come back on, as if normalcy had to do with streetlights and electricity. I saw some familiar faces at one of the teahouses, and they immediately asked me if I was at my service apartment when the IED went off. Some of them even laughed when they asked. I was also laughing by their laughs. They had also heard that it was a fifty-kilogram bomb and that there were no casualties. News had travelled fast.

After chatting with them for about ten minutes, I got on my bicycle and cycled to the old district of Muang Pattani, also called downtown. All the food stalls with kerosene lamps or electricity generators at the open-air night market were open, with a lot of customers. My friend kak Hah was busy stir-frying her famous *padthai* and *hoi tot* (oyster omelette). I was her busboy and dishwasher that evening because her husband and children decided to stay at home. When I asked her if she was frightened, she replied, "Takut, mana tak takut. Tengok, belum ada api." (Frightened, of course frightened. Look [pointing at the row of houses surrounding the night market], the electricity is not back on yet.) She somehow managed a smile as if to say, "Lives must go on." I smiled back. Before packing up, she fried me a plate of *hoi tot* with extra oysters. As I was eating, I thought to myself: "Am I the only one who is being extremely cautious and terrified of what has just transpired? Am I the only one thinking that this quick return to normalcy is absurd? Or, for that matter, the only one who is not yet *biasa* about the violence that has engulfed the region?"

On the day after the explosion the hotel owner, himself a senator, summoned together a construction crew to ensure that the repairs were done as fast as possible. Let me underscore: this was a day after the explosion. There was no further assessment of the explosion or any kind of forensics. One of the service-apartment staff members put it to me, sarcastically: "Ajarnn Kee, have you gone over to C.S.? There is an army of construction workers there. Khun Pong[6] [the owner] wants to be back in business as soon as possible. Even Khun Par [the owner's mother] and Khun Pat [the owner's younger brother] are there to supervise the repair crews. They want to get right back to making money." I walked to the hotel to see for myself. There was an army of construction crews. The owner, his mother, and younger brother were walking back and forth from one section of the hotel to the next, followed by an entourage of hotel staff members and construction supervisors. The hotel was back in business in less than two weeks. Conferences and workshops had already been booked, I was told, and they needed to be held. Normalcy had to be declared as soon as possible to avoid losing further revenues.

On the following weekend the hotel swimming pool was packed with children accompanied by their mothers, or, I should say, with Malay Muslim children. Prior to the explosion the swimming pool was usually empty because one had to pay to enter it. One of the service-apartment staff told me, again with a sarcastic smile, that the owners of the hotel had decided to allow Muslim children to use the swimming pool for free but only on weekends. He emphasized: "Yes, only Muslim children." Rumour had it that it was part of public relations. Others said that the kind gesture was out of fear that the hotel might be bombed again. I asked a few managers from the hotel but all I received were smiles.

Three weeks after the explosion at the hotel a group of armed men set fire to a Honda showroom in Pattani's Nong Chik district, destroying fifteen cars and two motorcycles. When Anusart Suwanmonkol (Khun Par), the managing director of Pattani Honda Cars Co. and part-owner of C.S. Pattani Hotel, was asked by reporters if his hotel and now his car showroom had become the insurgents' target, he deflected from the question by admitting that the general situation in the far south had become more violent and that these bombings had more to do with the intent of eroding public confidence in the economy of the troubled far south.[7]

The Routineness of Things

> The answer was simple: Because, with time, vigilance tends to relax, because all horrors are dulled by routine.
> – Roberto Bolano, *By Night in Chile*

After consecutive summer months of fieldwork in Muang Pattani I did feel a little calmer about the conflict. Although Muang Pattani had seen several bombings and shootings, the situation there did feel safer compared to other districts within the province of Pattani and, most certainly, when compared to the provinces of Yala and Narathiwat. However, I am not suggesting that, with time, as with the protagonists in Bolano's novel, my vigilance had relaxed, or that all horrors were dulled by routine. The fear that was not immediately perceptible to me was still there.

In Skidmore's detailed description of urban Myanmar landscapes towards the latter decades of the long twentieth century, she describes how the militarization of urban space serves as "means by which bodies are moved to different locations and restricted from others. This includes the bulletproof vests, bayonets, and guns of the soldiers and the crowd barricades, barbed wire, and roadblocks that limit pedestrians and vehicular access" (2004, 25). As mentioned earlier, I always had this uneasy feeling every time I encountered or approached any military accoutrements, not because of the battle readiness of these armed forces but because they had become the insurgents' hot targets. Paradoxically, the heavy military presence also made them vulnerable. The same was true for the pickup trucks that had their front, side, and back windows tinted black – and I mean dark black – which added an element of suspicion and fear as to who might be inside these vehicles. Government agents, insurgents?

I once asked a former army person why the windows of the military and paramilitary vehicles were tinted dark black, and the need for it, or why the *tahann* and the paramilitary personnel put on such heavy gear when patrolling the streets. He chuckled and responded with a catch-22: "When you have them on, they make you less vulnerable. But having them on, they also make you even more vulnerable. You become visible, a target." Such strange but familiar logic was being repeated daily for these military and paramilitary personnel in Thailand's far south or, for that matter, in any other insurgency-related zones. Pragmatically, it was in response to such catch-22 that most of my interlocutors, including myself, tried avoiding being near to agents of this strange and familiar logic.

To be sure, the C.S. Pattani Hotel bomb experience increased the level of my fear and unease and heightened my paranoia each time I encountered or approached these military accoutrements – Humvees, *tahann* or police station wagons, pickup trucks. The locals also shared the same unease and paranoia, but to them, it was *biasa*, or at least that was how they tried to project it. But I sensed *"biasa"* could also be a cover, a protective shield from something hidden underneath it. Let me elaborate. Once I was riding in the car with Pi Kun,[8] a Thai Buddhist – the owner of the restaurant across from my service apartment – to an open-air market. When her car stopped at a traffic intersection with a checkpoint on the left side of the road, a military Humvee immediately rolled up and stopped next to the left side of her car, on my side. As all traffic intersections have electronic timers that count down the seconds until the light changes, and this intersection took a full one-and-a-half minutes (ninety seconds) before changing from red to green, I had this intensely disconcerting feeling. I had passed by this intersection almost every day on my way to two of the open-air markets. This traffic intersection, like many other traffic intersections in Pattani, had become a site where life was constantly shot through with the anticipation of violence. Sensing that I had suddenly stopped talking, Pi Kun asked if I was scared. I asked if she was referring to the Humvee, to which she responded, "No, Ajarnn Kee, I am talking about bomb." She laughed but it was a nervous laugh. The sense of being at the wrong place at the wrong time rang loudly for us, something many of my interlocutors have also commented. Being safe or unsafe was dependent not only on some spaces, but also on time. One minute you were safe, the next minute ... When I think of it now, it must have been more disconcerting for

Pi Kun, even painfully haunting, considering how she must have been traumatized by the memories of her father's tragic death, something I will touch upon shortly.

I once asked Mariyei if she shared the same uneasiness and fear, even paranoia, each time she came close to a military Humvee or any of the other usual targets of the shadow insurgency. *"Inshallah!"* she said, "Our lives belong to Allah and no one else. I also have this feeling each time I am approaching those vehicles or when they are coming close to me, but what can you do? You just can't avoid them all the time. I am a pious Muslim, like all my sister *mak pasar*. We take our *salat* [daily prayers] seriously and we try to live our lives as morally right as possible." Somehow, I was not in the mood for getting yet another mechanical response that morning, and I chimed in: "Yes, I am aware of that, especially in regard to your *salat*, but don't you think your Islam has been hijacked by multiple agents, not only by RKK? Don't these people worry about going to hell when they die?" Mariyei gave me a long and nervous look. She remained silent for a while, before giving me a lengthy response: "We like to see ourselves as true believers of Islam, in the prophet and Allah. In the end, Allah decides whether we go to *syurga* [heaven] or to *neraka* [hell]. We are just ordinary folks, leading a simple but moral life. We don't like to talk about *syurga* and *neraka* as opposed to those who, like you said, are hijacking our religion. It's not just the RKK or whichever other groups are massed behind the current conflict. You have some *ulamas* and *ustaz* as well. You know the term *munafik*?" I was glad that Mariyei was not upset with me for being slightly impolite in my remarks.

And then she said something that I thought was spot on and made me laugh. "Besides, *syurga* has become so overrated by the frequency these people are invoking it." She proceeded to laugh but somewhat nervously as other *mak pasar* might have heard what she just said. She lowered her voice, saying: "Every time they talked about Allah, and about *syurga* and *neraka*, they would also, at the same time, talk about the manifestation of these or that *hantu* (ghosts) and all sorts of *roh roh baik dan roh roh jahat* (good and bad spirits or jinns) to scare people, especially at places that are historically significant in our struggle to retain our Muslimness. They have been saying for decades that Duson Nyior is full of this or that *roh roh*. Lately, some are saying this about Krue Se," at which point she raised her voice a little: "How can they even say that? Krue Se is *suci* [holy]." She continued, "Besides, *hantu* aren't attached to places but to people, to the living." I thought to myself, from her indignant manifesto, that she was spot on. She speaks to all of us. For me it was fascinating how the kernel of an analysis can be said so succinctly – indeed, a lesson to us academics.

Just at that very moment Mariyei looked over my shoulder and her facial expression changed. It turned serious. She said something elaborate in Arabic to a group of elderly men in white robes and headdresses, to which they reciprocated. Zainab also greeted them in the same fashion, and they reciprocated. When they left the market, I asked Mariyei to repeat what she had said, and Zainab to write it down in my notebook. Zainab said, "We greeted them with the blessing 'Assalamualaikum warahmatullah wabarakatuh' [May Allah bless you with safety and prosperity]," as she wrote it down, "and they reciprocated with 'Waalaikum salam warohmatullahi wabarokatuh' [May Allah bless you with safety and prosperity too]." That was a rather formal set of greeting and it was only after these men had left that I found out from Mariyei and Zainab that one of them was none other than Den Tohmena, the grandson of Haji Sulong, who like his grandfather was a highly respected figure in the region, one who was a powerful Malay Muslim advocate against Thai state violence and played a role as mediator for ordinary Malay Muslims (McCargo 2009). I thought to myself: "Wow! No wonder the fully elaborated Quranic greetings and what a coincidence that Den Tohmena would show up just as Mariyei was saying something about Dusun Nyior!" I was getting goosebumps. "The Haji Sulong Awakening," I thought, "has at least eradicated some of the traditional beliefs in ghosts, spirits, or jinns in the region, at least for Mariyei." Malay Muslims with whom I spoke confided in private that Haji Sulong had achieved almost mythical-like status in the three provinces for his reforms, and his advocacy for autonomy remains relevant to this day.

Erosion of Law and Order

Ever since two commercial aeroplanes flew into two tall buildings in New York City and kick-started the war against so-called terrorism by not only the US government – its chief architect – but also many other governments, we have been witnessing what Benjamin had described during his time: "there is something insufferably attractive about the margin of law where the state re-creates the very terror it is meant to combat, such that there will always be not only a military, but a paramilitary as well" (Taussig 2003, 202). As in many other violent sites, declaration of a state of emergency has been renewed each year in Thailand's far south since 2004, and draconian laws giving security forces extralegal power remain intact – a situation that fits Benjamin's well-known formula "that the 'state of emergency' in which we live is not the exception but the rule" (Taussig 2003, 392). This is very similar to

Pandolfi's description of the oxymoronic permanent state of exception in the Balkans: "Locked in this state of exception, the Balkans has become a site for the management of living beings through military intervention …, a process that places them in the midst of a permanent transition" (2010, 154).

To invoke Talal Asad (2012) once again, many scholars have underlined the role of fear and violence in theories of the modern state, in that part of the state's articulations of the law is premised on the fear of attack that only the state can curb successfully. Thailand's far south has been conscripted by a permanent state of emergency under the hackneyed trope of "security concerns," so much so that for those living in the region, fear in different forms remains widespread. Some fears – those relating to the insurgents and the militarization of their lives – were clearly visible and easy to articulate. It was, as some of my Malay Muslim interlocutors would say, rule by fear. This is less so for other kinds of fears that relate, for example, to the effects of neoliberal economic forces and their projects for social control, and thus to the disruption of daily life in conflict times. Asad also emphasizes that the most important political fear for many, especially in moments of conflict, "is not the state's continuous surveillance but its inability to carry out the basic task of ensuring security and orderliness" (2012, 272–3).

As killings have become a daily reality, and as law and order erode with every new incident that goes unpunished or unresolved, the population in the far south continues to lose more faith (not that they ever had any) in the government to handle the situation. Moreover, the indiscriminate killings of soldiers by roadside blasts and in ambushes further confirm that security officers themselves are seen as incapable of dealing with the violence. Such is the task facing ordinary civilians: not of escaping (since they cannot) but of inhabiting, enduring, and engaging with the difficulties of reality that constitute the geography of living in these conditions of not peace, not war.

Indeed, many ordinary Malay Muslims with whom I worked were fully aware of the inability of the government to manage their living conditions and they did not expect that any regime change in Bangkok, which occurred frequently, would make much difference to the grim slippage of their safety and livelihoods. As they so often commented, regardless of who or which political party (or an alliance of political parties) was in charge, it did not make any difference to the far south. For them, after each general election there had never been a new far south, but rather a neo–far south. And most of them would never bother to vote during the general elections, which, to them, were merely tired and ritualized exercises. It was as if they were saying, to invoke Sartre (1977), the philosopher of engagement, election is trappings for fools.

In their opinion, the government of the day had all along been mere subterfuge for the *tahann* to advance its interests. As Asad emphasizes, in most, if not all nation-states with a strong military, "[m]ilitary coercion is central to liberal governance, not only for defending the nation-state (and its citizen's rights against one another), but also, as in the US model, for defending 'humanity'" (2012, 279). This is certainly true for Thailand, especially if one considers the number of successful coups: nineteen since Thailand changed (symbolically, that is) from an absolute monarchy to a constitutional monarchy in 1932. The latest coup in May of 2014 was seen by many as the second attempt to complete the mission to restore the bureaucratic regime because the previous coup, in 2006, had failed to weaken politicians, notably those in former prime minister Thaksin's camp, and their political institutions.

Furthermore, my interlocutors repeatedly pointed out to me that even as each successive government recognized or allegedly declared that political solutions were needed to end the current conflict, there was no political will to put words into actions. To put it into perspective, since the latest conflict, which erupted in 2004, Thailand has seen the succession of five prime ministers. Thaksin Sinawatra from the Thai Rak Thai (Thais Love Thais Party), who won the second-term elections with a landslide victory, was overthrown by a coup in 2006, leading to the junta-installed prime minister Surayudh. Abhisit Vejjajiva from the Democrat Party won the 2008 election but lost to Thaksin's younger sister Yingluck Sinawatra from the Puea Thai (For Thais Party) in 2012.[9] In 2014 Yingluck was ousted in the latest coup. Moreover, the Democrat and Thai Rak Thai (later renamed Puea Thai) parties had formed on the basis of mutual hatred of each other, and, on top of that, the *tahann* hated them all. As such, not only was there no possibility of cooperation between these political parties, as well as with the *tahann*, but there was also the absence of any continuation of policies and practices between successive regimes on how to handle the violence-plagued far south.

As Askew (2010b) points out, a deal with the insurgents was highly unlikely during the Abhisit administration because the then prime minister's hand was tied by the *tahann*'s top brass and by the monarchy, which tended to strongly oppose the expansion of representative democracy. When Yingluck Shinawatra was elected the prime minister in 2012, she backtracked from her election campaign pledge to give some special autonomy to the far south, perhaps in part to avoid further fracturing her party's relationship with the opposition and the *tahann* on matters relating to Thailand's far south. In fact, the Yingluck administration was never particularly interested in the Malay Muslim insurgency and only made general remarks about the restive far south. The current junta-installed prime minister, General Prayut commonly dubbed by some of my interlocutors as officially the country's sole law enforcement officer, has been lukewarm when it comes to matters relating to the far south.

Moreover, many observers have pointed out that, so long as the conflict remains confined to the provinces of Pattani, Yala, and Narathiwat, and occasionally in a few districts in Songkhla, each successive regime in Bangkok remains content to assign all forms of counter-insurgency campaigns and strategies (if any) to the *tahann* (Abuza 2009; McCargo 2009; Askew and Helbardt 2012; Helbardt 2015). To be sure, each successive regime's lackadaisical attitude towards the conflict is not without notice from the Malay Muslim communities. As Ajarnn Abdullah and Sumree, the *mak pasar*, and other Malay Muslims often emphasized sarcastically, there were other more pressing issues in Thailand that flooded the national media imagination, like the border conflict with Cambodia, especially with regard to the Preah Vihear temple complex in the northeast; the farce of the yellow-shirt and red-shirt demonstrations; and the yearly floodings.[10] But most of all, running through all the fear is the suspicion and paranoia of having to rely on the government to protect them against the agents of violence that could very well be, as far as they are concerned, not just the shadow insurgents but also state agents.

Regarding the possibility of peace, on 9 March 2016 the government negotiators involved in peace talks made an announcement that they were preparing to publish a *progress* report in Thai and English outlining what they had (supposedly) accomplished in talks with the Majlis Syura Patanai (Mara Patani, an umbrella group comprising several current and former separatist organizations). When I saw the *mak pasar* that afternoon, they were quick to point out to me yet another blunder by state officials. Fatimah gave an analogy: "These officials are those who, when they see light at the end of the tunnel, go out and buy some more tunnels." That got us laughing. Pla and Nurul asked, "But why only in Thai and English? What about Jawi?"[11] Zainab immediately asked, while laughing, "Tell me, what has the stagnant peace talk achieved?" She continued: "They [the authorities] think they can cover the clouds with their hands. But with what they had done again and again, they simply can't. It's *biasa lah* [as usual]." Fatimah shared the same cynical sentiment, asking, "How *sombong* [arrogant] and *bodoh* [stupid] are these officials?" As Taussig emphasizes, while the "art" of assuming power "seems to be second nature to the magicians and sorcerers who have peopled history, it is not at all easy for modern state machinery to pull this off without looking gauche or stupid" (1997, 94–5).

To these *mak pasar*, the so-called peace talk and its intention to publish its report in English and Thai (and not in Jawi) was another indicator of pushing further into the future the negotiated end to the current conflict – another modus operandi for the story of deaths and miseries foretold. This is particularly true for the government's unabashedly arrogant approach to peace that can only be properly understood as placing a thin veil of deception over a concerted push to achieve a victory, while pretending to seek peace on the basis of a political compromise.[12] Contrary to many journalists and scholars, the *mak pasar* were not surprised when the Thai government and the BRN-C (a Malay Muslim separatist organization still somewhat active in Thailand's far south) signed an agreement to hold peace talks in Kuala Lumpur, Malaysia, on 28 February 2013. To them, the so-called peace talk, or stagnant peace talk as they put it, whether or not punctuated by sincerity was just one in a long line of faux peace processes that the state had initiated and presided over during the past few years. The aim was, as usual, public relations, nowadays playing to the international gallery and stalling the negotiation in order to keep the embers of conflict glowing.

Many Thais and Sino-Thais were equally upset with the government's decision to publish a report of the peace talk in English and Thai only. Pi Kun emphasized to me one evening: "The government needs to have more respect for the various communities in the far south ... the government needs to understand there are also those of us [non-Malay Muslims] living here. Okay, ... we might not be searched or become suspects, but the conflict is affecting us too. It is not just *them* and the *tahann*. Businesses are affected too. Look at my restaurant. I could barely survive without my regulars, and most of them are my husband's buddies." She said that the decision to publish only in Thai and English could only create more problems for all of them. It would incite more hatred. It would give further reason for the insurgents. Pi Kun went on to talk about some Thais and Sino-Thais she personally knew who had moved or were planning to leave the three provinces. She emphasized that these were established family businesses. It was a sacrifice they were willing to make. Pi Kun had also been thinking of moving back to Krabi where she once had had a florist business.[13] I sometimes wonder what prevented her from moving out of Pattani, considering how traumatized she must have been by the tragic death of her father, on which I shall now elaborate.

The Logic/Illogic of Arbitrary Reparation

I have known Pi Kun and her husband, Pi Beer, since 2009. I shared plenty of food and conversations with them, together with their regulars, which was why I was surprised, even disturbed, that none of the regulars knew about the tragic death of Pi Kun's father until one evening in 2013. It was like any other evening at the restaurant in that, at some point as I was having dinner with some friends and acquaintances, Pi Kun and her husband joined us as the evening progressed. But unlike any other evening, Pi Kun said something that stunned us all that evening. She started slowly, saying that her father was an assistant officer of a *tambon* (subdistrict) within the province of Songkhla.[14] I could see that her eyes were beginning to well up. She then said, "My mother and father were at a 7-Eleven when two masked gunmen entered the store and shot my father twice, right in the head in front of my mother." At that instant she took some napkins from the table to dry her tears. Her mother had never spoken about it since. And as with Zainab's brother-in-law that I mentioned earlier, the tragic death of Pi Kun's father was on 17 December 2003, before 1 January 2004, the arbitrary date set by the government for insurgency-related deaths to qualify for reparation. Even though her father was a subdistrict assistant officer and thus a *soft target*, and the assailants were clearly related to the insurgency, her mother was denied any right to file for reparation. All of us at the table were stunned. We were shocked not only with the knowledge of her father's death and the way he was killed execution style, but also because neither Pi Kun nor her husband had ever talked about this disturbing revelation in all these years we had made their acquaintance.

The silent was broken when at some point a military intelligence officer sitting at a table next to ours said that he could try to petition the government for some compensation since the death had occurred only two weeks before the reparation date and Pi Kun's father was a subdistrict officer. Pi Kun looked at him but remained silent. Her eyes were welling up. She tried to hide her pain and anguish, but the haunting suffering inflicted by the tragic death of her father was etched on her face. And then with an unexpected look of audacity, an almost devilish look of mischief came into her swollen, red eyes and she said, "You know, I would like us to have another bottle of whisky. Let's get drunk; it's on me." She called out to her employee, Ning, to bring us another bottle of whisky together with a pail of ice cubes. None of us talked about her father's tragic death for the rest of the evening.

As I now look at my field notes, I cannot help but wonder: What is the logic (if there is any) that those who died prior to the arbitrary date set by the government (1 January 2004) cannot be counted even though their deaths were clearly insurgency related? Is the qualification for reparation then part of the formula for counting death from a certain arbitrary date? I am fully aware of the politics of numbers. I do not want to reconstitute counting death as a sentimental artefact, an object to be smuggled into the already crowded room of my bad conscience. But I do want those whose deaths were insurgency related to be counted, only if they truly count; in other words, they must be known by more than just the number that was given to them – as in number 7257 (and 7258 for the next insurgency-related death, and a non-insurgency-related death that somehow also got counted, and on and on) – because otherwise the memories and stories of these deceased remain infinitely reproducible to the point of abstraction.

Taussig succinctly laments, with his usual cynical demeanour, the notion of honest statistics and numbers in a war zone, which applies to Thailand's far south and other forever-conflict sites:

> … statistical encounters with death and consist largely of squabbles with other people's measurements, which should, you would think, suggest that perhaps violence cannot be measured … In the end, the numbers numb, burning themselves up as soon as they appear in the dark firmament of our ignorance. They evade our grasp, eager to control reality through quantifying it. Worse still, numbers drain the meaning out of the stuff being numbered. How do you imagine the difference between 420 and 207 homicides per 100,000? [In the case of Thailand's far south, they were numbered as victim number 356 and 6578.] Moreover, the accuracy intrinsic to numbers is wholly belied in the case of death and violence by the devious, bloody and rumor-riddled society that brings those numbers into being. How could you possibly expect honest statistics in a war zone? Like corruption [which is also rampant in Thailand], numbers feed off truth. But unlike corruption, numbers flatten our understanding of the social world and the imagination that sustains it. (Taussig 2003, 86–8)

On the subject of not arbitrarily being counted as an encounter of insurgency-related death, I found out from Pi Kun several days later that the same tragedy had happened to Ning, her employee. Ning was a university student who shared a rented room with her mother and a younger sister close to the university. She had to work to contribute to her mother's income as a seamstress. Tragically the same style of execution happened to her father. Both her father and her mother were at a 7-Eleven when her father was shot and killed right next to her mother. And just like Pi Kun's father, Ning's father was killed before the arbitrary January 2004 date. Ning's mother filed for reparation but was denied several times. And as with Pi Kun, the same military intelligence officer offered to look into the petition of Ning's mother.

As uncomfortable as it was, when I approached Ning to ask about the petition as well as about the tragedy, she refused to entertain my questions. She forced herself to smile before walking away, as if saying, "Leave me alone." Proust once wrote that if the world of people we associate with bears so little resemblance to the way we imagine it, it would seem sensible to try and bridge the gap. But this is where the trouble starts. We cannot bridge the gap and, Proust insists, we do not want to. Since that evening, I realized I had no right to pry. The last time I was in Pattani was in February 2016. Both petitions for reparation were still pending, but I had the feeling they were not working out, judging from the fact that the military intelligence officer had avoided talking about the subject when I brought it up twice.

Chapter Six

Are We *Kon* Thai?

In my work with these *mak pasar* it was common to hear their frustration: "Are we *kon* Thai [Thai person] or not? Why can't we be *kon* Thai without being Buddhist? Why can't Malays be Thais? We do speak Thai, don't we? Why can't we be treated like the Chinese who have since become Thais?" I think they were saying: Why couldn't Malay Muslims be Thais without being culturally Thai and religiously Buddhist? Or, why was their Malayness an obstacle in the minds of the state to being Thainess, as was not the case with other minorities in Thailand, or even with other Thai Muslims in Thailand? Unlike the Malay Muslims in the far south, the Muslims in other parts of Thailand were not Malay and had accepted the creolized status of "Thai Muslim," one whose Muslimness is incorporated, if not subordinated, into a broader Thainess (or Thai identity), one who does not threaten the hegemonic racial and religious ideology of the kingdom (McCargo 2011, 839). Jory echoes the remark, that paradoxically, "Thai Muslims can even be seen as a lumpen category: within official discourse of Thai-ness ... there is a place for Muslims, it seems there is no place for Malays" (2006, 43).

Many of my Malay Muslim interlocutors were also asking why there must be a degree of Thainess. As McCargo and others have pointed out, "being a citizen of a country such as Thailand [and elsewhere in Southeast Asia] is not an either/or matter, but a question of degree, [one] fraught with ambiguity and complexity ... [whereby] some Thais are more 'citizenly' than others" (McCargo 2011, 841). Some analysts have commented on the parallels between the historical and contemporary dispositions of the Malay Muslims in the far south and the historical minority position of the Sino-Thais. However, while the legally conscripted, "hyphenated" citizenship experienced by the Sino-Thais may be a thing of the past, it continues to be the persistent reality for the Malay Muslims in the far south.

Mariyei once asked Fatimah and me, "Berapa lama lagi mesti wak wi jadi serupa mereka?" (How much more must we be like them?) I thought to myself, what does it take to convince the Thai state of the sincerity of their effort to be Thais and Malay Muslims respectively, if not simultaneously? However hard they might have tried, they failed to lose entirely their identity of old (and why should they?) and to be unreservedly assimilated; they were looked upon as foreign bodies (remember the label *khaek*), and it was probably this uncertain status, the lack of a well-defined identity, that enabled them to see more, to question more, than those who were satisfied with their politically inherited and natural sense of belonging. The position of a minority offers them a cognitive privilege. However, paradoxically, the Malay Muslims do not succeed and cannot succeed; under the cover of their "optimism," if any, one can easily detect the hopeless sadness of assimilationists.

Zainab once said something that I found to be profoundly ironic and troubling: "We wish the political parties in Thailand were race-based, like in Malaysia. There you see political parties looking after their respective races. They have a political party that looks after the Malays, a party looking after the Chinese, and so on. Are we correct, Ajarnn Kee?" Fatimah quipped, "And like Aceh, they now have freedom." I controlled my emotion. How could I blame them? After all, their consciousness was informed by what they heard or read. The late Irish poet Seamus Heaney put it best in his acceptance speech for the Nobel Prize in Literature (1995): "Without needing to be theoretically instructed, consciousness quickly realizes that it is the site of variously contending discourses."

Concerning Malaysia, I wanted to tell Zainab and Fatimah that what they had said was not only prereflexive but also preliterate and ahistorical. I wanted to tell them that it was precisely because most, if not all, political policies and practices in Malaysia were race-based, or race- and religion-based, that the very fabric of multiculturalism in Malaysia that was once the status quo had become a thing of the past. I wanted to say that the concept of a race-based political party was a product of British colonialism, and that race, if not religion, had been constitutionally politicized since 1971 in Malaysia with the implementation of the National Economic Policy to divide the nation along racial (and thus religious) lines. I also wanted to tell them that the Malay government ministers and rich businessmen, irrespective of their races and religions, would rendezvous and talk about contracts and deals to enrich themselves; there was no race or religion within the confines of their VVIP rooms. In short, race and religion have been, and still are, adjuncts to class politics. It is all about money, about how much these government officials and their business partners can continue to plunder the wealth of the Malaysian nation-state until one day there is nothing left. I wanted to tell them about the 1Malaysia Development Berhad scandal. Concerning Aceh, I wanted to tell Fatimah that ever since Aceh had achieved so-called autonomy from Jakarta, it had become one of the most conservative, if not the most ultra-religious, province in Indonesia. I could go on. But I kept quiet.

Reflecting on it, I remember the same scenario I encountered back in Borneo when my Hakka interlocutors – former communists or labelled as communists by the government – would often compare their dispositions to those in Indonesia, in short, to a comparative view of things. As with those Hakkas, my Malay Muslim interlocutors' theme of comparing their own dispositions in Thailand's far south to that of the Malays in Malaysia was a constant throughout my fieldwork, especially for those who had either dual citizenship (Thai and Malaysian, even though it is illegal to have dual citizenship in Malaysia) or relatives in Malaysia. It was common to hear them talking about the political and economic power of the Malays in Malaysia as if, by making comparison to the privileged position of the Malays in Malaysia, they were making claims or excuses of how they should also enjoy such privileges referentially. I should state that the comparison with Malaysia is also part of the separatists' assertion: to tell the Malay Muslim population that they would be better off to be part of Malaysia rather than Thailand. Therefore, to hear my subjects making this comparison is a reflection of not just their specific dispositions but also those of the separatist rhetoric.

On Muslimness

Much research from around the world has highlighted the effects of political violence and the production of bifurcated social identities, especially, in the context of this ethnography, of being Malay Muslim in Thailand's far south. From the Thai state's perspective, the Malay Muslims in the far south are often divided into suspects and non-suspects. Similarly, insurgents are equally suspicious of Malay Muslims who do not espouse their cause, or, worse still, for being state informers. Consequently, such narrowing of social identities also tends to impose the adjective *Islamic* as the only determinant of their identities, thereby reducing their multifaceted culture to its religious dimension. This is a kind of logic or illogic in which a social category such as Thai Malay Muslim, their marginal socio-economic status, and their diverse ideological, religious, political, and business affiliations, as well as rivalries, are reduced (or made to appear as homogeneous) to a binary set of denominators – suspects or non-suspects. Indeed, in the highly charged atmosphere of the unrest, reification of the Malay Muslims was the norm among not only state officials but also their own so-called Malay Muslim leaders, as reflected in their habitual use of the standard phrase *our culture and religious way of life* as a summary for an irreducible Malay Muslim identity in Thailand's far south.

As in other conflict zones, the pervasive feature of distrust of the others, the fear that someone could be an undercover state agent or an insurgent, meant that people "were constantly on guard as they navigated the treacherous reality of their social life" (Thiranagama 2011 38). Consequently, as Skidmore points out in parts of urban Myanmar, "nothing creates more self-censorship and fear than the possibility of one's actions and words being reported to the regime," (2004, 76). In the case of Thailand's far south, it is fear of being reported not only to state agents but also to the shadowy insurgents. As a result, when my interlocutors chose to talk about the current shadow insurgency, albeit reluctantly, they confided to me the discomfort they felt, unsure of who were the RKK and who were not, and even unsure if the RKK were solely behind the insurgency. "There is no trust [*kepercayaan*] among us Malays any more" was a frequent refrain, and they spoke of how this had negatively affected the level of *muafakat* (the means of living together) not only between the multi-ethnic and multi-religious groups in Thailand's far south but also among the diverse Malay Muslims.

Writing in the context of a new understanding of the Middle East, renowned political sociologist Sami Zubaida calls for a desacralization of the region, which deserves to be quoted in full as it applies to Thailand's far south and other Muslim countries:

> [We need to question] the predominant role attributed to religion in so much of the writing on these histories and societies, where the adjective "Islamic" is applied to every aspect of culture and society ... Religion is an important element in Middle Eastern societies, as indeed it is, or was, in Europe and elsewhere. But it is one among many factors, and one with varying inputs into social forms. Those social forms, however, are only explicable in terms of politics, sociology and economic and cultural processes, just like any other social formation. Within these configurations religion is "materialized" or "embedded" in social institutions and practices that are open to determination by economic and political factors. (Zubaida 2011, 1)

My own experience in Thailand's far south does not allow me the luxury to reduce them in any simple terms of what it means to be Muslim, Malay, or Thai. In my working relations with the *mak pasar* and other Malay Muslim interlocutors, I see similarities as well as differences among them. To quote Norbert Elias, "societies are nothing other than figurations of interdependent people ... and individuals within a figuration can be amicable as well as hostile to one another" ([1969] 1983, 18, 161). Ultimately the project that I am interested in is not the collection of individuals but a collective assembly in which "the joins, the disagreements, are allowed to show" (Buse et al. 2005, 39). For example, for those who regarded the Thai state as the perpetrator of injustice, there were others who resented the insurgency. For those who would constantly stipulate the history of the glorious Patani kingdom in the historical present, there were many others who professed no interest in that past or that any instrumental use of that past was ultimately a trivialization. This is not to say that ordinary Malay Muslims are not critical of the Thai state. The majority of them are critical of its immense bureaucracy; endemic corruption; the insincerity of its promises in delivering development and other services to the region; the staging of their history and their cultures; the lack of resolution of the Krue Se mosque and Tak Bai incidents; incidents of disappearances; and the purposefully prolonged peace talk, to name just a few.

To drive home the point about the state of endemic corruption not only in Thailand's far south but also in Thailand generally, Ajarnn Abdullah was laughing hard while getting his point across. "Fighting corruption in Thailand," he said, "must be one of the biggest jokes of the year, which ever year you care to pick. Take [the then prime minister] Yingluck, for example. The anti-graft agency is investigating her for corruption and abuse of power in her role in the rice pledging scheme.[1] They called it a scandal. But to us Thais, that was not a scandal. The scandal is that Yingluck's personal and political trajectory suggests it is impossible for anyone in Thailand, no matter how well meaning – and I am not suggesting she is – to get elected to public office and govern from that office without actively playing the corruption game. This is not a secret. Everyone knows about it openly.[2] That is the very scandal in Thailand. Welcome to Thailand, the Land of Smiles!" He continued laughing. It is crucial to grasp the sentiments contained within the appellation *Smiles* here, a sarcastic dialogic enshrouded in a chronotope composed of both contempt and laughter, something inseparable from the imputation of subjects that remained backwatered and denied coevality to this day.

To be sure, the unsettledness of being Malay Muslim in Thailand's far south was further exasperated by the coup in September 2006 that I touched upon earlier. Initially, most Malay Muslims back then thought that perhaps the coup could bring some hope and thus their moral imperative to forgive, albeit paradoxically, before justice arrived.[3] After all, the general who led the coup, Sonthi Boonyaratglin, was a Thai Muslim (note that he was not a Malay Muslim), and the then interim government did signal a willingness to talk. But such hope has since dissipated. As in the past, the then interim government resorted to the establishment of loosely regulated armed proxy groups working alongside paramilitaries to flush out so-called Malay Muslim extremists. Hanisa, a beverage vendor, had this to say: "Sonthi and Surayud's *hati* [hearts] lie somewhere else. Not here. The real *kuasa* [power] is in Bangkok and they don't care about us. We don't count."[4] In other words, in a Rancièrean (1999) sense, the ordinary Malay Muslims in Thailand's far south are the parts that have no part to play in the configuration of Thailand's socio-economic and political discourse.

In consideration of Hannah Arendt's reflections that rage arises "when there is reason to suspect that conditions could be changed and are not," did the 2006 coup create "an imaginary of hope" that quickly turned into rage (1969, 63), an explanation for the surge in violence in that very same year in Thailand's far south? Could rage be seen as potentially a productive analysis of identity, one that led to political awareness and activism? Could they be seen as spontaneous action to injustice, one that transgresses the "law" that has become (or had always been) an empty signifier in the far south? In some ways the sequence that marked the illusive experience of hope after the 2006 coup united some of these Malay Muslims as they shared a "lived relation to cycles of hope, then to cycles of discouragement, and on to the displacement of hope" (Ross 1991, xxii).

Experience with the cycles of hope, discouragement, and rage was especially unsettlingly for Malay Musim young men and boys. Their fear that was tinged with anxiety, menace, uncertainty, and certainly rigidity and vulnerability could also lead to rage. Indeed, as violence and political strife became the norm, many of their youth turned to that singular political demonic identity – insurgent – attributed to them by suspicious security forces and unfortunately also by so-called terror experts. As echoed by Abraham and Nakaya, "in some cases, adoption of such singular identity happens as a reaction to anger, humiliation, and confusion; in others, it may happen due to exposure to and indoctrination from genuine insurgents that takes place in jail cells and police lockups" (2007, 2308; see also Askew and Helbardt 2012).

Kratom Leaf *(Mitragyna speciosa)*

As I have mentioned many times, one of the major concerns of the *mak pasar* was their sons, grandsons, or brothers being recruited by the insurgents or getting into trouble with the authorities. On top of that, another concern was the dramatic rise in the consumption of kratom leaf, especially among their unemployed men and their youth. Kratom leaf (*Mitragyna speciosa*) is classified in the same category as cannabis and magic mushrooms. It is illegal to possess, distribute, sell, or consume this addictive substance. But the law is not effectively enforced because the plant is indigenous to the region. To be sure, consuming kratom is nothing new to the region, but it was the increasing number of local Malay youth consuming kratom in recent years, especially since the start of the current conflict, that was striking and, for some, a shocking new development.

Fatimah emphasized: "Recently more and more of our youth are drinking kratom, even here in town. It used to be a village thing. Nowadays, you see *them* hanging out by the shacks at night ... see, those next to the road, right there [she pointed to a few shacks down the road from the market]. They drink [kratom tea] from plastic bottles and they smoke. Some of them are only twelve or thirteen years old. What have become of our youth? Where are their parents?" Zainab shook her head and said, "Those are one-litre plastic bottles, one-litre Coca-Cola bottles," at which point Pla interjected: "Once I walked to their shack. I walked close to the shack to see if these boys are afraid of me. I saw not one but at least four or five one-litre plastic bottles of kratom on the floor. And there are several bottles of *ubat batok* [cough syrup] as well.[5] They looked at me as if I wasn't even there."

When I asked if the use of kratom at their villages was getting out of hand, they went quiet until Fatimah responded in the affirmative: "Yes, it is a problem back at my village. It is a problem because of the *tahann* [presence]. And of course, now that we are living in the township, ... we are not home to watch over them," she sighed. They all sighed. Mariyei sensed that the situation was only getting worse. She said: "It never used to be so bad. Sure, young people were consuming kratom even when I was just a little girl, but now this is something new. It has gotten worse since the start of the current conflict. And it's not just kratom. These kids, some of them *dek ponoks* [students who attend the religious boarding schools], are taking all sorts of *barang* [stuff/things].[6] They are spiking their drinks with all sorts of *barang*. I often wonder where they get the money for all these *barang*." "From the *tahann*, of course," Fatimah interjected. "They are the number one kratom consumers."

Most of the *mak pasar* I asked confirmed that the *tahann* stationed at their villages were the main customers of kratom. It is, however, quite difficult to confirm exactly how the role of the military presence is exacerbating kratom consumption among their own youth. It is quite difficult to distinguish between political violence and this kind of intercommunity violence, meaning between the soldiers and the youth at the village level. When I asked if these *dek ponoks* were taking drugs at their *ponoks*, Mariyei responded, "No, not at their *ponoks*." And then she laughed before continuing: "Most of them don't even have their *ponoks* any more. They have been shut. There were so many of these idle teenagers at my village the last time I went back. I worry for them." Fatimah, Pla, and Zainab agreed with Mariyei, and almost in unison they uttered: "*Inshallah!* May Allah help these *dek ponoks*, may Allah help us all."

Fatimah (and many other *mak pasar*) was thinking of moving back to her village even if that meant she would have to deal with the precarity of travelling during the *waktu geriya*. As she puts it, "the current situation with *kratom* and other *barang* our idle teenagers are taking is too much for me. And not just that, they do nothing but *lepak* [lounge] all day in the house and stay out late at night. These are just kids. What will become of them when they grew older?" Most of the *mak pasar*, including some *ustazs* and *ulamas* I spoke to, were worried that kratom consumption had gotten worse with the presence of more soldiers in the region. As Anusorn Unno (2010) points out, kratom has become a lucrative business since the start of the current insurgency, in part because it was spurred by the presence of soldiers stationed in the region who have become not only regular customers but even "protectors" of the illegal business.

A *ponok cikgu* said he was not surprised that there had been no serious effort by the government to curb the growing consumption of kratom generally or by the foot soldiers. He emphasized: "After all, [most] of these foot soldiers are minorities, just like us. They are from Isan, from the northeast, another backwater." Besides, it had not passed without comment by the local Malay Muslims that there was something amiss in having these foot soldiers from another cultural and geographic area who would be slow to grasp events in the far south. The *cikgu* continued: "Do you know that these soldiers, where they came from, were once labeled as *thin thai dee* [a region of good people] during the Second World War. I heard that Isan people are more Khmer than Thai. And what about us? We were labelled as *khaek*." He held up his arms, as if telling me how baffled he was, before continuing: "In the first place, we don't like to be called *khaek* … We call each other *orang* Patani. We are the locals, the natives, but we are up against a long-standing effort by the Thai state to reduce our physical and political presence in what was historically our land, the land of *orang Patani*." He smiled and looked at me before continuing: "I have a Chinese friend, a Thai Hakka. She is the wife of the famous *radna* noodle shop in downtown. You know this place?" I nodded. The *cikgu* continued: "She once told me *khaek* is a derogatory term that is usually labelled for the Hakkas, whether here in Thailand or in China and elsewhere. She told me a *khaek* is a person driven to seek refuge outside of his/her own territory ... With us here in the far south, the term *khaek* has no meaning at all. We did not seek refuge outside from what was once the Patani Kingdom. So, why are we called *khaek*? ... Does that mean we are the lesser minorities than those from Isan? Why are we not Thai enough? And even treated as enemies within Thailand?"

In *Siam Mapped* (1994), Thongchai convincingly argued that it was not possible to conceive of an "enemy within" Thailand until an answer could be given to the question "Within what?" This is especially true when the geo-body of Thailand has many contenders and the fragility of the kingdom was and is constantly used, paradoxically, to perpetuate the terms of national unity or, I should say, the fiction of national unity whereby this story of national unity does not and cannot exist apart from the contexts in which the state and its agents simultaneously declare their own existence and appear to do their own work. The cikgu was not alone in feeling insulted at being called khaek. He asked rhetorically: "Do you think the government cares about our youth? Or even their soldiers? What does that tell you about Thailand?" And this is really what concerns the mak pasar: the lives and future of their sons and grandsons, should the fear about Islam continues unabated or when these teenagers have no idea why they are being sought after or whose interests they are serving. These are some of the local faces of the war on terror.

Separatism, Exiles, and the Battles for Islam

> The exile's trade is: hoping.
> – Bertolt Bercht

When I met up once again with Ajann Abdullah and Sumree in 2013, they both pointed out to me, as they had before, that the political situation in the far south had reached a stalemate. Ajarnn Sumree asked, somewhat rhetorically: "We just had the last coup not so long ago. Do you think it is the insurgents that are keeping the region in conflict, or the *tahann* and other interests now massed behind it?"[7] I could not tell whether to believe him. On the face of it, it was incredible, but he told it with a half-smile that inclined me to doubt him. But, more importantly, he asked: "Regardless of the status of these self-professed leaders and their alleged involvement in the current shadow insurgency, why shouldn't the current conflict not be seen as a *pembangkitan* [resuscitation] of the long history of struggles for justice?"

At this point Ajarnn Abdullah offered some scathing remarks on the local elites: "They are usually the people who talk about defending Islam and yet they behave like *munafik*. They think just because they performed their obligatory *salat* each day and they dressed up like Arabs, they will go to heaven." And then he brightened up and made the same comment I mentioned earlier as coming from Mariyei, "Anyway, heaven is overrated," before laughing mischievously. He did not stop there. As for the leaders of former separatist organizations who were now living in Malaysia and Sweden, he offered this remark, which I thought was spot on:

Separatism from the 1960s onwards was a Malay elitist movement with diverse – sometimes mutually contradictory – interests and values. That's why you have the PULO [Patani United Liberation Organization], PLA [Patani Liberation Army], the BRN [Barisan Revolusi Nasional], and the list goes on. When these so-called leaders ... whether PULO, PLA, or BRN, resided in Malaysia or Sweden, they became nobody. They no longer existed. In the minds of some, they were old champions, even communists. In the mind of others, they were a vague memory of the sixties', seventies', and eighties' hopefulness, they were picturesque. Some had died, some disappeared, and others had made public apologies and started new lives.

Ajarnn Sumree smiled and tapped his colleague's shoulders for saying it so succinctly. Ajarnn Abdullah added more:

There is a difference between living here and abroad. While here, the authority could clamp down on them. But most of these exiles left voluntarily. They would voice their feelings once in exile. But what is considered a matter of life or death here is of nobody's real concern over there. These exiles are, on the one hand, unable to address those who care at home and, on the other hand, able to address those who do not quite care overseas. Besides, their knowledge of everyday life over here eventually faded away ... they lost the concreteness of the situations. If you read about those who now live in Malaysia or Sweden, are they exiles or expatriates? They are not even refugees. They have a choice. They are not hapless. If so, why are they treated like heroes? It is ironic."[8]

Ajarnn Abdullah looked at his colleague, and they were both smiling. Once again Ajarnn Sumree tapped his colleague's shoulders and clapped his hands. I did the same. Well said, I thought of both their reflections on, for lack of a better description, the symbolic transposition of reality and the moral torment of the many so-called past leaders who now live in exile or are dead or are living as expatriates elsewhere. These exiles are or were essentially political figures because they belong to a proscribed category simply because of their ethnicity, religion, or class. By some sort of levity of conduct or looseness of tongues they had incurred the displeasure of the state, a political crime against the tyranny of the state. But, ironically so, their sacrifices and courage, once the exiles transported to foreign lands, became subjects of romanticization, of pity, or, as Breytenbach, an exile himself, ironically put it, "a meal ticket."[9]

"What about the current insurgency? Will some of them also end up as exiles some day? And is their cause Islamic?" I asked. "Well ... we don't know since we don't even have the slightest clue who they are. Is their cause Islamic? Well ... yes and no, ... Perhaps Islamic nationalism?" answered Ajarnn Sumree.[10] Ajarnn Abdullah chipped in:

> It has something to do with 9/11 and the "war against terrorism." Images of Iraqi prisoners being abused and insulted by American soldiers are easily available on social media, and Israel's occupation of Palestinian lands is interpreted by some as a threat against Islam, even though I cannot agree with such interpretation. It's about land expansion, expansion eastward. And we hear about American secret prisons, even here in Thailand. And when you have a past like ours, the abuses in Iraq and in other Muslim societies can easily be internalized, especially by our youth. So, you see, it is both a local and a foreign problem ... It's a very sad situation."

Both Ajarnn Sumree and Abdullah said that even though the current conflict had reached a stalemate, they believed it was only going to get worse. Ajarnn Abdullah emphasized: "Here in Thailand's far south, as in the Middle East, terrorism is never about religion, never about Islam. And it is very difficult to defeat terrorism. In the beginning the government talked about defeating these insurgents militarily, which only led to more violence." Ajarnn Sumree interrupted to correct his colleague: "No, in the beginning they were never called insurgents, even today, at least officially. In the beginning the government called them bandits, terrorists, militants, gangsters, even drug addicts. Remember what [former prime minister] Thaksin said?"

Ajarnn Abdullah laughed and said: "Yes, in the beginning the government talked about defeating these bandits, terrorists, militants, gangsters, drug addicts militarily ... even fighting ghosts. And then they talked about defeating them psychologically." Ajarnn Sumree once again interrupted, to ask, "By psychologically you mean getting the Muslim communities to side with the government?" "Yes, they talked about getting the Muslim communities to help them defeat these gangsters, drug addicts, bandits, terrorists, blah, blah, blah, ... they are just names," Ajarnn Abdullah responded. He then asked emphatically: "But who are they? Do we really know who these agents of violence are? For all we know, they might really be, like what the *tahann* have been saying all along, *hantu* [ghosts], *hantu lawan hantu* [ghosts fighting ghosts]," which prompted all three of us to laugh. I felt I had become like them. We laughed even though we were dealing with a frustrating situation, a situation that had no end in sight. Laughter was one tactical way, an antidote to the stresses, worries, and fears, of trying to live sanely in an insane world that was, dialectically, at a standstill.[11]

To be sure, names make identity an issue: gangsters, drug addicts, bandits, terrorists, or even ghosts. Besides, is there an ideology behind the latest conflict? Is religion even part of it? I took out my notebook and glanced through the notes I had written during previous nights, before asking:

> If you would allow me to speak some of my perspectives about terrorism or, to borrow a term in vogue lately, *jihadism*. I want to ask, with what Ajarnn Abdullah said earlier that terrorism is not about religion, not about Islam, wouldn't you agree that these terrorists, whether they are of the Wahhabis or neo-Kharijite traditions, or those who subscribed to the Bin Laden doctrine, are themselves products of certain Islamic history and tradition, certain history and tradition, who want to assert their orthodoxies, their versions of Islam?[12] Let us say they possessed certain pathological mindsets where their interpretations of Islam were used to justify their unjustifiable, their violent, actions against those who did not subscribe to their one and only orthodox interpretation of Islam. If so, wouldn't you agree that the fight against such history and tradition, or terrorism or jihadism as it is being construed today, is also ultimately an internal Muslim fight, an internal Muslim struggle? Indeed, it is a fight and struggle for the very soul of Islam? Of course, terrorism or jihadism, however defined, is a problem to which the West too has to react, more or less on a case-by-case basis, but it is primarily "a Muslim problem," and diminishingly it falls on the shoulders of Muslims in the areas where it is waxing. Obviously, the answers to many of the problems with Islam lie also in the West, in changing their minds – a daunting task, I admit. Both you and I know there is a tremendous need to debunk their monolithic thinking of Muslim societies, their generalizations that are so totalizing as to erase all possibility of nuance. At the very least, it will serve the purpose of

bringing these long-stereotypical depictions of the Muslim world out into the open where they can be freely discussed.

Ajarnn Abdullah and Sumree both wanted to say something, but I asked them to let me finish:

> And yes! I am in complete agreement with both of you that this struggle has been hijacked by the rhetoric and military strategy of the war on terror and that it could only feed the monster of what it most desires: more violence. I agree with that. The war on terror, not that I agree with this phrase, cannot be a militaristic war at all. It has to be a reasoned war, a reasoned engagement with certain history and tradition whereby all Muslims will need to examine their words, deeds, moralities, and, most of all, their interpretations of Islam. They have to be ready for opposing views and interpretations. Otherwise, they would be behaving just like those who are possessed with a pathological mindset. One last point I want to make is the referent *Muslim world*. Do you agree, once you designate certain societies, or communities, nations, or regions, as a *Muslim world*, you are reducing a multifaceted political and social culture to its Islamic dimension? You don't mind the equivalent of a Christian world, at least not in the contemporary sense, or a Jewish, Buddhist, or Hindu world, do you?

Ajarnn Sumree wanted to say something, but Abdullah beat him to it: "You are absolutely right, Ajarnn Kee [and they stretched the word *Ajarnnnnn*], and thanks for giving us a 101 about Islam and the Muslim world." I laughed and *minta maaf* [offered my apology]. Ajarnn Abdullah smiled before continuing:

> We must not be hijacked. At least there are Muslims like us who know that we must not be hijacked by the rhetoric and military strategy of the war on terror, you know, George Bush, *lah*! And we also know we must not be hijacked by the Wahhabis or the Kharijites, which, by the way, came out from the same pathological mindset, same tradition. Do you know that, as far as Islamic history is concerned, the Kharijites were defeated before, defeated by the humanistic and rationalist traditions of Islam. Unfortunately that kind of mindset was not completely erased. They came back. In fact, the Wahhabis, Muslim Brotherhoods, the Taliban, or the Bin Ladens were offshoots of the Kharijite traditions. Yes, this is an internal struggle within Islam, and a military strategy is not the way to defeat them. As I said earlier, it will only lead to more violence.

Ajarnn Sumree interjected:

> You see, the problem is not only within Islam ... or with Islam. You see it in other religions as well. Look at the way Buddhism is practised in Thailand, a deep and unfeigned reverence for Buddhism exhibited by the government regardless of which political party is in power, and the generals, not forgetting the monarchy and Thais Buddhists in general.[13] It is the same in Buddhism in Sri Lanka and Myanmar. And what about Hinduism in India? What about non-religious institutions, the so-called secular societies, even in the university? What is strikingly odd to me is that you only see the proclamation of a war on terror when it comes to Islam. When it comes to Thailand's far south, all the so-called efforts so far have not stopped the violence one bit. And this anti-terrorism phobia has turned into an anti-Muslim phobia. The planes that flew into two tall buildings in New York City, and somewhere in Pennsylvania as well the Pentagon, gave a lot of political mileage to many in the West, and here in Thailand as well.

"Wait, was that a plane that hit the Pentagon?" Ajarnn Abdullah asked. We all laughed, before Ajarnn Sumree continued:

> Thaksin, the first one in Southeast Asia to jump onto the war-on-terror bandwagon and who believes what has happened to America could easily happen in Thailand, is long gone. And the SBPAC he dismantled has since been reinstalled. And still peace is nowhere to be seen.[14]

Ajarnn Abdullah interjected:

> Now that Thaksin has been ousted and, with it, the business-like CEO, Thaksinism has become a *wasm* in Thailand, everyone (except Thaksin's supporters) is wondering what all the fuss was about. In Thailand's far south, the term means nothing, except to some local politicians and academic analysts who think it was Thaksin's dismantling of the SBPAC that angered the Malay Muslim populations in the region, and consequently the revival of a recurring conflict.

Ajarnn Sumree agreed with his colleague's assessment:

> And speaking of peace, what about the peace talk? First, they got the Malaysian authority to act as liaison, then some BRN representatives or exiles living like expatriates in Malaysia got on board [we all laughed], and now you have MARA Patani, and who are these MARA Patani representatives? Do they represent the insurgents on the ground? Why MARA

and not BRN in the peace talk? Are they trying to purposefully ignore the existence of the BRN, or are they saying the BRN is no longer influential in coordinating the activities of the RKK militants? And why so many preconditions ... like rejecting BRN's demand for a neutral third-party mediator and international observation? Where are we now? But the most important question remains: why are ordinary civilians not invited to participate?

It was Ajarnn Abdullah's turn:

> Why can't we just call those behind the current conflict separatists or, better still, freedom fighters. You and I know all too well how dissenting voices were not only sidelined and marginalized, but at times also criminalized in our country. Haji Sulong and his movements were one among many. As such, why can't we see the many who felt disempowered at that time and those who have currently joined the insurgency as a means of regaining a sense of relevance and citizenship? Can we not say that they are beginning to assert themselves rather than be bystanders of their own history? And this is the truth: whatever you want to call them, they are very difficult to defeat because they can appear anywhere. Because of this, when you go against them, you become their target. Like what my colleague here points out, why are ordinary civilians not invited to participate in the peace talk? The overwhelming majority of casualties were ordinary civilians, even as some of them were part of the voluntary defence forces. And why are academics not invited?

At that juncture Ajarnn Sumree interjected and bemoaned: "Actually *one of us* here at the university was invited. His expert opinions on the conflict are being sought by the authority all the time at the peace talk." Ajarnn Abdullah and Sumree both looked at each other and laughed. There was a silent speech between them, but I knew why they were laughing and who was this *one of us*. Suffice to say here, this person was not a Malay Muslim. Ajarnn Abdullah continued:

> Look at who among the Malay Muslims are being killed. They are mostly the rangers, civilian defence volunteers, village chiefs and their assistants, the usual victims. Quite often they were ambushed when suddenly a motorbike would show up alongside them on the road, and BANG! BANG! BANG! What about those killed while tapping rubber? Those were mostly Malay Muslims, the civil defence force.

I felt that I needed to say something else:

> Please correct me if I am wrong. I think it is common knowledge to both of you that the range of debate on matters relating to what is happening

to Islam, hijacked that is, is far more wide-ranging in the Muslim world than in the West, which brings me back to something I said before: one of the solutions to the problems of Islam lies in changing Western minds. I would like to add that it lies also in changing the minds not only with the West but also within the non-Muslim, non-Western world. Otherwise you will run the risk of alienating indispensable allies, for example your Buddhist friends and neighbours.

Ajarnn Sumree and Abdullah both looked at me but remained silent. I felt as if I had spoken overly directly about something, even accusatory to their taste. Perhaps I had touched on something that was ultimately too sensitive, something too real that they could not, or had not been able to, comprehend, especially coming from someone who was not only, literally speaking, not Western but also not Muslim.

After a moment of silence Ajarnn Sumree said something funny, perhaps to overcome the sensitivities: "The government must also understand you cannot defeat them by handing out guns to civilians, at Buddhist villages ... even teachers or Buddhist monks. Who will they be handing guns to next? Doctors, nurses, ... next thing you know they might be handing out guns or M16s to your *mak pasar*!" That got all of us laughing again. Seriously, I could not fathom seeing the *mak pasar* arming themselves with guns, let alone M16s. Ajarnn Sumree continued: "Anyway, M16s are overrated, completely outclassed by the AK-47s during the Indo-China war. Everybody knows the Kalashnikovs are way superior, and what a name. But seriously, as it is, Thailand already had too many guns even before the current conflict. Now it is only getting worse. You don't have to apply for a permit. You don't have to pay for the guns. They are handing them out to you. When will this madness end?"

We sat there in silence, at a loss as each of us knew this shadow insurgency was going to drag on indefinitely. And just like the *mak pasar* and other Malay Muslims and non-Malay Muslims to whom I have talked over the years, all three of us knew there was no end in sight.

Perhaps exhausted from talking about the dire situations, Ajarnn Abdullah and Sumree both said they should get going, as we all sat there in our exhausted state of mind. The sun was setting; the *waktu geriya* was about to take over. That evening at my service apartment, as I went through our lengthy conversation, I realized that they both had not responded to my comment about the problems of reductionism relating to the term *Muslim world*. But then again, reductionism is not unique to the term *Muslim world*. The world is suffering from reductionism, and there is plenty of that to go around within the academy.

Freedom, Freedom, Freedom …

In working with my Malay Muslim interlocutors over the years, I have been struck at how little space for freedom their accounts seemed to offer. In fact, when it came to their intemperate social and political dispositions, the opposites were true. What is also truly painful for me is not only the idea of their helplessness but also their realism that would not allow them to entertain for a moment the utopianism necessary to save their world. They remind me of Ernst Bloch's book *The Principle of Hope* (1986). To paraphrase Bloch, the most tragic form of loss is the loss in the capacity to imagine things could be different. Amina was one exception. She was only twenty-two years old when we met on a minivan ride from Hatyai to Pattani in 2010. Amina had a bachelor's degree in English and History from Chulalongkorn University in Bangkok, one of the top universities in Thailand. Even with such an achievement she was unable to secure a teaching position in the far south, leaving her to give private English tuition to a few students at her parents' house.

Frustrated with her lack of success, she told me on several occasions about her intention to open her own school. She had ambitions, yes, but there were also obstacles, obstacles that I will call "tradition." In our discussion on the possibilities of setting up her own type of Islamic primary school, and in her refusal to conform to the traditional type of Islamic boarding school, she talked about the immense difficulties of her idea being accepted by the local Muslim communities, especially among the conservative *ponok* communities around her village. Her refrain, first spoken out loud and clear, was, "What infuriates me most is our *tradisi* [tradition] … so much restriction, suspicion, jealousies, rumours" when her father heard about her plan to start her own school, and then she muttered more or less throughout the exchange: "Freedom, freedom, freedom … I want freedom to set up my own school, my kind of school." She felt incandescent at the way things were so restrictive and conveyed that frustration with a raised voice: "I feel as if I am an exile in my own backyard … I want freedom. I will keep pushing … how do you say it? Our *tradisi* is holding me back, holding us back. I am tired of being a victim of my own *tradisi* as if I have committed a crime for having a dream. I feel like an outsider to my own *tradisi*. I am tired of engaging an elsewhere, but I will keep trying as if my hope could someday be reached. Let's take bigotry and politics out of education."[15] As frustrated as she was, she was brimming with pride with what she had just said.

Amina was one who speaks out. She felt alienated by her own tradition. I understand the conditions of her virtue that were called her crime.

Although *alienation*, as a philosophical term, is no longer in vogue, perhaps it is safe to pick it up again, if only for a moment. The ways she talked about the trappings of her *tradisi* remind me of what David Scott emphasizes: to understand "'tradition' in a far more critical sense, following Alasdair MacIntyre (1984), we have to remember the contradictions within any tradition, namely and simultaneously that 'tradition cannot have a life without density, without conflict, without alteration, without intensity, and without instability'" (Scott 1999, 10). Amina's frustration with her *tradisi*, or in her attempt to evade it, as endless as Sisyphus's, is a reflection that many times individuals are constantly being trapped in a net of rituals that reaffirm tyranny, and that these rituals, however minor or major, are intimate in nature. Amina's own principle was to stay clear of orthodoxies, as though by her determination she could oblige the "as if" to come true. Facing these obstacles requires great and scrupulous determination on her part. "I refuse to conform to any type," she said. "I refuse to be pigeonholed. I refuse to be a victim." Raising her voice, she asked, "What is my crime? I want to have the freedom to move beyond the clichéd social binaries that are tearing us apart. My journey is to end up at a haven where class, ethnicity, and religion no longer matter. My journey is to come out of the first bigotry of our societies, our *tradisi*." She smiled and looked for my reaction.

She continued: "You know my major at Chula was English and History. We read Dante. To me our *tradisi* is like Dante's Hell, the First Circle. No, it's more than that. It's a kind of Hell that keeps renewing itself." I laughed at her last point, but she wasn't laughing with me. She was clearly frustrated. "When I was at Chula" she said, "my two most hated subjects were political science and history. I cannot believe I survived those history courses. I only took a poly science course as an elective. You know why? I learned from taking one poly science course that politics are inevitably based on distrust. Of course," she laughed, "I did not say this to the professor. And history? A Chinese friend of mine at Chula, a bookworm, is into Chinese philosophy. He said something from Confucius that I will forever remember. I even wrote it down in my diary, no, diaries." She showed me the notes in her current diary: "According to Confucius, there is no justice in history, and that the inevitability in politics in generating distrust is bigger than the greatness of truth." She continued: "To me I feel the same about Tradition, with a capital *T*. Traditions tie us down, ... they generate jealousies, distrusts, inequalities. Perhaps as a student of history my view of history has gradually changed. History, especially Thai history, in every sense of the word, *is* so cruel [emphasis mine]. It doesn't give them a story that is just. It didn't give people time to mature."

Amina was not only exceptional but also incredibly competent and articulate in expressing her thoughts and her refusal to be encapsulated. She refused to sit on the sidelines, nursing a wound. Amina has cultivated a scrupulous (not indulgent or sulky) subjectivity. Such is a person who would find it impossible to derive satisfaction from substitutes furnished by illusion and dogma. I do not deny that overcoming the obstacles requires great determination on her part, or, for that matter, on the part of anyone who possesses such scrupulous subjectivity. Amina reminds me of the difficulties and the great determination and boldness of spirit she adopts in living in isolation from her society, her *tradisi*. I think it took a lot of courage and integrity for her to find her own voice and ways to express not only her feelings but also the reality of the setting she was in. Her optimism, indeed, was admirable, even if she said so herself. And can you imagine what a welcome experience it would be, it will be, for her to see with her own eyes what she has already looked upon in her imagination? I wish there were more Aminas in the world we live in.

I always make it a point to call upon her each time I am back in Muang Pattani, or I will contact her by videoconference. Aside from asking about her and her family's well-being, in various conversations I hinted to her that she might, even remotely, be interested in pursuing graduate studies. She told me she still hoped to open her own school. I could not muster up the strength or courage to remind her that her hope and desire could also be a trap, a burden in lieu of the challenges: the jealousies, bigotries, politics, her *tradisi*. I also have to say that her wishes are not something taken right out of the neoliberal playbook that transforms precarity into individual agency, or desperation into entrepreneurship.

On another occasion Amina told me she wanted to write a short story of her life which would bear the title *The Pleasures of Living in Thailand's Far South*. There is obvious irony to the title, made all the more significant because she was addressing her disapproval of the government(s) that marginalizes her communities. Her disappointment and ironies are understandable. What is more, she could no longer embrace this formal and familiar relationship with her *tradisi* without a certain disdain, without cynicism, one that creates so many obstacles for her as a young Muslim woman – or even as a young progressive Muslim woman, if that term is applicable at all without any sense of political cynicism. The *tradisi* she was confronting was not a pleasurable relationship but more like "pressurable," if it could ever have been described in that way.

She once looked at me and then closed her eyes for a few seconds as if in contemplation, before she found the courage to ask: "Has anyone ever told you about what happened to Haji Sulong, about what happened to him, his son, and a few of his associates? I mean, how they died? May they rest in peace, *Al fatihah*!" She shuddered before looking down, as if her spiritual resonant was not completely at ease with what she had just asked.[16] "*Sangat sangat sedih* [So, so sad]. How tragic. What a loss to suffer. We grew up as much as we lost. Or at least I grew up as much as I lost," she continued.[17] I shuddered as well, not just by what she said but by the sadness in her voice.

Amina once again closed her eyes as she mustered more strength to continue. She took a deep breath.

> Even after Haji Sulong was released … the community knew it was coming but not the tragic way he died … also how he was betrayed by his own people … by certain *ulamas* and especially the *orang kaya* [rich Malay elites]. This was what I was told by my parents. Sometimes when I think about their tragic deaths, it makes me afraid to endure any more. But we must, I must. When you told me certain elites here in Pattani said to you Haji Sulong was a Wahhabi, you have no idea how much that infuriated me. I told my parents after that. Haji Sulong was sacrificed. They were sacrificed. These elites have no values. They are the ones who remind me I must endure. It's as if Haji Sulong and their *disappearance* never happened, as if his only value was to teach these elites how to forget. Haji Sulong was aware of his tasks, and people were waiting for his words, but he was forbidden to speak. Nowhere was he free to speak, and there are some of them who never listened or chose to forget what he had spoken. Not for us. Haji Sulong and those who died tragically that day have not been forgotten. Their deaths, their absences, filled my life, our lives. Indeed, the rumour about the manner of their death is something we will never accept. To hear about and recall their tragedy … that they were given pork and stuffed into barrels filled with cement and thrown into the sea – I still have shivers running up and down my spine when I think about it. The way they were killed or disappeared is to me the deepest possible form of exile, deepest possible exile of their souls. We won't accept that version of their deaths. Or at least I won't. For me, we are also what we have lost, what we have been told about the death of Haji Sulong. I refuse to accept that, the way he died, they died. I refuse but it is also what I have become; what is lost to me has become part of what I am. Even though they are no longer with us, their absences are ghostly present to us all, to us … who have been denied our rights for so long. *Innalillah*.[18] May Allah be with them! May the soul of Haji Sulong and those with him that day be blessed!

She paused and was again in deep thought for a few minutes of reflection before she once again mustered the strength to speak: "I feel the same when I think of the obstacles I am now facing, in thinking and trying to set up my own school. My father once said to me that I am safe so long as my aspirations are in the realm of the dream, but when I must bring them back to the world, I am in danger. His advice has been haunting me since, for what he said reminds me of Haji Sulong. Haji Sulong was the beginning of a movement but …" She did not finish the sentence.

I asked if I could meet her father. She laughed. I never did meet him. The images of how Haji Sulong and his followers might have been killed more than sixty years ago sticks in my mind as an image not only of precarity but also of the worst form of human brutality. As Amina put it so hauntingly, so violently, it was "the deepest possible form of exile, deepest possible exile of their souls." I have to say I am deeply impressed by the ability of Amina – who was then in her early twenties – to comprehend the outer limits of human brutality. We shared the same feeling that the legacy of Haji Sulong and his call for a modernist Islam had achieved little to emancipate the Malay Muslims in Thailand's far south or to get rid of superstitions, bigotry, jealousies, betrayals, and suspicions among the diverse Malay Muslim communities in the region, especially those with religious and political power. Her anguish is a clear challenge to any naïve and simplistic rendition of a collective "we" among the Malay Muslim population in Thailand's far south, a collective and homogeneous "we" that is manufactured by the state, by the so-called Malay Muslim leaders and some conservative *ulamas* and *ustazs* in the region.

Repeatedly Amina reminded me that when I would write about the current recurring conflicts in Thailand's far south, I should elaborate upon their diversity, if not the rivalries and competitions among the Malay Muslims. It is worth quoting her in full:

> Your readers are in North America and probably Europe. Surely most of us won't be reading it if you publish in English. Besides, most of us cannot afford it. But make sure you elaborate on our diversity, including the past and current rivalries amongst us. This is important. Treating a people as homogeneous has many consequences, usually bad consequences. The world has let a lot of atrocities happen by treating a group of people as the same. The world watched as bad things were happening in Cambodia. What about Rwanda? And now, look at the Rohingyas. The Rohingyas might be worse off than us but we are not that far behind. And what about the Yahudis [Jews] and what happened to them in Germany?

Are all Yahudis the same, all of them rich? And how ironic it is the way they are treating the Palestinians. I am sure Ajarnn Kee can come up with many other historical and contemporary examples of what happened when people were grouped as being one and especially when they were the minority.

Once again, I was astounded to hear that from her. As Alan Klima puts it, "the deaths of countless people in our world that were sacrificed in the past in the name of religion, nationalities, race, ideologies, and so on can be brought to consciousness in a new global community only on the condition that the community can no longer remember the conditions that put them where they are, or can stare back at them or even speak on their behalf, since they are buried in time and cannot speak themselves. And this only on condition that the conditions that buried them there are no longer remembered as present, in the present" (2002, 15). I was so proud of what she said, but all I could muster to ask at that moment was, "Did you learn all these from your history classes at Chula?" I smiled. She laughed at my smile and stressed that all the history classes she took at Chula were about how great Siam, and later Thailand, was, that it was the only country during the long European colonial encounter that was not colonized, in part because of the diplomatic skills of its kings, starting with Chulalongkorn. She added: "It was not hard to figure out, once I understood, once I got it from what I read at one of my history classes, why the movie *The King and I* was banned in this kingdom. Sometimes it takes a minority, a minority with a minority perspective to get it." I was beaming with pride. Her minority perspective, her hope and imagination, might very well be the only sustainable hope for the heterogeneous Malay Muslims in Thailand's far south.

Amina was not alone in feeling betrayed by her own people, but she was far more outspoken about it, about being betrayed. Similar to what Vincent Crapanzano (2011) writes about the Algerian Harkis in France, the belief in the vantage point of the collective "we" among the Malay Muslims in Thailand's far south is more or less intentionally lost with this sense of betrayal. Despite the long history of the conflict between *orang* Patani and the Thai state, the belief in a collective "we" among the diverse Malay Muslims is more or less relinquished with this sense of generalized and historically layered betrayal by their so-called elites and conservative *ulamas* and *ustazs*. This might explain why reiterated calls for autonomy are at best ambiguously felt in the region. Even those expressions of a collective hope for some form of autonomy, or the occasional invocation of Patani's glorious past, are murmured with a half-smile, narrated as if emptied of life and saturated with doubt.

Repetitive Temporality

Writing on what the Israel's endless occupation does to Palestinian subjectivity, Kelly (2009, 2013) asserts that one of the crucial tasks of anthropology is to elucidate the limits of endurance, its elasticity as well as its limits, and that what makes violence so violent is the consequences from the exhaustion of enduring and engaging with the difficulties of reality that are without end. This is similar to Thailand's far south with its recurring episodes of violence in that they have not only hardened ordinary Malay Muslims' sense of reality but also produced a sense of profound scepticism of any future when the communities continue to be engulfed by a "tiresome, weighty now," to use a phrase underscored by Adam Reed on the temporality of prison inmates in Papua New Guinea, one that was structured by repetition (2003, 100).

Thinking about violence that is not only recurring but also without an end in sight, indeed, temporality that is not linear but repetitive, poses a conceptual challenge to an anthropology that tries to accommodate agency and that of any imaginative future. The difficulties of reality in Thailand's far south since the days of Haji Sulong were symptomatic not of change (since change has yet to arrive even though it is overdue) but of repetition, violent repetition admittedly but repetition nevertheless, for the diverse Malay Muslims living in the region. As I have already emphasized, they were waiting not only for change to arrive but also for violence to erupt once again. It is as if violence were the eggs of danger that were always incubating and then would hatch in a matter of time. In other words, it is as if violence and its irruptions are only a matter of time.

Picking up on Julie Peteet's term "terrorology" (2010), in the aftermath of 11 September 2001, Al-Marashi (2010) suggests the phrase "banality of terrorology" as a more appropriate reference to the barrage of concise titles and catchphrases like "New World Order," "axis of evil," "War on Terror," and "Operation Iraqi Freedom" invoked by the then Bush administration, terms that have become so pervasive in the media and the entertainment industry as they seek to create an identifiable enemy bloc. Al-Marashi points out: "The problem with these concise, catchy titles is that they repackage complex phenomena into deceivingly simple components. A war on terror implies that terror is something that can be targeted, fought, and defeated when in reality such a title is so broad and so ill defined that it becomes essentially meaningless ... [However, t]here were those in the Bush administration who wanted to target not just al Qaeda but Iraq and Iran, and a war on terror gave them free rein to justify any military action in the name of seeking out terrorists wherever they may be" (2010, 165). In other words, in characterizing the enemy (whoever they are), one lends it an essential identity, an essential identity that is essentially meaningless.

The conflict in Northern Ireland and other conflict zones has strong echoes with what is happening in Thailand's far south.[19] They have protracted conflict involving insurgents and counter-insurgents, they mostly have ethnic and religious components, and they have struggles for autonomy. But, most important, in each of these conflict zones the so-called enemy within the language of the divisive "we" and "them," depending on which sides one is seeing, "is not a 'counterrevolutionary,' a 'wild man,' or an 'infidel' but a fellow human being who is attempting to live meaningfully in a world filled with hues of gray" (Hinton 2010, 52).

Thus, this contradiction or uneasiness of a hope has proven to be impossible, to me and I think to my Malay Muslim interlocutors to consolidate the realism of what we call change.

Scores of writers and poets have written about such hopelessly impossible change in other conflict zones. This is a passage by Irish poet Seamus Heaney's Nobel Prize acceptance speech that applies to Thailand's far south: "The violence from below was then productive of nothing but a retaliatory violence from above, the dream of justice became subsumed into the callousness of reality, and people settled into a quarter century of life-waste and spirit-waste, of hardening attitudes and narrowing possibilities that were the natural result of political solidarity, traumatic suffering and sheer emotional self-protectiveness" (1995).

That change might happen in Thailand's far south is not only impossible but also necessary had me thinking of what was formulated by Derrida, namely the paradoxical calls for justice that are premised on the idea of the impossibility of justice and on its necessity (1994). It is one that creates flashes of awareness that forestall perpetual national consensus or, to put it slightly differently, a consensual public that is also founded on exclusion and violence.[20] Following this, it is one that makes impossible demands that refuse the terms of the fiction of national unity, a national unity that allegedly distributes equality for all of its citizens.[21] At the same time, it is with this simultaneous calling for recognition and the impossibility of recognition, this impossible situation, in mind that we should think about the temporality of violence and our subjects' endurance as repetitious or, in the words of Das (2014a) and others, as habitual in the quotidian sense.

However, this does not mean that every aspect of their quotidian lives is enacted dramatically. Indeed, if there is any future, it is mainly an aspect of the present. Being captives of the present and living for the moment are in no way unique to ordinary Malay Muslims in Thailand's far south. They are characteristics of marginal people as a result of the insecurity, instability, and poverty inherent in their life's worlds (Day, Papataxiarchis, and Stewart 1999). It calls to mind Orwell's observation in *Down and Out in Paris and London*, which could apply to violence: "the great redeeming feature of poverty is that it annihilates the future ... You think vaguely ... And then the mind wanders to other topics" (1986, 16). This is perhaps as close to the meaning as I could sense when my interlocutors explained that they were *biasa* with the conflict, and that its actualized or potential violence had almost seemed uneventful, an aspect of "ordinary life that is imbued with the presence of violence, but is, at the same time, generally uneventful" (Povinelli 2012, cited in Buch Segal 2016, 17).

By saying that they were *biasa* gestures towards an uncanniness of a political, social, economic, and psychological fatigue that is repetitive, of their daily endurance and engagement with their difficulties of reality. Even if the current conflict should end one day, and I realize I am sounding wishful, I am immediately reminded of their notion of "waiting": that they would be waiting for violence to recur, just like they were waiting for violence to recur prior to the latest conflict that has been simmering since the year 2000 and exploded in 2004. As in the past, the overall Malay Muslim populations in Thailand's far south have become sceptical of any durable solution to the current shadow-insurgency quagmire. And just as it was in the past, the response to the latest insurgency is mostly military, committing the same mistake and disastrous outcome as in Vietnam, Iraq, Afghanistan, Argentina, and elsewhere. The state has still not learned (or perhaps refuses to learn) that in any counter-insurgency war the "people's hearts and minds are never won militarily but only politically, economically, and socially" (Robben 2010a, 18).

It also seems to me that, if the legacy of Haji Sulong and his awakenings is to rediscover its politics in the historical present, a starting point would be the assertion that life for the diverse Malay Muslim communities in a modern Thai Buddhist hegemonic regime remains a maelstrom of violence, with the most marginalized at the sharp end. Or is it a paradox of separatism or political emancipation (not that many of my Malay Muslim interlocutors sincerely believed the current conflict to be about that) which the struggle for autonomy brings starkly into focus, that oppression must be met with self-affirmation, as in "I have dignity. You will not overlook me. Do not insult my dignity, my morals. I am a Muslim. *Allahu Akhbar*! [God is great!] To vacillate is political and moral death. No second thoughts. No room for doubt or the day-to-day aberrations of being human"?

At times, reading the narratives collected from my field notes, I have felt that the range of utterances my Muslim interlocutors are permitted narrows them into a stranglehold: "I feel discrimination." "I suffer as a Malay Muslim." "I am proud to be a Malay Muslim." "Why can't I be a Malay Muslim and also a Thai?" "I am *orang* Patani" (I am a Patani native). These sorts of utterances, while they sometimes promote strident ethnocentrism, also give rise to investigations of selves that inevitably go far beyond such a simple and positive fact as "ethnicity." For example, there is the self-consciousness of an individual trying to understand why the histories of the Malay Muslims in Thailand's far south have certain pattens to them; why, in spite of the oppression and the violence of assimilation, a particular ethos remains alive within a recurring violence that has become one of the longest-running but least-known conflict in Southeast Asia.

I think this might be the reason why I often get the sense of there being parts of the story that do and do not want to be told, moments that reach the surface only to be brushed aside or forgotten in the forward march of narrative time. In holding onto the rails or pigeonholes of identities that are conscripted by normality – normality being constructed by the state, by some conservative *ulamas* and *ustazs*, as well as by some male Muslim elites, and by, let us not forget, their *tradisi* – we foreclose the possibility of analysing desire and motivational complexity in a manner that adequately describes the multiple contradictions of individual lived experience. Like any story of a person's life, all the messy stories I have discussed are ensnared in histories that are not of their own choosing. But they needed to be told.

Chapter Seven

War on Terror?

Well rehearsed since the day that two commercial aeroplanes flew into two tall buildings in New York City, the George W. Bush's administration's (hypocritical) unilateral declaration of a global "war on terror" (or sometimes "war against terror") in the name of "humanity," "freedom," and "democracy" came with a clear binary choice – "Either you are with us or you are with the terrorists" – thereby shaping the discourse that is largely based on the threat of an imaginary, fabricated, or exaggerated political enemy.[1] The Bush administration's post-9/11 interventionist posture towards the Middle East represents a long-standing bellicose US foreign policy and the country's endless pursuit of war. Before there was terrorism, there was communism. And just as communism during the Cold War was a wildly imagined and exaggerated threat against a certain imperialism more than sixty years ago, the war on terror (or war against terror) is, in practice, an American imperialism, including its allies, against a largely imaginary set of enemies over expansive and diverse transnational geographies (Khalidi 2005, 2010; Bradley 2009; Yong 2013; Vine 2021).

However, it is important to make the distinction. In *Anthropology and the Colonial Encounter* (1973), Talal Asad describes colonialism as a foreign presence with possession of and domination over allegedly bounded local peoples and places. And as Engseng Ho (2004) emphasizes, with our current emphasis on transnationalism and globalism, the distinction between imperialism and colonialism is critical. The term *imperialism* is more appropriate as it refers to foreign domination over expansive multiple transnational spaces without the necessity of presence or possession. If we want to invoke Foucault's governability, the space is governed at a distance. Since the Cold War and currently the war on terror marshalled by the United States, the appropriate term is not *colonialism* or *post-colonialism*, but *ongoing imperialism*. The political enemy is also indeterminate in the sense that it is never given any formal or legal channel in which to surrender. To be sure, the current war on terror – now that the Cold War has allegedly ended (even as people still die or are maimed in parts of Southeast Asia by previously undetonated Cold War bombs and mines, and let us not forget the effects of Agent Orange) – is, once and for all, to consolidate and solidify only one kind of economic method, the neoliberal globalization economics and their long-standing (thirty-something years and counting!) blind eye towards it, both theoretically and practically. Never mind neoliberalism's contradictory definitions and unfulfilled promises or its incompatibility in non-Western settings.[2]

Since 11 September 2001, words like *militant, extremist, terrorist, Islamo-fascist, radical Islam, fanatics*, and so on have become the political lexicon for talking about the indeterminate enemy within and without the Muslim world. In many ways, the discourse on the war on terror is predicated on a truism of a certain cultural and political theory that goes something like this: the more modern (read: Westernized) a society becomes, the more its religious tradition declines or, at best, is privatized. In such a view of historical development, what it obscures is the wellspring of religiosity running through all societies, including those in the West.[3] Moreover, the root cause of terrorism, or whatever other names one wants to call this indeterminate enemy, has nothing to do with religion or Islam but with decades, if not centuries, of Western imperialism and its installation of puppet regimes across the Middle East and elsewhere.

To further emphasize that the war on terror is a form of ongoing imperialism or economic imperialism, let us think along with Carl Schmitt, namely, that to go to war in the name of humanity is not only absurd but also denies your enemy its humanness.

> Humanity as such cannot wage war because it has no enemy (it is supposed to be universal), at least not on this planet. The concept of humanity excludes the concept of the enemy ... When a state fights its political enemy in the name of humanity, it is not a war for the sake of humanity, but a war wherein a particular state seeks to usurp a universal concept against its military opponent. At the expense of its opponent, it tries to identify itself with humanity in the same way as one can misuse peace, justice, progress, and civilization in order to claim these as one's own and to deny the same to the enemy ... The concept of humanity is an especially useful ideological instrument of imperialist expansion, and in its ethical-humanitarian form it is a specific vehicle of economic imperialism. Here one is reminded of a somewhat modified expression of Proudhon's:

whoever invokes humanity wants to cheat. To confiscate the word *humanity*, to invoke and monopolize such a term probably has certain incalculable effects, such as denying the enemy the quality of being human and declaring him to be an outlaw of humanity; and a war can thereby be driven to the most extreme inhumanity. (Schmitt [1932] 1996, 54)

Besides humanity, the worst confusion arises when concepts such as justice and freedom are used to legitimize one's own political ambitions and to disqualify or demoralize the enemy. Ironically, as Hobbes emphasized time and again, "the sovereignty of law means only the sovereignty of men who draw up and administer this law. The rule of a higher order ... is an empty phrase if it does not signify politically that certain men of this higher order rule over men of a lower order. The high points of politics are simultaneously the moments in which the enemy is, in concrete clarity, recognized as the enemy" (cited by Robbins 2006, 67).

When the keys of the White House changed hands from George W. Bush to Barack Obama, one of the most salient aspects of Obama's foreign policy, one could argue, was his gradual retrenchment in the Middle East, where the United States had been hopelessly overstretched. Instead, what we were and are seeing is the focus on Asia, where booming economies and a rising China are threatening to reshape the global economic order. Asia is simultaneously a region where there is the greatest opportunity for expanded trade and investments, and where the United States confronts its greatest rival, China. In economic terms, China is the leading trading partner of almost all East Asian countries, while it is set to transform into a pillar of infrastructure development in Asia and elsewhere, thanks to major development initiatives such as the Asian Infrastructure Investment Bank and the Maritime Silk Road plan. China is hoping to be the new economic pivot around which Asia and elsewhere revolve, namely through its overly ambitious Belt and Road Initiative (BRI), and it is seeking to advance business opportunities through the Free Trade Area of the Asia-Pacific and the Regional Comprehensive Economic Partnership. As such, it was not surprising that President Obama, who was raised in Indonesia and Hawaii, had visited Asia more than any of his predecessors, and the United States was and is beginning to establish cordial ties with former foes such as Vietnam, Cambodia, and Myanmar and to have upgraded high-level dialogue with China, while courting and cajoling support for its major regional trade pacts with the now debunked Trans-Pacific Partnership Agreement as the US firewall against China's BRI.

At the same time, it was moderation season once again when leaders of the developed Western world were on the lookout for moderate Muslim states and leaders to engage in dialogue as their strategic, economic, and political allies and partners (Mamdani 2002). Needless to say, some governments of the Muslim world were equally pleased with this open invitation and were prepared to bend over backwards to accommodate the demands of the man who was residing in the White House. It ought to be noted that the honour of being anointed as a "moderate Muslim" leader is something that most Muslim leaders would wish for and cherish above all else, cognizant of the fact that such an anointment would be followed by a blanket support of their own domestic policies as well as lashings of economic, political, and military support to boot. During the bad old days of the Bush administration, countries like Thailand and Australia were given the dubious honour of being seen as the closest allies of Washington in Asia. Thailand was given the title of being America's "number one non-NATO ally in ASEAN," while Australia (or rather the then Howard government) was dubbed America's sheriff in Asia – a dubious recognition indeed that merely compounded the image that both states were anti-Muslim and anti-Islam.

In terms of Southeast Asia in the post-Bush era, Malaysia comes to mind as the prime candidate for the top slot of "most moderate" Muslim state even though the country is not exactly a beacon of freedom and democracy. The prime minister of Malaysia, Najib, even flew to Washington to play golf with President Obama (and he later played golf with President Trump). Talking about playing golf, let us not forget Erving Goffman, who capitalized on one's stigma and "played golf with it." If Islam is currently seen as somewhat of a stigma within the lexicon of the war on terror, those leaders who come from the labelled "moderate" Muslim countries can use their Islamness to make a career out of their Muslimness. To achieve political agency, they could reckon their religiosity opportunistically. In other words, under the present political atmosphere on Muslimness, Muslimness demands as much as it enables.

Meanwhile the governments of Myanmar, Thailand, Cambodia, Laos, Singapore, and the Philippines must be cursing their bad luck for not having enough Muslims to make the rankings and to play golf with it. What about Brunei? Perhaps it was disqualified when it became the first country within ASEAN to introduce the sharia law, one to which is subjected (arguably so) only its tiny citizenry and the mass of foreign workers working on its rich oil fields.

What exactly are the criteria for selecting a moderate Islamic state, if there are any at all? Take Indonesia. It has had a long record of strife and political violence, much of which was sanctioned, if not tacitly approved, by the United States and the international community, who are guilty of condoning the rise of political gangsterism in Indonesia in the past. It was well known that during the bloody counter-communist putsch in 1965, thousands of suspected communists of the Parti Komunis Indonesia and their sympathizers, and the commonly scapegoated Indonesian Chinese, were summarily wiped out by right-wing religious elements of the Nahdatul Ulama, with the tacit support (or at least non-interference) of the West. During the violent annexation of East Timor in 1974–5 it was also the governments of the West that turned a blind eye to the violence, on the grounds that East Timor might become the new "Cuba in ASEAN," and it was thus seen as the "red threat" to countries like Australia and to ASEAN. Let us remember one of the late Desmond Tutu's famous statements: "If you are neutral in situations of injustice, you have chosen the side of the oppressor."

Or perhaps history is not important in the selection criteria. Despite three decades of violent and arbitrary dictatorship under Suharto and his generals, commonly duped the Berkeley Mafias, Indonesia has now developed to become one of the few *less-managed democracies* in ASEAN. Its press has become freer, relatively speaking, than the press of its neighbouring countries. We should also remember that so many of the *reformasi* leaders who brought down the government of Suharto and his army were former student activists who were themselves Islamic activists and intellectuals. Today, Indonesia's Islamic universities are at the forefront of modern Islamic education and are producing Muslim scholars who have developed a rational, objective, and critical understanding of religion per se. Yet almost none of these developments features in the international media, which continues instead to harp on the idea of Indonesia being the hotbed of radical Islamist terrorism.

Conversely, next door in Malaysia we see a totally different framing of Islam altogether. Malaysia was one of the longest-serving *managed democracies* in the world prior to 2018 when the Barisan Nasional Alliance was finally defeated, after more than six decades, in the fourteenth general elections. For decades Malaysia had been cast and recast as a model moderate Muslim state for others to follow, notably by the international media whose own exposure to the living social realities of Malaysia might have stopped at the poolside of the five-star hotels in the capital city, Kuala Lumpur. Yet a quick survey will give a very different picture of the state of normative Muslim praxis in Malaysia. This is a country in which, until the last general elections, book banning was rife, and opposition members of parliament, civil rights activists, and comedians were selectively charged with sedition. Despite having a semi-new government, Malaysia is still a country with its morality religious authorities (at both the state and federal levels) that have become a law unto themselves, and even criticizing these religious authorities and their fatwas is considered high treason and blasphemous and could land one in a rehabilitation centre, on trial in court, or in jail. This is also a country in which feminist Muslim organizations like Sisters in Islam, transgender communities, and other vulnerable minorities are constantly persecuted and demonized.

With the Malaysian authorities' embracement of a religious totalitarianism in recent decades, the space for Muslim thought, expression, and social life has been shrinking, and what is worse is that the ultra-conservative religion of the Malaysian Muslims seems to only be fuelling hatred, bigotry, prejudice, and ignorance among the increasingly ultra-religious and ethnocentric nationalist communities. This is especially so of the altered version of Shafi'i Sunni Islam that is being practised by the ultra-conservative Malay Muslims in Malaysia. Yet despite all these developments, Malaysia is still cast in a more positive light compared to Indonesia.

As Mamdani (2002) and others have pointed out, such a binary and essentialist way of framing issue(s) – in this case of describing Muslimness (whether moderate or otherwise) – often ends up offering cultural explanations ("culture talk") of political outcomes that tend to avoid certain history and issues. As I have pointed out earlier, in the case of Thailand's far south such "culture talk" could very well be called a "leveling crowds" discourse, to borrow the term coined by Tambiah (1996), targeting the diverse Malay Muslim communities in Thailand's far south with antiterrorist rhetoric, in essence treating Muslimness as an object of criminality. However, what is equally crucial is an analysis not of the origin of binary representations of so-called secular and religious societies but of "the forms of life that articulate them, the powers they release or disable" in the concatenations of "the new concept of 'religion,' 'ethics,' and 'politics'" (Asad 1993, 2–7), which brings me to the Islamic boarding schools in Thailand's far south.

There Are Ponoks, and There Are Ponoks

Summarily labelled as bastions of religious conservatism, most Muslim religious boarding schools – (madrasah, *ponok*, *pondok*, or *pesantren*)[4] – from Kandahar to other designated Muslim sites have been accused of being contemporary "dens of terror" or potential "jihad factories" since 9/11. They have become one of the metaphors for Islamic extremist religiosity that the West has to confront – singularly the most dominant metaphor for evil. In predominantly Muslim countries in South and Southeast Asia such as Pakistan, Bangladesh, Indonesia, and Malaysia, as well as in Thailand's far south, many Muslim religious schools have been policed and raided. Some have been forced to close.

As mentioned earlier, following the Bali bombing in 2002, Thailand's then prime minister Thaksin was one of the first leaders in Southeast Asia to jump on board the global war on terror, unleashing Thailand's security forces on a hunt for alleged Islamic militants or terrorists in the far south. Meanwhile, the rest of the ASEAN member countries were curiously silent about Thaksin's bloody campaign as they too were likewise engaged in their own anti-terror campaigns. At the same time there was a proliferation in the vast corpus of literature – many of them bestsellers – on Islam and Muslims that sought to locate the basis of Muslimness in some primordial essentialist value that was a menace to civilized life and humanity – an antithesis to the so-called modern neo-liberal ethics that served Samuel Huntington, and those who followed in his wake, a way of essentializing the Muslim world and its diverse subjects, and thus its legibility.[5] To be sure, the hysterical global mainstream media is adding more fuel to the fire with its spurious claims about terrorists and terrorism.[6]

Even though Huntington's *Clash of Civilizations* (1998) that demonized Islam in its entirety has been increasingly discredited, it has been replaced with a modified view that terrorists are predominantly linked to Wahhabi Islam – never mind its ludicrous interpretation of Wahhabism. This view claims that Wahhabism, predominantly from Saudi Arabia, has been exported to Afghanistan, the United States and elsewhere in recent decades (Mamdani 2002, 766). Since then, Muslims all over the world have been not only increasingly essentialized but also "Arabicized" and radicalized. It is as if Allah is making a comeback, albeit in a very post-modern ecumenical way, so much so that our imagination and understanding of Islam have been increasingly restricted to a few religious lexicons, attire (as in the full-faced niqab worn by Muslim women), and gender segregation. What is missing is the pluralism of Muslim politics, its diverse and competing visions of Islam and nations among and within the Muslim world (Hefner 2002). As I mentioned earlier, it is most unfortunate that many conservative *ulamas* in parts of Southeast Asia have also, unhelpfully if not incorrectly, accused the revival of modern Islam since the beginning of the twentieth century as being a form of Wahhabism and its extremism.

Lost in the midst of all the paranoia about Islam and Muslims is the economy of the war on terror – the enormous profit for the producers of arms, the private security industry, surveillance technologies, and kickbacks given to governments and political elites. The world was still reeling from the East Asian financial crisis of 1997 when the war on terror was declared, which demonstrated in no uncertain terms the vulnerability of a global financial system that was operating with almost no legal and institutional checks and balances. In many ways, the war on terror can be seen as a godsend to many liberal-economic capitalists in both the developed and the developing world, manifesting, among many things, the development and expansion of an anti-terror industry.

So, once again enters another chapter for the international community, the crepuscular West continuing to give lessons in good management and good behavior to the rest of the world. It is like the Cold War all over again (as if the Cold War had ever ended in the first place); those hot battlefields live on for parsing reality, with Western military hardware and intelligence, economic aids and assistance, violently inscribed (read: violent gifts) onto the rest of the world to curb the spread of no longer communism but terrorism.[7] It should also be clear that despite all the sound bites and talk of mutual partnership and assistance, the power differentials between the donors and the receiving countries of such violent gifts in the war on terror are painfully real and terrifying. In some cases, it is not entirely clear if the donors are working for or against the receivers' interests.

Allow me to reiterate: the most recent layer of aggression against the Muslims in Thailand's far-south – whether social, economic, political, or religious – had roots in the monarchical tradition of Thailand. During the European colonial encounter, in an effort to avoid being colonized by Western imperialists, King Chulalongkorn (Rama V) signed various treaties with Britain and France and pursued a policy of modernization (read: internal colonialism) through which the entire kingdom was consolidated under a policy of centralized bureaucratization and administration (Che Man 1990). After the 1909 ceding-territory treaty with Britain a series of stringent assimilation policies were to follow. In 1929 Bangkok insisted that Islamic family and inheritance laws be codified into Thai language, which, if successfully implemented, could be interpreted by Muslim subjects as usurping the sacred ground of the sharia – the moral code and religious law of Islam – and establishing Thai as the language of Islam (Surin Pitsuwan 1985, 136). The notorious Thai Custom Decree (Rathaniyom) imposed Thai "modern" behaviour and dress on the minorities, and an allegiance to the trinity of Thai's nation, king, and Buddhism became the cornerstone of Thai patriotism. Following the Second World War, the king of Thailand was established as the patron of Islam according to the Patronage of Islam Act and the creation of the Chularajamontri (or Shaykh al-Islam), the Central

Islamic Committee of Thailand under the minister of the interior. Since the 1960s the *ponoks* in Thailand's far south have been forced, through legislation, to register as "Private Schools Teaching Islam" and to teach, besides religious subjects, the Thai national curriculum (Madmarn 1989, 2003). As if to add salt to the wound, the Thai government constructed several mosques in the far south with their minarets resembling Buddhist lotus flowers (Surin Pitsuwan 1988, cited by Joll 2011, 41).

All these efforts resulted in the state having not more but less control over its diverse Muslim subjects. They also resulted in a dramatic increase of those who pursued Islamic education in the Middle East and South Asia. To be sure, the exodus coincided with a range of global developments that have often been unhelpfully bundled together as "Islamic resurgence" – with its genealogy to the Iranian Islamic revolution and Shiism on the one hand, and the countering of it by the newly acquired economic power of Saudi Arabia in the form of Wahhabism, on the other hand.

Dek Ponoks (Ponok Boys and Girls)[8]

It is against such historical background and the current paranoia surrounding Islam that I met Nar, a fifteen-year-old Malay youth. It was a stifling hot day in July 2014. I was waiting for a van at the border town of Sungai Kolok (Kolok River) in the province of Narathiwat, one of the most violent sites in the far south. Like many Malay Muslim boys and girls in the far south, Nar went through the *ponok* system. He was the fifth of six children in his family to go to a *ponok*, but unlike the rest of his siblings, he was the only one enrolled at a prestigious madrasah on the other side of the Kolok River, at Kota Bahru, the state capital of Kelantan, Malaysia. This is the religious seminary boarding school managed by Nik Abduh, the son of Nik Abdul Aziz, or the Tok Guru in Malay (Great Teacher). Nik Aziz was also then the leader of a Malaysian opposition party, Pan Malaysian Islamic Party (PAS), and chief minister of the state of Kelantan.

Perhaps because my image of *ponok* students had been affected by what had often been broadcast by the media, I was pleasantly surprised when I found out that Nar was just the opposite of what I had imagined. He was sporting tight-fitting dark jeans and a black Metallica T-shirt, wearing Ray-Ban sunglasses (possibly imitation), and smoking under the cloudless sky and somnolent hot sun. It did not occur to me that this was a *dek ponok*. When I asked him how long he had been smoking, he smiled but did not offer an answer. He was quick to point out, however, that he only smoked when he was back in Thailand

and not at the prestigious madrasah where he was then enrolled. He laughed when I asked him if he was a heavy-metal fan. Still laughing, he asked if he could roll a cigarette with my Drum tobacco. We shared a moment of silence while we both rolled our cigarettes. After taking a few puffs, he said that my Drum tobacco was better than any Thai cigarettes.

Since we were talking about smoking and cigarettes, he told me he learned to smoke during his *ponok* school days mostly because, like many *dek ponoks*, they were bored out of their minds. Nar told me they would rather be playing soccer or the local favourite, *sepak takraw*[9] than be inside the classroom – much like any other schoolchildren at our so-called modern secular schools. He said the *ulamas* and *ustazs* at his *ponok* were aware that some of their students smoked. Nar explained, "There were traces of *daun ro'ko* [leaves of rolling tobacco] and cigarette butts everywhere within the compound." He went on to say that the only thing their *ulamas* and *ustazs* could not tolerate was students smoking in their presence. I would say that the *ponok* is more "liberal" than the elementary and high schools I attended if the only restriction the *dek ponoks* had to observe was to refrain from smoking in front of their teachers. I took down Nar's telephone number because we were taking different vans. I was heading to Muang Pattani, and he was planning to spend a few days with his sister at Muang Narathiwat before going home to Pattani for two weeks. It was their mid-year recess period.

Two months later I met up with Nar at my service apartment. After breakfast he took me on his motorbike to his former *ponok*, which was located about half an hour outside of Muang Pattani. He had already spoken to the headmaster about my visit. Ustaz Sulaiman, the headmaster, and two of his colleagues were waiting for us at his office when we arrived. They were happy to see Nar and immediately asked him what I gathered must be the usual questions: what was he learning at the prestigious madrasah? And, in particular, how was the Tok Guru's health?[10] They proceeded to talk about their own experiences at this prestigious madrasah and the invaluable *nasihat* they had received from the Tok Guru.[11] They were proud that one of their very own, Nar, was now enrolled at the madrasah. I later learned from Ustaz Sulaiman and his colleagues that, apart from the standard fare of religious subjects ranging from the Quran to the Hadith, religious law (*fiqh*), exegesis, ethics and morality, mathematics, geography, and history were also taught at their *ponok*. I forgot to ask him what kind of history. The headmaster told me to feel free to chat with the *dek ponoks* as he had to attend to some matters.

When I left the headmaster's office, I could not help but smile when I saw not only traces of cigarette butts on the ground but also some *dek ponoks* and Nar smoking under the shade of the trees. Eager to make contact with the stranger, these *dek ponoks* asked Nar a series of questions: "Bang ini dari mana? Apa nama nya? Buat apa di sini?" (Where is uncle from? What's his name? What is he doing here?) As soon as I had given them the standard replies, I was bombarded with other queries. Calling me *ajarnn*, they asked about what it was like living in North America, what it was like having snow, whether we had tsunamis and *ponoks*, and so on. Muhammad 1 and Muhammad 2 playfully asked if I was FBI. I was pleasantly surprised that they even knew about the FBI. And like any boys, they giggled or laughed loudly, and screamed almost hysterically when the subject of the opposite sex was brought up. Soon Ustaz Sulaiman came to give me a tour of the girls' section of the *ponok*, a gendered space separated from the other half where the boys were. I noticed that it was much cleaner and there were no traces of cigarette butts, but it was just as noisy. And like the boys, these girls asked me the same set of questions.

As Ustaz Sulaiman and I were heading back to the boy's section, young Ibrahim 1 and Ibrahim 2 tagged along and joined the other *dek ponoks* who were sitting on a bench underneath a tree. Soon the girls brought tea and a variety of *kuih kuih* for their teachers and the anthropologist before heading back to their quarters.[12] Ustaz Sulaiman asked if I was familiar with the *kuih kuih* and the ingredients in each of them. He said that some of these *kuih* we were eating were once only served inside the palace. The rest of the *dek ponoks* listened attentively as Ustaz Sulaiman and I were conversing in a clumsy creole (Pattani and standard Malaysian Malay) – or, more accurately, as Ustaz Sulaiman waxed about the glory days of the Patani kingdom. By that point I had already been introduced again and again to their selective remembering of their history, their midwives of history, so to speak. He seemed inclined, like many others I had met, to return to a certain nostalgic past in order to escape, albeit momentarily, the squalid and difficult realities of the present. Perhaps his nostalgia of a certain past was also invoked by the *kuih kuih* we were having that day, those only served inside the palace. I forget who once told me this, but it makes sense: "Food is a recipe for nostalgia."

When I asked about the current conflict and his concerns about the closing of several *ponoks* in the far south, he paused to think and carefully chose his words because he was responding not only to my question but also for the benefit of the *dek ponoks* who were listening attentively. He then said: "The conflict that is happening now is a recurrent theme in the region. This is because the government has always believed or chose to believe that all Malay Muslims are the same, that we are suspects of this or that violence. For the government these insurgents and us are like fish and water, inseparable." He smiled before continuing: "They don't understand, or perhaps they don't want to understand, that we belong to neither side. You see here, Ajarnn Kee, there is no side for us, at least not since after the days of Haji Sulong. After Haji Sulong, most of us had never been the *water* to PULO, BRN, and now, whoever these shadowy insurgents are."[13] Note that his comment "there is no side for us," because it has been chosen for them, is repeated many times in this ethnography.

With a melancholy look on his face, he turned to look at his *dek ponoks* as if pondering what would become of these young boys should the paranoia and fear of Islam continue unabated. "The government has never wanted our *pandungan* [opinions]," he continued, "and they don't care about our *perasaan* [sentiments/feelings] ... If they cared, if they listened, we would not be having these recurring conflicts." He asked if I had heard of this saying "Perasaan rakyat awam seperti buluh. Dan bila angin tiup, buluh pun akan membengkok" (The public sentiment is like a reed. And when the wind blows, the reed will also bend). "Surely," he said, "the government must be familiar with this saying."

I think he was also telling me and the *dek ponoks* that the Malay Muslims in the far south had become the infinite others who see without being seen, who hear without being heard. For these reasons I feel that the category Malay Muslim fails to adequately capture the complexity of the relations of power that oppress them, or the resourcefulness and fortitude with which they struggle. To reiterate, the diverse Malay Muslims in Thailand's far south have no part to play in the configuration of Thailand's socio-economic and political discourse, and history. Consequently, their interest falls beyond the pale of concern and, as such, beyond the hope of acquiring some measure of what they seek.

Ustaz Sulaiman went on to say that what happened at Krue Se mosque and Tak Bai only proved his point that the Thai government had never cared about the *perasaan* of the Malay Muslim communities. He asked, "Ajarnn Kee, you know about the tragedy at Tak Bai?" I told him I had read about it. "Just because some of those killed or arrested that sad day were former *dek ponoks*, the authority conveniently concluded that their *ponok ustazs* and *ulamas* were the instigators. Now you tell me, does the government realize how many of our youths went through the *ponok* system? The *ponok* system has always been one of the fibres of our communities. Surely the government is aware of that, or is it because they prefer not to? It is as if they want to further provoke our frustration and anger. It is as if they want the current conflict to prolong as long as possible."

Forgive me for repeating but this is important. The insurgents are also prolonging the conflict. Thailand, with its strong security apparatus, is seemingly helpless in dealing with the latest insurgency or identifying the insurgents (Helbardt 2015). Or perhaps being "seemingly helpless" is the intention. Not only is civilian lethality much higher in contrast to previous insurgencies, but also more Malay Muslims are killed than Buddhists are. It begs the questions: who are these insurgents? What are their motives or ideologies, if any? Are they really connected or an offshoot of the armed wing of the BRN-C, as many observers contend? Are they engaging in a "bleeding war," similar to what the Front de Libération Nationale (FLN) did in Algeria or what the *mujahideen* did to the former Soviet Union in Afghanistan? Or are we dealing with what Appadurai (2006) calls a Dadaist nightmare, the kind of violence that has neither a definable sender nor a decipherable code.

Ustaz Sulaiman emphasized that the participation of women in the Tak Bai protest was significant, particularly in a culture where women are often denied autonomy. I nodded meekly but told him that their participation was a choiceless decision, a burdened agency. He was in deep thought. I continued, "Perhaps some of the youth that were arrested at their village were their sons or brothers?" He gave me a look and agreed with my assessment. As for the closing of several *ponok* schools in the region, Ustaz Sulaiman looked at the *dek ponok* before saying, "The *ponok* system has always been a thorn in the side of the Thai government." He paused before continuing with what I thought was a really succinct statement: "You see, Ajarnn Kee, there are *ponoks*, and they are *ponoks*." He paused to see if I had understood what he had just said. I nodded. "You see, they are many kinds of *ponoks*, but what is often missing from their [the government's] stories is the multiplicity of *ponoks*, as would be the case for the multiplicity of *anuban* [kindergartens], *prathoms* [elementary schools], *matthayom* [secondary schools], and *mahaawittayaalai* [universities] in Thailand or any other country. And in every of these you also find a multiplicity of students. Take Chula and Thammasat [Chulalongkorn and Thammasat universities in Bangkok]. Everyone knows Chula is more conservative and Thammasat more progressive. Most of the student protests in Thai history have come from Thammasat. It's the same with the *ponok*. Some are conservative and traditional, others are modern. Many *ponoks* have gone through transformation since Haji Sulong. Inshallah! May Allah be with him in Jannah [Paradise]." I immediately asked, "Yes, Haji Sulong, I read something about him. What about him?" The *ustaz* smiled and was glad I had read about Haji Sulong. He went on to explain that since the days of Haji Sulong many *ponoks* in the far south had adopted a modernist, more progressive teaching of Islam, one devoid of all the traditional superstitions, and had included mathematics, geography, history, and science in their curriculums.

Then the *ustaz* said something I was already familiar with. He said: "But it has always been difficult to be a progressive Muslim in Thailand. We have government after government that seem determined to dismantle the progressive Islamic institutions because they lump these as part of the conservative *ponok* system, and therefore not Thai enough, not *modern* enough. The conservative *ustaz* and *ulamas* cannot help the situation because to do so would compel them to abandon much of what they believe, from the belief in all sorts of ghosts and superstition to this or that charm, even magic potions that could make one not only strong but also invincible." He asked if I had heard that some of the young Malay men who participated at the Tak Bai protest had drunk holy water laced with something, believing that that might make them bulletproof. He shook his head in disbelief and once again looked at the *dek ponoks*. "But the government has never bothered to find out what we are teaching, but instead hold onto their conviction, not even their suspicion, that all of us are either a bunch of traditionalist and backward education outfits or sympathetic towards separatism, even terrorism. To this day, they continue to believe that all *ponoks* are the same ... Like I said, there are *ponoks*, and there are *ponoks*. To them [the government], we are either *jihad* factories or potentially *jihad* factories, or *ponoks* of traditionalism."[14]

Since he was on the topic of Haji Sulong, I asked him about the authority's claim that Haji Sulong and company had just "disappeared" that horrific day. Ustaz Sulaiman laughed and then in a serious tone said: "While their claims may pull the wool over the eyes of those who are not familiar with the law of this country, it has not fooled us at all. Do you think the police who escorted Haji Sulong and his associates acted in the interest of the law back then, or even today? There is no greater failing than a dereliction of their duty. Kalima: la ilaha illa Allah, Mohemmed rasul Allah [There is no God but Allah, and Mohammed is His Messenger]." I gave him my notebook so he could write it down. He noticed I was smiling. Perhaps he was aware he was being mechanical. He proceeded to write down his recitation and gave the notebook back to me.

In the social and political context, Ustaz Sulaiman's view on the tragic faith of Haji Sulong, the recurring conflict, and the closing of several *ponoks* indicated that the welfare of the Malay Muslims in Thailand's far south (like other marginalized minorities elsewhere) was not only contingent upon a racialized and religionized division of space and time but also articulated by the exclusionary power and impunity of the state to exclude those affiliated with a chronology of certain problematic and unusable pasts – of an allegedly glorious history and later on as part of the 1940s Islamic Awakening, followed by the elitist separatist movements from the 1960s to the mid-1980s, and now the shadow insurgency. In short, they were all lumped together and charged under one temporal logic and problematic, that of *baeng yaek din daen* (separating the land).

When I asked the *dek ponoks* why they were enrolled at the *ponok* instead of the government schools, they all gave me an empty look. Ibrahim 1 gave a short and straight-forward response: "Nak belajar" (To learn). Realizing that my question was rhetorical, Nar saved me by intervening, "Their parents, brothers, and sisters, just like mine, went through the same system." This prompted Ustaz Sulaiman to declare: "This is our *tradisi*. Most of our children began attending the *ponok* at five years old. Within a year most of them could recite a portion of the Quran in Arabic, although it wasn't clear to me how much they understood" (which prompted a few nervous chuckles from the *dek ponok*). He continued, "Each *ponok* has coexisted harmoniously with its surrounding community for a very long time." He paused for a few seconds before reemphasizing his point: "We never forget we are part of the community, partly because we are all equally poor." It is true that being in one of the backwater regions of Thailand, the *ponok* system is still the cheapest learning institution for ordinary Malay Muslims to get an education. To reiterate, Ustaz Sulaiman continued: "There has always been a bond between the *ponoks* and their communities. This was a kinship built upon being poor, about pain, loss, love, humiliation, and survival." I have often asked myself, Why can't the authority get it? Or was it because, like what Ustaz Sulaiman and others said, the government has never cared about the Malay Muslims' *perasaan*.

Ustaz Sulaiman prevaricated when I asked him about smoking among some of his *dek ponok*. He brushed aside my question by saying that there were bigger concerns like joblessness, alcoholism, drug addiction, the recent upsurge in violence, and the militarization of their lives. And, of course, just like the *mak pasar* and other Malay Muslim interlocutors with whom I worked, Ustaz Sulaiman was equally concerned about the recent and shocking kratom phenomenon and all the other *barang* (stuff) their youth were consuming. He was concerned that kratom consumption was getting worse with the absence of law enforcement officers in the region, especially after sunset. He then corrected what he had just said: "Actually it is not the absence of law enforcement officers but the presence of too many of them. The villages down the road are full of *tahann*. Full of them who are making kratom a lucrative business. Full of *tahann*!" he said with added emphasis.

Bang (Big Brother) Mann accompanied me in his 1950s Toyota classic to this same *ponok* on my second visit.[15] Like many Malay Muslims, Bang Mann was not only a product of the *ponok* system but interested in this particular *ponok* from the stories I had told him. Once again Ustaz Sulaiman was waiting for us when we arrived. He was with a young colleague. The headmaster introduced him as Ismael. Like Nar, Ismael was also once a student at his *ponok* and had just graduated from the prestigious madrasah in Kota Bahru. "Inshallah!" Ustaz Sulaiman exclaimed, "for Allah is almighty for us to have Ismael back to serve his community." Once again, the headmaster and I strolled over to the benches underneath the trees where the *dek ponoks* were congregating. The *dek ponoks* were happy to see me again, especially with the goodies I brought along – biscuits, chocolate, and other snacks. Before I could even tell them that half of the goodies were meant for their sister *dek ponoks*, young Ismael and two girls came with a large tray of *goreng pisang* and some ice-syrup.[16] He said that the girls wanted to show their gratitude to an overseas *ajarnn* who not only came for a visit but also shared their concerns about the state of their *ponok* system. I felt grateful. Bang Mann felt the same. "What about you boys?" I asked the Muhammeds and the Ibrahims and other *dek ponoks*. "What have you brought for me?" They laughed and giggled. Some pretended not to have heard my query by staring up at the clouds with a distant look in their eyes.

Soon the two girls left, and as Bang Mann and I were eating the freshly fried *goreng pisang* and sipping our iced-syrup, the boys were busy devouring their half of the goodies, mostly the chocolate. I asked Ustaz Sulaiman and young Ismael if they had heard of the alleged cooperation, however covert or silent, between agents of the shadow insurgency and the local mafias and drug dealers. Ustaz Sulaiman asked if I could elaborate. I told him I had heard, as well as read in the newspapers and a PhD dissertation, that the authorities had noted that drug dealers had hired insurgents to retaliate each time their drugs were confiscated. Furthermore, the authorities had also noted that for the local mafias to claim ignorance of who these insurgents were, even on their own turf of operation, was not only suspicious but also interesting. It was interesting because if the allegation was true, it suggested that there must be certain silent cooperation between them. At the very least, it would suggest that the local mafias were afraid of the insurgents and avoided any open confrontations with them. Moreover, if the allegation of cooperation was true, would that undermine the self-perception of these insurgents not only as devout Muslims fighting for an Islamic order but also as agents condoning the spread of drugs, extortion, prostitution, gambling, and other moral disintegrations of society?

Ustaz Sulaiman pondered my questions. He looked at young Ismael and the rest of the *dek ponok* to see if they had been listening to what I had said, before he dissected the allegations I had heard or read. "First of all," he said, "I have also heard of these allegations but, like I said, they were allegations. It could be true that the drug dealers, who could also be the local mafias, do hire the insurgents, or call it whatever you like, to do their retaliations. It could also be true that the local mafias are scared of these agents because they could be anyone, lurking in the shadows. And they are getting so good at killing, at making and detonating IEDs. And they are armed with Aks and M16s. It was the same with the communists back in the days. They were guerillas, just like the current insurgents, and they lived amid the *rakyat* [the populace]. And just like the communists then, did the local mafias reveal their whereabouts? No! They were afraid of the communists back then, just as they are afraid of whoever these shadowy agents are. All that the local mafias and drug dealers care about is business, about getting rich at the expense of the *rakyat*; they are not like the communists."

I sensed that Ustaz Sulaiman was satisfied with his analysis, judging from the acknowledged nods and smiles from Bang Mann and Ismael, which prompted him to continue. "As to your point or question that if there was cooperation between the agents of the shadow insurgency and the drug dealers or the mafias, like what you say or read, would that undermine their moral indignations as true Muslims: First of all, I have yet to read or hear of any declaration by these insurgents, militants, stating that what they are fighting for is acting in the faith of Islam. Sure, I heard that the RKK had issued warnings against Muslim businesses that open on Friday as being unholy, but where in the Quran does it say that Muslims cannot open their businesses on Friday? ... The current conflict is not about Islam. It is about fighting for respect, for dignity; it is about fighting to be heard, to be counted. That is what I think it is."

He paused before continuing. "Actually there is more. Here, like the other border regions of Thailand, it is almost like a lawless territory ... being notoriously good for those seeking fortunes through illegal and immoral means. Like the Golden Triangle ... we also have plenty of drug dealers, smugglers, mafias, prostitution, gambling rings, even human trafficking. Have you not read about the discovery of mass graves ... of the Rohingyas along the Thai-Malaysian borders? Not far from here. From what I heard, some top brass military generals are complicit in it. They [the Rohingyas] look like Indians but are Muslims living in a Buddhist country. I hope we will not become like them in Thailand. Not only are they internally displaced and often without *bantuan undang undang* [legal recourse], but also there is a *kekosongan pengadilan* [judiciary vacuum] when it comes to the Rohingyas, more so than other minorities in Myanmar. And when they fled Myanmar, they ended up in a lawless territory, finding themselves, once again, in a situation of *kekosongan pangadilan*. *Kesian!* [Pitiful!] Justice is something foreign to them. I heard they are listed as the most persecuted peoples in the world by the United Nations."[17]

Once again, he looked at the *dek ponoks* to see if they were listening to what he had said. Seeing that some of them were listening attentively, he continued: "But unlike other border regions, here in the far south, when crimes are committed, they are usually attributed to the insurgents. It was the same back then [during the Cold War]. It was either the separatists or the communists. We know many of the crimes had nothing to do with the current insurgency but were labelled as such. Now, why is that? The government says the current insurgency is a shadow insurgency … as they commonly would say, fighting ghosts. Why ghosts? What ghosts? Why not fighting the RKK? Or is it because by invoking 'fighting ghosts,' it allows the *tahann* to prolong the conflict. Separatism or insurgency are catch-all terms; they give the *tahann* and police an excuse to ask for more money, more equipment. It is about *fasifikasi* [pacification], a form of violence directed at the uncontrolled borderland populations that are liable to erupt again and again. What they [the *tahann*] are doing here is not about peace or any of your Western versions of *humanitarianism*" – he laughs as soon as he utters the word, and I laugh with him as well – "but about the logic of the will to dominate, to *fasifi* [pacify].[18] By calling it an insurgency, it promotes fear, and fear is money. It's business." He smiled. "Here in the far south there is no legitimate or hegemonic *tahann*, just a few hundred thousand conscripted minorities or, you might say, those committed to certain state ideology and in turn receiving their salaries. There are conflicts not only in the far south but all over Thailand. And to be a *tahann* is to have the best job and a lucrative one. So do tell me, Ajarnn Kee, who is sustaining the conflict?" And just like what I had heard from others, the headmaster asked: "And do you know most of these *tahann* stationed here are from Isan? Just like us, Isan is also one of the backwaters of Thailand. So you have it, using minorities to battle with minorities." All the while, Bang Mann was listening attentively, watching with his eyes and nodding his head. After that, for weeks, if not months, he reiterated to me and his daughter, and to the delight of the regulars at his garage, what the headmaster had said. Each time, he would repeat, "Fear is business." At one point he asked me to explain *fasifikasi*.

Since my introduction to this *ponok* by Nar, and after my second visit with *Bang* Mann, I went back a few more times with my friend Faosee, the university student. On these visits what I saw at this *ponok* was a rather different picture from what has commonly been portrayed about the *ponoks* as rigidly strict and pious or as the playground for radical Islam. Similar to Farish Noor's observation of the madrasahs in Afghanistan, Pakistan, Kashmir, Java, Bali, and southern Thailand (2009), while it is impossible to deny that militant groups might have infiltrated some of the *ponoks* in Thailand's far south to recruit young members, one should not generalize that making bombs and shooting guns are part of their standard curriculum. As the title of this section alluded, "there are *ponoks*, and there are *ponoks*." The arrival of the current wave of horror, perhaps even to claim these playful children who are still oblivious to what had re-emerged, reminds me of Shahla Talebi's recollection about the terror during the Shah's reign and later the Islamic regime in Iran as "this contaminating power of violence and money, of the way they both often spoil whoever or whatever comes their way" (2011, 11). This brings me to the story of another *ponok*, the one that Zainad's son attended before it was shut down by the authorities.

A Ponok in Narathiwat

Located somewhere in Narathiwat is one of the largest *ponoks* in the far south. Like any other *ponok*, it is not just a religious boarding school but also the home to the headmaster, teachers, *ulamas*, *ustazs* and their respective families, and close to seven hundred boys and girls. The government closed it down in July 2007.[19] What initially prompted the government to accuse this *ponok* of all sorts of crimes was that two of its *ustazs* and two of its male *dek ponoks* participated in the infamous Tak Bai demonstration. Just like the *mak pasar*, the headmistress of this *ponok*, Puan (Madam) Shafikah, and her *ustazs* and *ulamas* all struck me as welcoming when I first met them to ask about the fate of their *ponok*. But beneath the measured tone of our discussion lay a deep and sinister view of their *ponok* and what the future held, if anything, for their students. Puan Shafikah talked about the frustration each time she ran into the parents of her *dek ponoks* as she could not offer any reassurance about when their children could return to school. She said that she and her staff would never forget the sarcastic smiles of the police officers when they came to question and later arrest two of her students and two *ustazs*. She said, "Polis itu jahat, kejam [those police were bad, diabolic]. The two *ustazs* and *dek ponoks* were from the fishing village where the authority arrested some of their youth." Shafikah reminded me that that was the time when not taking part in the Tak Bai protest for that village community was itself an anomaly, if not immoral.

After the students and *ustazs* were taken away, the first question the police officers asked as they began their interrogation was about the financial situation of the *ponok*. To be specific, they wanted to know how the *ponok* managed to operate when it was only charging a meagre 150 baht (C$5) per *dek ponok* per term. Puan Shafikah felt that the police officers either were playing dumb or had not done their homework. As she put it to me, "everyone here knows that most, if not all, *ponoks* receive some form of financial assistance, whether it came from the Middle East or from some local Malay Muslims who prefer to remain anonymous ... Sometimes we received donations without knowing who were the donors. Some were *wakaf* [religious donations]. You tell me, can we reveal to the police our donors even if we know who they are? The police would go after them. That would be wrong, *tak sopan* [immoral], of us."[20]

After the *ponok* refused to divulge any financial information, more police officers arrived to search the school. The raids continued for months, usually unannounced. Less than a week after the first visit, the police made an accusation that the *ponok* was a bomb factory because they found cooking gas tanks (liquefied petroleum gas cylinders) in the communal kitchen. With their hands held up in the air to express their exasperation, Puan Shafikah, the *ulamas*, and the *ustazs* pointed out to me that it was not only a horrendous but also an illogical accusation. "How else are we going to cook?" the headmaster asked before continuing: "This is a *ponok*. We live here. Those children, they live here, study here, sleep here, wash their clothes, they cook here." She was fuming. To calm down the atmosphere, if only just a little, one of the *ustaz* interjected: "One of the moral values they receive at our *ponok* is *nasihat*. This is something that the authority never understood or refused to understand." The police officers dropped their initial accusation but insisted that the cooking gas tanks could potentially be used as bombs. Throughout a series of unending accusations, the headmistress *ulamas*, *ustazs*, and some *dek ponoks* were interrogated, and to this day the charges against them are still pending in case the government decides to enforce them.

Besides the police, the *tahann* were eventually called in. To make matters worse, on one occasion they dug up some graves in the *ponok*'s cemetery on the allegation that weapons were hidden underneath them.

This was not only a sign of disrespect but also a violation of Islam (or, for that matter, any religion), something that enraged the residents at the *ponok* and the entire Malay Muslim communities in the area. The news reverberated throughout the far south. Even though no weapons were found in the cemetery that day, it did not prevent the authorities from staging further raids. It got worse. On one of those raids they ordered everyone to evacuate the *ponok* compound while they conducted their search. Sure enough, how coincidental it was that the *tahann* did manage to recover illegal weapons. The locals were not amused by it at all. On the contrary, they were outraged. This is a common expression I often heard when they lamented their disposition: "Kalau kerajaan tak adil, hidup tak senang" (If the government is not fair, life will be difficult).

The last straw happened when the *tahann* arrested a few *dek ponoks* at an abandoned *tadika* (kindergarten) and also dug out several graves. After that, the *ponok* was closed, and with its closing, the state created a situation of joblessness for the headmistress, her *ustazs* and *ulamas* (and their respective families), and left the *dek ponoks* without a school, a home, and a community. Many parents in the surrounding area were enraged at the closing and worried that their children could become *mat lepak* (young and idle) and indulge themselves in drugs, alcohol, and gangsterism and, worse still, be recruited by agents of the shadow insurgency.

Whenever I visited this *ponok* in Narathiwat, I would make it a point to stop by a teashop down the road, not just for drinks and food but because I liked talking with the owner, Hamid. My friend Faosee, the university student whom I mentioned earlier, would take me there on his newly acquired second-hand (or third-, fourth-, fifth-) classic Vespa, one of those with its exhaust pipe producing the classic *peang, peang, peang* rhythmic sound![21] On one of our visits Hamid asked: "Why is it only of late that the government believes the *ponok* is preaching hate? Why not in the past? Why not before 9/11, before the war against terrorism?" "Besides," as he put it, "these mysterious militants, whatever you want to call them, they are the minority. And they are killing not only state agents but also ordinary Malay Muslims. They don't represent us, but we are blamed for their violence."

As we were sipping our sweet coffee and tea and watching and listening to Hamid's songbirds, a convoy of American-made General Motors pick-up trucks and Humvees raced past his shop, bearing men in various uniforms: counter-insurgency units, jungle police, paramilitary, paratroopers, and kratom military commandos. There was also a helicopter in the sky, which prompted Hamid and his wife to laugh. It reminds me of the aesthetics of vulgarity that Achille Mbembe (2001, 2019) attributes to the condition of the post-colony in parts of Africa: these top brass travelling with heavily equipped escorts as becoming childlike instruments for the celebration of status – much like events medievally coeval for the era of chieftains, complete with magicians and acrobats chasing citizens out of the way in parts of Africa. Part of the subtext here is that the apparent folly of these military top brass is inseparable from their appetite for, in the Bataillian sense, a sumptuous unreproductive expenditure (Bataille 1991).

I asked Hamid if some top brass were visiting the nearby military camp, to which he responded, with a bit of sarcasm: "Yeah … sure look like it. But this kind of display, show of force, is *biasa*. We are used to it, checkpoints, army garrisons, what have you. *Biasa*." I sometimes wonder if these military top brass as well as other state agents have any concerns about being parodied, of not being taken seriously. While he was feeding one of his songbirds with the expensive banana, he gave me this half-smile look and said: "But such show of force is only for the daytime. Not at night." And then the common refrain: "Day and night is a different world around here. One is *waktu tahann*, the other is *waktu geriya*." Faosee, who had been very quiet during the entire afternoon, interrupted Hamid and asked something I had heard on so many occasions from my other Malay interlocutors: "Are we *kon Thai* or not? Can we be *kon Thai* without being Buddhist?"

"Concerning the hours of the guerillas … are you not afraid of the RKK?" I asked. Hamid gave me this uncomfortable smile before responding, "Of course, I am. I don't know who and what are the RKK," he whispered. He pushed his chair closer to Faosee and me before continuing, "Everyone here is afraid of the RKK or whoever is doing all these killings." He leaned further forward as if he were about to divulge something secretive and dangerous. "You just don't know who they are and what might one's action be that could be construed as being against them. And when they might just show up … at your house, on the country road, or while you are tapping rubber. So many of us have stopped tapping," which prompted him to laugh. He continued with a repeated refrain: "But what is the point? Three kilos [of latex] for 100 baht." He paused and looked around as if he had an uncanny feeling of being watched, as if there were some ghostly and shadowy insurgents present in his house listening while their fingers wandered over the smooth barrels of their Kalashnikovs. Spooky! He continued, silently, cautiously: "Almost every time the *tahann* raids or captures one of them, you can almost guarantee they will retaliate, either against the *tahann* or some *orang kampong* [villagers]." He lowered his voice even more before adding: "As with most separatist movements, the RKK, or whichever separatist movements in the past, have to be ruthless. It is not enough for them to be unafraid. They must instill fear."

I should have let him talk more but I interjected: "But from what I heard and read, most of these villagers that were targeted were either village chiefs or their deputies, or those who volunteered for the civil defence, or worse, as rangers or paramilitary," I also lowered my voice even though there was no one else except the four of us. The closest house was at least fifty metres away. Hamid looked uncomfortable as if what I asserted was a public secret and dangerous, especially about the paramilitary, about which I will elaborate in the next chapter. I looked up and noticed that his wife was also uncomfortable. Faosee, who usually just sat and listened also smiled uncomfortably, but he said something this time: "To me, the only movement that is truly genuine was Haji Sulong in the *empat puluhan* [1940s], and look what happened to him. We never found his body." Both Hamid and Faosee uttered almost at the same instance: "*Kesian*" (Truly sad). Faosee continued: "The rest of the callings for autonomy, as much as I know, which is not a lot, were from these *ketuas* [leaders] – I personally don't know who they are. And each of them proposed the use of violence to stop violence. And now RKK. I don't even know who they are but it's the same: violence and fear."

We were all quiet. What Faosee had said was, I thought, so succinct as his reflection was not the first or the last to lay claims to the precarious reality in the far south. The RKK, in the opinion of my interlocutors (as well as mine), seem like the latest actualization of long-standing fear and paranoia that have preoccupied the back of people's minds for as long as the region has known. Hamid's wife went inside and came back with a bat. It looked like a tennis bat, but it was not. This was a bat charged with enough electricity to electrocute mosquitoes, flies, and just about any insects. The recent surge of dengue fever and malaria was a real concern. Hamid's wife told us that her nephew who lived in Yala had been diagnosed with dengue fever a few months ago. The fever had contorted and hurt all his joints, so much so that he laid motionless on the hospital bed for weeks. He eventually passed away.

Sure enough, the mosquitoes were swarming. I was always the only one complaining about being bitten by mosquitoes. It seems to me that the locals have this apparently infinite capacity for tolerating the intolerable itches from mosquito bites or, for that matter, the recurring conflict that has inflicted the region. "What about *waktu nyamok* and *waktu geriya* [the hours of the mosquitoes and the hours of the guerrillas]?" I asked them. They laughed but seemed resigned. Perhaps *resigned* is not quite the word. It was just an old and new normal for them, as cliché as it might sound. But then again, has not violence, and all that is associated with it (as in the declaration of a state of emergency), become routinized during the past few decades throughout the world? Faosee suggested we should be leaving. Darkness was falling and the *waktu geriya* (and *waktu nyamok*) was approaching. "Selamat jalan! Berhati-hati ya?" (Safe ride. Be careful okay?), Hamid and his wife said as we rode off, going *peang, peang, peang*, that classic exhaust pipe sound of a vintage Vespa.

By Way of Concluding

Maurice Freedman (1975) once pointed out that culture (and here I add religion) is not like a homogeneous substance with the power to spread, but that is how Muslimness and Islam in Thai's far south and elsewhere seem to be presented: as a pattern of seepage, of slow overspill. Freedman points out that there is a tendency to look for order and concurrence once we use these words, blinding us to all its ambiguity, movement, and complexity, and, in the case of the war on terror, focusing on a collection of stereotypical values and behaviours that have been made into this fearful fantasy in the war on terror.

Of late, all across the world, and even among Muslim countries in Southeast Asia, the governments seem to be obsessed with the threat of Islamic terror. Lost in humanism at a time in history when we insist on the outer binary signs of international conflicts are the inner struggles and suffering of civilians, each taken individually, who are the unbreakable core of what really matters. In the case of Thailand's far south and elsewhere, the fact that *ponoks*, like so many other religious boarding schools, were more than conduits of religious education, that they also maintained a wide range of social and economic functions, was never really appreciated or understood by the authorities, both historically and in the contemporaneity of the war on terror (Madmarn 2003; Narongraksakhet 2005; Liow 2009). Since 9/11, *jihad factories* or *dens of terror* have described the intended, the metaphoric, and the symbolic function of the *ponok*, obscuring other possibilities that these terms might entail. With the heightened surveillance and/ or closing of several *ponoks* in the far south, and thus depriving many of a source of affordable education, many of *dek ponoks* were forced to seek other alternatives in getting a decent education or dropped out of school altogether.

Of those who dropped out, many became entangled with all sorts of delinquent activities, including the possibilities of being recruited by militants. Much to the encouragement of their parents' choiceless decisions, or their own, many Malay Muslim youth escaped from the violence by doing the thirty-day-visa hop to Malaysia, only to end up being exploited at the *tom yum* restaurants and other job sites. Like the *ponok*s, the *tom yum* restaurants in Malaysia, perhaps because they were operated by Malaysian Malay Muslims, were also accused by the Thai authorities of being complicit with the current insurgency, of donating part of their revenues to the insurgency (see Helbardt 2011). It seems like the generalization did not stop with the *ponoks*.

Recalling my earlier conversation with Ajarnn Abdullah, one of the main reasons the insurgents are using to recruit angry young Malay Muslim men and boys is the underlying poverty and the neglect that the far south has suffered for so long, whose scars run deeper than what is visible. Malay Muslims are fed up with talks about development and all the benefits of mega projects that have not trickled down. As a matter of fact, in the atmosphere of profound scepticism, if not cynicism, many ordinary Muslims to whom I spoke were not interested in talking about mega development projects. And if they did, they joked about them with the acronym NATO (No Action, Talk Only). In other words, these were projects that expressed intentions and aspirations rather than actual practice. King (2005) has also made the same reference to the (broken) promises of development in the region as *NATO*. I must also add that not all of these were broken promises but rather promises that did something else, something far from what was advertised. I will elaborate on this point in the next chapter when I talk about a mega development project, Halal Industrial Park.

More importantly, the perils of the long-standing assimilationist politics were laid bare in the historical present, and the costs of the *denial of coevalness* (Fabian 1983) to ordinary Malay Muslims as historical agents were high and can be virulent. Central to these neglects was precisely the cultivation of an agonism, a decidedly young male population (or boys) who refused the disciplined body of the state, who refused to be docile bodies available to be worked over by the state, to be worked over by the *tahaan* and the police, or to be counted by the statistical ideologues of representative democracy. To make their point, some government schools were burned by these angry and hardened youths who had turned their backs on dialogue because they were never listened to in the first place. Festering with political impotence, these angry, hardened, frustrated, and disenfranchised youth were being held captive by, and were absent from, the narrative of the discourse on the war on terror. It seems to me that these were individuals who were trapped in a set of rituals that reaffirmed tyranny, a set of rituals that were so interconnected that they became, over the decades, a system of ensnarement. The evasions of these individuals were as endless as Sisyphus's. In my opinion, it is necessary to make sense of this set of rituals and its system of ensnarement in order to clarify any knowledge we might have of the logics of "resistance," "disorder," and "conviviality" inherent in Thailand's far south and elsewhere.

In my mind, to miss this is to misrecognize the puzzle to the whole equation as to what is happening in the far south, that quaint little war that hardly, if ever, makes any headlines in international news coverage, let alone in Thailand.[22] It also seems to me that the answers are there, but the questions have yet to be asked. To reiterate, this is what concerns me: the lives and future livelihoods of these *dek ponoks* and their teachers, should the fear about Islam continue unabated, or when these children have no idea why they are being sought after or whose interests they are serving.

Chapter Eight

The "Halalness" of Things

Since the middle of the twentieth century the West, the North, the First World, the rich and developed countries – call them whatever you want – have unilaterally decided to develop the poorer, less-developed countries, the non-West, or the South (again, call them whatever you want). And all these "developments" can also mean underdevelopment, or stages of stagnation and deterioration, for the latter countries, which the First World disdainfully feels can have no bearing on the course of its own history. Indeed, it even seems to be saying that there are no histories without the First World. However, recent events after events – for example, the political, economic, social, cultural, religious, climate, and industrial refugees (and the categories keep piling up) – show that it is foolhardy for the so-called First World to close its eyes and close off its heart behind the pretentious bulwark of the perceptual horizon of the North.

When I asked the *mak pasar* and other interlocutors about the much-publicized mega-development projects of the Indonesia-Malaysia-Thailand Growth Triangle (IMT-GT) that started in the 1990s, they responded with slight smiles on their faces as if I were asking the obvious. They sarcastically asked if I was talking about Hat Yai or Phuket, referring here to the development of sex tourism. I was taken aback at this question coming from Muslim women who prayed five times a day and wondered whether I was being teased. In a funny way I felt as if their reference to what was *development* made them feel deprived, on the one hand, but also liberated in equal measure, on the other hand. Suraiya looked into my eyes to see if I understood the emotional content of the violence behind the not-so-subtle socio-political messages of the IMT-GT and the way they were being manifested and staged.

The Growth Triangle development project is part of a trend in Southeast Asia in which territorially adjacent provinces of neighbouring countries are targeted for integrated socio-economic development. It was initiated by Singapore, this city-state that is forever starving for and aggressively reclaiming more land. Thailand participated in one of these GT projects, the Indonesia-Malaysia-Thailand development project, in 1993 and it was celebrated as a commitment to address poverty in its proverbial backwaters, Thailand's far south. Malay identity was presented for the first time as a form of social capital to be exploited with partners of similar ethnic, linguistic, and religious persuasions in Malaysia and Indonesia. However, as Phil King (2005) points out, cultural identity was a "public transcript" when the "hidden transcript," to use James Scott's term (1992), revealed that fifteen of the twenty-one IMT projects were concentrated in Songkhla, the only non–Malay Muslim majority province in Thailand's far south. Similar to Phil King's observation, I often heard the *mak pasar* and others using the following metonym in reference to development (or the lack of it) in Thailand's far south: NATO (No Action, Talk Only). To them, the IMT projects, like other development initiatives, were basically the carrot and stick of capitalist hegemony.

Critiques of development, or the political theories for talking about development – modernization theory, dependency theory, world system theory – and the corresponding violence of developmental discourse are well documented, and to rehash them would be superfluous. Simply put, an entry point for an analysis of the role of development is the mantra that modernization is the only force capable of eradicating poverty in Third World countries despite its social, cultural, and political costs. The ingredient for modernization (i.e., exporting agricultural cash crops, industrialization, and urbanization) is capital, and capital has to come from somewhere, from abroad; local governments and international organizations need to take an active mediating role in establishing a set of capital relations. In other words, development is a discourse. To understand development as a discourse, one must look not at the elements themselves but at the system of relations established among them. It is this system that allows the systematic creation of state-inscribed spatiality or territories, objects, concepts, and strategies; in other words, the system of relations establishes a set of rules on who can speak, from what points of view, with what authority, and according to what criteria of expertise, and through these rules the discourse moves across the cultural, economic, and political geography of the Third World. As Cooper and Packard (2005) point out, development as a discourse is very much part of the modernization theory even as the latter has been effectively discredited. The ethos of development always has its targets or, as Escobar (1995) calls them, "abnormalities" –

a certain ethnic group, indigenous peoples, the community, the village, the local. Indeed, the very idea of defining a "target population" harks back to the very notion of evolutionism, whether explicitly or inexplicitly. Yet, despite these critiques, the processes that encouraged the development of authoritative regimes that have bred corruption, weak civil societies, nepotism, a military culture of violence, and an infrastructure of impunity have not gone away. This is what is happening in Thailand's far south and elsewhere. Under the IMT project and its commitment to address poverty in the Malay Muslim proverbial backwater, it comes as no surprise that one of the development projects is the industry of halal food, food prepared to prescribed Muslim law and practices. The idea is to produce halal food locally instead of having to import it from Malaysia or Indonesia.[1] One of these modern halal industries is located at Talukhan, a subdistrict of Sai Buri in Pattani. It is called, rather generically, Halal Industrial Park.

I visited this facility in July 2010 with a group of *ajarnn*, their students, and two human rights NGOs from Bangkok. We were greeted by a group of villagers at the cultural centre at Talukhan. They were waiting to tell us about this development project, to bear witness to the mountain of grievances that this project of modernity has unleashed upon them. As it turned out, the location where Halal Industrial Park was constructed used to be their land before they were tricked into selling it, and at below market price. The village chief was so upset that he could not muster a single word throughout the entire meeting. He just sat there with this angry look, a look of someone struggling to contain his emotions. The villagers were filled with bewilderment and dread and occasionally shook their heads for they knew that their village chief would normally say something unless he was that upset, because he felt solely responsible and to blame for the fiasco that had befallen his village. *Fiasco* is perhaps a misnomer; *enraged* seems more accurate after we found out what had happened. It was the deputy village chief who broke the silence and told his fellow villagers that the whole purpose of our visit was for them to brief us on what had gone wrong.

As it turned out, none of the villagers, including the village chief, was informed or consulted by any government agencies of the intention to build a halal industry park at Talukhan. However, a few paramilitary personnel from Talukhan knew about the scheme through their connections with the *tahann*. And when there is wealth to be made, a chain reaction occurs, proving that behind paramilitarism there is something other than an altruistic interest in counter-insurgency. This is the basic "something other," and in their land-grabbing scheme, these paramilitary personnel cajoled some of the locals, some of them their own relatives, with lies and subterfuge into selling their land, and that at below market price. They told their fellow villagers that property prices across the violent far south had been falling and would keep falling with the ongoing conflict that had no ending in sight. They further reasoned that with the falling prices of rubber latex, things were only going to get worse. These paramilitary personnel were even competing with each other to buy up as many plots of land as possible at the location gazetted for the construction of the halal industry park. Some of them even paid cash. Some villagers at our meeting even claimed that these paramilitary personnel were responsible for encouraging the government to build Halal Industrial Park at Talukhan. If that is true, this was where "the economic" and "the political" were not only dependent but also manipulable. This would be a case whereby Halal Industrial Park was, in every sense of the word, a carefully spatialized and choreographed sleight of hand, evoking the presence in absence of the hand of the state and the sliminess of the paramilitary.

Speaking of sleight of hand, not all the villagers were cajoled into selling their land, especially as rumours started making the rounds about the construction of this development project. However, by that time it was not only too late for those who had sold to rescind the sale of their land, but also too late to stop the construction of this modern halal complex and its paramilitarization. Modernity and its consequent violent gift had already arrived. The modern Halal Industrial Park under the GT development scheme, or should I say its underhanded scheme, that was supposed to benefit the Malay Muslim populations at Talukhan had arrived. Soon government agents started making offers at market price to villagers who had earlier refused to sell their lands to their own relatives, the paramilitary personnel. With these purchases, together with those the government bought from paramilitary personnel, the construction of Halal Industrial Park was a *fait accompli*.

"How was this possible?" these villagers were asking us during the meeting, as if the entire thing was a nightmare. They were still genuinely incredulous. "Some of our very own were doing this to us? How was this possible?" they repeatedly asked themselves. At that moment the village chief, who had said nothing throughout the meeting, grimly shook his head, signalling that there had been no mistake. We all sat there, looking at each other, in silence. When we were about to head to Halal Industrial Park, only one villager accompanied us. The rest suggested to us that it would make things *susah* (difficult) if they were to come along. We were puzzled. I sensed something, as if a thought was there shimmering on the horizon but would not divulge itself.

When we arrived at the main gate of Halal Industrial Park, we could see paramilitaries guarding the compound, perhaps the same agents who had cajoled some of their own villagers into selling their land. From where we stood, I could see that they were armed with the usual M16s. For someone who absolutely hates guns, each time I see these armed personnel with their M16s, I say silently to myself, "At least the shadowy insurgents know better; they much prefer the AK47, and who would not when it is also called the Kalashnikov?" These paramilitaries were sitting on a row of cement stools in their usual camouflage uniform, but none of them had those shiny boots or deadly efficient-looking pistols in a webbed holster on their hips. In fact, all of them were barefoot as they sat there, smoking. Some were wearing sarongs. They felt very much at home, or so it seemed to me. But it was their M16s that spoke loudest to me, in case there was trouble.

It took some negotiations before we were finally allowed to tour the brand-new modern complex. From the unrelenting looks of these paramilitaries, I do not think we were welcome. The villager who accompanied us introduced one of the paramilitaries as his *pakcik* (uncle), but it was a coldly civil introduction. I think we all understood then what the other villagers meant when they said it would make things *susah* if they were to accompany us. We all had this terrible sinking feeling that something unpleasant and unwarranted had penetrated this tiny village of Talukhan, one that had produced a cloud of unwanted emotions that they would struggle to amend for months, even years to come.

Speaking of paramilitaries, the state seemed to have had no trouble in recruiting these personnel during the troubled history of Thailand's far south. These were soldiers who were not really soldiers but armed like them, killed like them, and, given the circumstances, benefited like them for being part of the powerful *tahann* machinery. They were not just part of a "war machine" but also part of the pack that was the war machine.[2] As Taussig delights us in several of his ethnographic exposés on paramilitaries and (X)paramilitaries in Latin America, the paramilitaries "are the wild component of the law, its necessary underside" (2018, 76). In the case of Talukhan, they provided the sleight of hand for state agents and institutions to achieve their economic development machine in what was supposed to be halal.[3] The irony is obvious as the entire development project was premised on an adherence to some Muslim law in order to commodify it as both thing and spirit, as reification and as fetish. In other words, religion has become a jargon, and things halal have become objects for sale. And I say this with a grave sense of irony. We take these concepts and ideas for granted;

they became our nature, and their underlying assumptions recede into dogma and orthodoxy. To refuse this state of affairs is a denial of noting the discrepancies between various concepts and ideas and what they are producing.

Halal Industrial Park at Talukhan is a huge and modern facility, consisting of several large buildings for processing halal food, a management building, a modern mosque, a few dormitories, and even two huge modern lecture halls. I was not entirely sure what were the functions of the lecture halls. They looked like those one would find in any modernly equipped convention centre with all the sophisticated amenities. While some of our group were chatting with the paramilitaries, I asked one of the activists from Bangkok if some of these paramilitaries could very well have been the ones who cajoled some of their own villagers into selling their land. She smiled and then said, as if daring me to ask, "Why don't you ask them?" I took up her challenge and asked, "Were some of the lands in this facility yours before you sold them to the government?" That got some members in our group quite uneasy, judging from the looks on their faces. The paramilitary guards laughed but did not answer. There was something sinister about the way they laughed. Two of them lit their cigarettes and looked away while the third walked away, still laughing. I felt that the way they laughed was not only disgusting but also violent. I was perhaps being too bold, even careless. During the entire time we were there, these guards treated us as if we were not even there. They acted so nonchalantly. They conversed among themselves, all the while smoking and laughing, and even when my eyes fell upon them, they would look past me as if I did not exist. Their M16s were always by their sides, as if translating the force of arms into the force of legality and reason – this "dense interweaving of arms and law" (Taussig 2003, 92). I recalled what the *mak pasar* had said: "It has always been profitable to be a *tahann* in Thailand."

Thanks to the Saltwater

After that initial introduction and an immensely forceful and sad awakening visit to Talukhan, I went back several times accompanied by Faosee on his vintage Vespa and once with Bang Mann in his classic Toyota. As I found out, the construction of the industrial park without the locals' prior knowledge and consent was not the only reason they were so upset, if not enraged. The violent political economy that came with the logic of the development was the other reason. To make the facility run efficiently, economically, and competitively, it was necessary to put a few logistics in place. First, the raw materials to the facility, as well as the finished halal products from the facility, had to be transported by ships instead of lorries. For that to happen, Halal Industrial Park had to have a seaport close to the facility, and one that was deep enough. While the complex was under construction, the authorities started the project of building a jetty near the facility. To have a port deep enough for the ships to moor alongside the jetty, huge rocks were laid around the outer circumference of the beach without any consideration of how ecologically unsound it might be. As it turned out, the construction of the jetty and the laying down of huge rocks not only changed the ecology of the beach but also adversely affected an area much wider and further from the beach. With the deepening of the water level by the beach, seawater began to rush inward and contaminate the rivers beyond Talukhan, destroying the local cultivations of freshwater cockles, shrimp, and fish along the rivers, together with those whose livelihoods and survival depended on these industries. It also affected their capacity to use the river water because it had now been affected by saltwater.

My last visit to Talukhan with Faosee was in February 2016. It was through the village chief's recommendation that I managed to speak with Mokhtar. Prior to being a freshwater shrimp and fish farm operator, Mokhtar used to be a fisherman. He started by telling me that his families had been fishermen for generations and that he had no regrets in giving up that kind of livelihood. In fact, he sounded almost apologetic when he said: "My previous three generations were fishermen from Pattani. It was never easy. We caught fish for a living, but in the end we killed to make a living ... each time we released the net. Too many buried sins that cannot be paid off. Besides, I didn't need my wife and children to wait for me each time there was a storm. I just want all of us to have a meal together. In 2542 [1999 CE], I was forty-five then. That was when I decided to give up being a fisherman and start my own freshwater fish and shrimp operation. Moreover, there were less and less fish each time we hauled up the net. The Japanese [trawlers] killed them all. Besides, there are too many fishermen in Thailand. Just look at the number of fishing boats we have, not just in Pattani. As fishermen, once we are beached, we are all dead, at least some part of us." And then, poetically, he said, "I am not the same me any more once I stopped being a fisherman. At least I am not the same me I was. I feel less guilty."

I was not entirely sure why giving up being a fisherman would make him feel less guilty when he switched from catching to farming them. At the end of the day it was still killing. But I kept quiet. Instead, I told him I was very touched by what he had just told me, the way he had said it. He looked at me and forced a smile, and then he continued: "We were doing okay with the freshwater farm. It was a family business. Me and my wife [now deceased], and my children were working at our farm. I have three sons and a daughter. She is the youngest [pointing to her in the kitchen]. But now they have all gone, *habis* [finished]. Not just our farm but many others. Thanks to the halal project, really. They kept telling us the project was for our benefit, to *bangunkan* [develop] the area. They even had the audacity to say the paramilitaries, some of them our very own villagers, had asked the government to build the project here at Talukhan. It was they who asked the government to develop the area." He was no longer smiling. "And thanks to their saltwater," he raised his voice, "each time I see this halal logo, it leaves me with a bitter taste in my mouth." He showed me a packet of sugar with the halal logo at the bottom righthand corner of the plastic bag that said *Buatan Malaysia* (Made in Malaysia). I wonder if any of the villagers at Talukhan and beyond benefited from Halal Industrial Park, or other development projects, if any, and they used the narrative of development, a narrative that obscures and diverts attention from the use of paramilitaries, to trick their own fellow villagers into selling their lands. But then again, the story of development has already been well documented. It is, as always, the story of a violently inscribed gift or, as Klima emphasizes, "the story of massive, growing, left-out underclass, which can only spell I-N-S-T-A-B-I-L-I-T-Y" (2002, 263).

After Mokhtar lost his freshwater farms, all three of his sons went to Malaysia. Mokhtar's youngest son started off as a rubber tapper in Kelantan before joining his eldest brother at a construction site in Johor Bahru. Mokhtar emphasized, "Itu jauh [That's far]. They are at the southernmost part of Malaysia." The middle son worked at a *tom yum* restaurant in Kuala Lumpur, and his sister might be joining him. Mokhtar managed a smile before saying, "The restaurant needs someone who can make a proper *son tam* [papaya salad], and my son told them his sister makes the best." Mokhtar confided to me, and he was not proud of it, that the remittances from his sons (and soon his daughter) had become the main part of his household income. I suspect this will also be the case for the other villagers whose livelihoods have been wrenched from them by the storm troopers (aka paramilitaries) who worked hand in hand with the development of Halal Industrial Park. They too have been sending their sons and daughters and, I heard, their wives and, who knows, even their grandmothers to look for work in peninsula Malaysia.[4]

With the Malaysian currency (ringgit) at its all-time low and falling, however, Mokhtar felt he had to do something to supplement his household expenses. Remorsefully he said: "The last time my son came home, my second eldest, was just last month. He could not even use his ringgit to purchase groceries at the local stores. They are no longer accepting ringgit, not when it is so weak, not when the ringgit would fall even further." Then he laughed and smiled mischievously. "It is the same in Hatyai. In the past Malaysian tourists never had to change their ringgit to Thai baht when they were in Hatyai. Not any more. Even the *ayam* are not accepting ringgit any more."[5] His eldest and youngest sons had not been back for almost two years, not even for the Malay New Year. "Sangat jauh" (Too far), he said. "What about their work permit? Are they there with work permits or the usual thirty-day visa?" I asked. "Mana ada permit? Biasa lah! 30 hari. Ada duit kasi, okay lah. Ada jalan lah." (What permit? The usual 30-day visa. If you have money, okay *lah*! They are ways *lah*!)[6]

When I asked Mokhtar how he might supplement his household income now that the Malaysian ringgit has become so weak, he gave me a grim smile before responding. "I have been doing some tapping [of rubber] of late but … You can't even get 100 baht for three kilos. Furthermore, many were killed at their gardens. What if they mistook me?" He then confided to me: "I spoke with my brother. He has a spare pickup truck … You know Sadao is not too far away from here. Even Padang Besar."[7] He laughed, asking if I knew what he was insinuating. I nodded. He told me that the secret is to adapt, adapt like a chameleon. Again he smiled as he tried to maintain his sunny disposition despite life's vicissitudes.

The differences in diesel and petrol prices between Malaysia and Thailand have made it common for Thais to fill up their tanks whenever they cross over into Malaysia. In fact, it has made Malaysian oil a favourite target of Thai smugglers and their powerful backers who score huge profits by reselling it illegally in the underground markets in southern Thailand. These smugglers employ drivers with modified gas tanks on their trucks that make several runs per day with the full knowledge and cooperation of the Thai and Malaysian immigration and customs officers. I observed them many times when I made my cross-border trips. In fact, the cheaper, smuggled oil came not only via modified pickup trucks crossing the Thai-Malaysian border but also through oil-laden fishing trawlers that got the "supplies" from ships parked in international waters.

For years the Thai authorities have been struggling to stamp out the flow of cheaper oil smuggled from Malaysia. The industry has generated a lucrative but illegal multibillion-baht black economy in Thailand's far south. Much of the reason for the Thai government's failure in curbing the illicit business has been due to the involvement of powerful local politicians and influential people who have been accused of running the illegal oil-trade cartel. To be sure, this illicit trading has also had a negative impact on the local economy and "frightened" genuine businessmen. The prospect of competing head-on with oil smugglers who offer petrol and diesel fuel at a much lower price is not an enticing proposition for businessmen wanting to set up licensed petrol stations in the far south, especially when these oil smugglers have the backing of powerful people.[8] To be sure, the elasticity of these smuggled commodities from Malaysia to Thailand's far south stretches beyond diesel fuel and gasoline. The prices of sugar and monosodium glutamate, as well as the entire list of halal merchandise, are also lower in Malaysia, in part because the latter has a much more established halal industry than Thailand has and because of the weakening ringgit. Once back in Thailand, these drivers sell the contraband gasoline and other merchandise to the margins of the commodity outlets across the entire far south and perhaps even further north.

Over the years I have made acquaintances with some of these drivers and their outlets at Muang Pattani. They were always in a hurry to dispense some of their smuggled oil into large plastic containers before driving off in their modified-gas-tank pickup trucks to get rid of their remains elsewhere. As soon as they left, the owners of the outlets would set in motion the routine of filling glass bottles with the gasoline and always adding a little water before selling the bottles to customers at other outlets, or, in the evenings, teenagers sold them by the roadside. It is just another way of making a living on the margins. "Making do" (*buat saja*) was their way of describing their economy, and they could care less if it was shady or not. It was life. It is a business that strikes a nerve that goes deep into the shady ethos present in today's recurring conflict in the frontier provinces of Thailand's far south.

To further add to the irony of it all, there is a running joke that this diluted petrol or diesel fuel will give one's motorbike the propensity to *kentut* (fart). Trust me, I often heard this farting when the motorbikes sped past me. During my reconnaissance visit in 2005, I bought a bottle by the roadside, thinking all along that it was the refreshing sugar-cane water. I was about to drink from the bottle when one of the teenagers who sold it to me shouted, "Tak bolih minum Bang! Tu minyak" (Cannot drink, uncle! That's gasoline). They were chuckling, and I was not even sure if I should be embarrassed. I gave the bottle back to them and walked away. I did not even ask for my money back. Mokhtar was laughing so hard, almost to tears, when I related my story to him, and then he turned serious: "What other options do I have? I am almost sixty. I can't be going to Malaysia to look for work but at least I can still drive there."

Although the procurement of this merchandise is deemed illegal as far as the Thai authorities are concerned, these transborder transactions paint a sordid picture of bribes and scams. Or to put it slightly differently, they were carefully not regulated, and facilitated by the reality of neglect in these frontier provinces. Thailand's far south is where the historical violence of frontier provinces is worked out, where the material inequalities between Thailand and Malaysia are experienced on a daily basis, where living and dying take place in the shadow of the border. At the same time, without romanticizing poverty, although there is a lot of inequality in Thailand's far-south frontier provinces, there are also examples of human creativity and resiliency regardless of the illegality. To turn to Taussig once again, making sense of why Mokhtar was considering getting involved in the procurement of illegal merchandise from Malaysia means having a willingness and an instinctive capacity to identify, even appreciate, it, from the perspective of one not identified with a nation or with a people but "through the soulness philosophy of commodities" (1987, 19).

As with most development projects, what we witnessed at Talukhan and beyond were the violent and uneven penetrations of capitalism, with the blessing of the state and of the capitalists from abroad. Halal Industrial Park is more than an industrial park; it is a mini-state knitting together the free market and the private property through the interface of deceit and violence. To put it slightly differently, Halal Industrial Park can be seen as an extension of the body of the state, which, like God, is making the paramilitaries in its own image. There is no metaphor or pun intended here. The construction of the industrial park has benefited some (those higher up within the *tahann*, and local paramilitary personnel, even those who later sold their land at market price to the government) but not the majority of the villagers where the plant was built or those whose livelihoods were destroyed by the extended logistics of Halal Industrial Park. The construction of the industrial park (and the ways that enabled it to be constructed) points to its fate or destiny to become the showcase for state planning of an industry sans the residents of Talukhan but with plenty of saltwater. It is not only a form of violence but also the violence of displacement of the locals and the freshwater farmers from their lives and livelihoods. All these deceptions become "washed away" by the sludge of state machinery (which includes the paramilitaries) in the name of development – in the name of the development of the halal industry when "the most important exclusion …," as it turned out, "was and continues to be, what development was supposed to be all about: [the] people" (Escobar 1995, 91).

Even though I do not have any empirical evidence, I wonder if the spike of violence at Talukhan and the adjacent areas in the subdistrict of Sai Buri had anything to do with the messy and violent debris produced by the construction of Halal Industrial Park, and not forgetting the competitions and rivalries between the two Islamic councils of Sai Buri and Muang Pattani (if the competitions and rivalries were true). It was no surprise that the complex was heavily guarded by paramilitary personnel equipped with M16s. I wondered if any of these personnel had become targeted victims in the surge of recent violence in the subdistrict of Sai Buri since the construction of Halal Industrial Park.

Cultural Spectacles

Besides the talk about development, one also finds similar carrot-and-stick situations in the constant staging of cultural events that have taken place since the start of the current conflict. Each summer when I was in Muang Pattani there were at least three or four cultural festivals across from the township's municipal ground each month, such that they had become more like cultural spectacles, a fetish. The same was true for the townships of Yala and Narathiwat. In a week-long state spectacle under the banner "Culture for ASEAN Peace," organized by the Ministry of Culture and the Southern Border Provincial Government in Pattani, a *teh tarik*[9] beverage vendor asked (as many others had similarly been asking), in between making the delicious drinks, why the opening ceremony – like any other state-sponsored cultural spectacles with their never-ending "opening ceremonies" – was being held during their Waktu Maghrid (sunset prayer). Encouraged by my listening, he said: "They are here organizing these cultural events but heavily guarded … the *tahann*, police. Who are they guarding, ordinary people or the VIPs, the VVIPs? And why do their opening ceremonies always have to coincide with our [Maghrid] prayer? Do they know anything about Islam? Is this how they intend to win our hearts and minds? … They keep repeating the same arrogance. And Bangkok admitted that development is one of the solutions to the conflict. Are these spectacles development? … And what is this AEC?" I asked if he would make me a cup of *teh tarik* with ice.

ASEAN Economic Community (AEC) has been the latest buzzword throughout Southeast Asia in recent years. It is part of an effort to internationalize to the world a regional cooperative economic community. In Thailand's far south it is marketed as such: under the

AEC, people across Southeast Asia will anticipate an era of greater prosperity, high economic growth, and unity, which should see citizens turning their backs on the insurgents. When I asked my interlocutors (both Muslims and non-Muslims) what they thought about how the AEC had been marketed as one of the solutions to resolve the current conflict, most if not all of them would ask if I was trying to humour them. This reminds me of what Lawrence Cohen (1998, 28) once remarked, that invoking terms such as *unity* and *economic progress* in the cultural field were good examples of an excess of language that "far [exceeded] the simple act of its signification," that it was also a game that more than one could play in order to ensure that this access of language did not fade into the unconscious realm of hegemony. In other words, the marketing of the AEC is rather like Dorothy's Wizard: its power to command those whom it addresses rests upon their belief in its omnipotence and their taking seriously its sinister authority or reprisal should they refuse to obey. However, this omnipotence and its effect collapses should anyone pull back the curtain, should anyone refuse to play along. This bears a prima facie continuity with the phenomenon of the "carnivalesque" famously discussed by Bakhtin ([1965] 1984) – by way of Rabelais – wherein laughter, mockery, indifference, and the like are used to "profane" the authoritative order of rules, roles, and norms that allegedly govern everyday life.

As Rosalind Morris (2002) has noted, the state-sponsored cultural spectacles were new inventions for Bangkok bourgeois entertainment, one that had enormous appeal in urban areas where working-class audiences internalized them in their longing for cultural capital. It would seem that these rituals constituted an ironic source of their own legitimacy and had little effect on the ordinary Malay Muslims in Thailand's far south who refused to have their culture and heritage fetishized by the state. To put it another way, they refused to endorse the performativity of these never-ending cultural spectacles or, rather, cultural spectacles as performativity (that is, cultural spectacles as something that exposes culture as a masquerade for all to see), something that verges on critical perversity.

Just like the never-ending state spectacles in Myanmar, Malaysia, and elsewhere, to the Malay Muslims in Thailand's far south the terms of the state cultural discourse have shifted dramatically into an elaborate staging of their tradition whereby each minority group is enlisted and transformed into a "commodity-on-display" or "body-as-commodity" (Benjamin 1983, 256), a discourse that seems to be founded upon the spectacular that has all the signs of being theatrical and thus citational.

Worse still, the spectacles are seen as patronizing Malay Muslim culture and heritage. It was impossible to ignore just how absurd they were, and, as far as the Malay Muslims were concerned, absurdity abounds in Thailand's far south, or perhaps in the entire country that seems intent on parodying itself, much to the delight of certain segments of its population, as well as the *farangs*.

In fact, most ordinary Malay Muslims have been questioning the excesses of these cultural spectacles, and it has also become increasingly embarrassing for them to have to witness these Narcissus-like engagements with their culture and heritage. Their disinterest or absence from participation in these never-ending state spectacles can be interpreted as another common way to resist the state. Even seemingly inconsequential, such refusal to participate constitutes a form of resistance not only materially (without bodily presence) but also mentally. It represents a conscious decision not to accept the mandated form of their presence, the marketed rhetoric of being part of the ASEAN Economic Community and, more important, its purported future. When one stands back and reflects on it, these cultural spectacles and their rhetoric come across as theatrics in which its actors indulge in some sort of make-believe that everyone knows, including the actors themselves. It is a public secret. But then again, do the state and its agents even care? After all, seeing nuance and thinking historically and critically are not among their priorities as they indulge, in a Bataillian sense, in these sumptuous, unproductive expenditures (1991). The local senator once said to me: "This is Thai politics for you. View everything ahistorically, and then selectively when it suits your agenda."

As I have mentioned so many times in the pages of this ethnography, what truly matters most to the ordinary Malay Muslims is not the institutional excess of the state's cultural discourse that has seeped into their landscape of fear and paranoia but the bread-and-butter issues. I often heard these disquietudes from the *mak pasar*: "It is getting harder to *cari makan* [earn a living]." Like many ordinary Malay Muslims that I met, these *mak pasar* were not in the least interested in the frequent staging of their culture and heritage. They too would laugh about the institutional excess of these cultural discourses that have gone beyond the boundary of their legitimacy. Ironically, even as their poking fun at the absurdity of the never-ending state spectacles could be seen as a way to forge camaraderie, they were inadvertently hijacked by violence that was affecting the economics of their lives and livelihoods. It would seem, paradoxically, that culture (and religion) limits economy, but economy also limits culture.

Conscripts of Modernity

It is even an exaggeration and one of the most pervasive fictions of modernity when borders between nation-states remain porous and a subset of their citizens exhibits an ambiguous feeling of belonging. Many Malay Muslims in Thailand's far south are not known to have much respect for national boundaries as they cross back and forth over the Thai-Malaysian border. In both acceptance and refusal of Thai authority, many of them see themselves as Thais, and not Thais, or as Malaysians, and not Malaysians. Mostly they see themselves as Thai Malay Muslims, or as Malay Muslim majorities in the three far south provinces – but paradoxically also as minorities in a modern Thai Buddhist kingdom. Perhaps this is one of the reasons it was not uncommon to come across many who would sometimes call themselves *orang* Patani (inhabitants of Patani) or *orang* Melayu (Malays who transcend the conscription of any single nation-state to that of the entire Archipelagic Southeast Asia).

Where Bangkok and Kuala Lumpur would classify Malay Muslims as Thais (more like hyphenated Thais) and Malaysians, respectively, to defy the binary trapping and self-fashioning of their porous relations to both nation-states, these inhabitants have the pleasure of calling themselves *orang* Patani. In fact, some of them told me that this was one of their greatest freedoms, that one of the greatest pleasures of falling outside the national norm was the freedom to pile category upon category. These are identities that persist and on which a new layer, a conscription of citizenship, would be added. Hence, where Bangkok and Kuala Lumpur see them as faraway subjects in backwater provinces, the communities in these places regard their location as one of many nodal points of a maritime trading network within the Malay Archipelago that predates as well as transcends the constricting official national territories. Theirs are places that are regional in outlook, a fact often glossed over by state agents and the media, as well as within the academy. One might even say, in a typical Schmittian thesis on sovereignty (2010), that this can be seen as a reprisal to the state because the Malay Muslims have retaliated for the primacy of the national borders as a point of concentration of decision and power by calling themselves *orang* Patani or *orang* Melayu.

Despite this mobility, imagined or otherwise, however, they are not completely exempt from state control. Their identities and cultures, indeed their life ways and subjectivities, have changed in relation to the Thai-Malaysian state agenda, particularly in relation to the two nation-states' colonial policies regarding the majority-minority problematics.

To reiterate, since the Sultanate of Patani was formally annexed by Siam, and with the consent of colonial Britain, the diverse Malay Muslim societies in Thailand's far south have been destroyed and remade by the political, economic, and ideological forces unleashed by Siam's appropriation of European modernity. To state it somewhat differently, while the Malay Muslim cultures in Thailand's far south have been invented and reinvented over the past one hundred years, they have been conscripted by modernity's project that has irrevocably altered the conditions of that invention. In short, the Malay Muslims in Thailand's far south were conscripts – not volunteers or resisting agents – of modernity and the nation-state.

Years ago, Talal Asad made the following vivid remark about history and change: "Historical conditions change like landscapes created by glacier – usually slowly, always contingently – on which old paths that followed old inequalities simply become irrelevant rather than being consciously rejected" (1987, 607). The geological metaphor is instructive for thinking about the transformations that constitute the making of communities who find themselves conscripted by their respective nation-states. For Asad, therefore, if there is a story to be told about the choices people made in the course of acting historically, there remains nevertheless "the story [that is] not of people's choosing, but within which they must make their history" (607).

What these *mak pasar* and others offer is an expression of that story, serving as witnesses to how a modern Buddhist state and the series of unsuccessful insurgencies, and thus their lack of a usable past, have reorganized the conceptual and institutional conditions of possible social action and understanding. They have this almost nihilistic perspective on the nation-state whereby their subjectivities are utterly compromised at the origin as they remain haunted by the spectre of nationalism and military power, corruption and nepotism, and the recurring conflict. At this moment, as in the past, the staging of the cultural events in Thailand's far south signifies the degree of aloofness that state actors have towards the sensibility of these diverse Malay Muslim subjects. This was echoed by many *mak pasar* and others who felt that such half-measured cultural spectacles were performances that hoped to evade the real issue – that the Malay Muslims have been denied coevality by the state. As they put it to me on many occasions, the cultural spectacles amounted to nothing other than *katok langik denga tapok tangae* (hiding the clouds with the palms of your hands). To borrow from Das, these theatrical performances of the state rituals have become "grounded in the routines of everyday life [so much so] that it brings the whole domain of infelicities and excuses on the part of the state into the realm of the public" (2007, 163).

Seen in such light, the Growth Triangle development projects, as well as the staging of the cultural spectacles, amount to nothing but a scandal. This ethnography has elaborated on many other scandals or blunders made by the state. My use of the word *scandal* here is influenced by a Nietzschean reading of the notion of "promise" in the violent "progression" of history. Nietzsche delights in showing us that it would be more accurate if we consider ourselves as "promising animals," and essentially history as a series of broken promises ([1874] 1983). In such reading of history, history proceeds from the scandalous promises made by leaders of nation-states and its chief executive officers. My reference to former prime minister Thaksin should be obvious.

To my discussion of the lives and livelihoods of these *mak pasar* in conflict situations, I also want to give voice to the border crossers – Thai Malay youth (and even mothers and grandmothers) who are now working in Malaysia and elsewhere – subjects who are locked in an economic relation in which they serve as raw materials for the refinement and subjective value of capitalism's progress. As Klima (2002) has noted, these are stories about imperialism and neoliberal economy that are replicated in countless other places, so much so that "there is an immense debt hanging over the new world order, ... a violent history replicated but hidden in the cleanliness of the moment" (54). Following the calls from Klima and others, we need to cultivate a habit of making them accountable – in all their diverse and messy articulations – to the contextual unevenness it occludes.

By Way of Concluding, *Biasa*

> Bombings: the usual pattern. By a clever trick. First, a small bomb explodes. A crowd gathers, or were tricked to gather since there were chaos and panic in the air. Police, explosive experts, fire men, ambulances arrive. Then a much larger bomb explodes, killing more. There are no explanations for any of these bombs, not even an attempted explanation. (Taussig 2003, 3)

As I turn the pages of my field notes and diaries from the years of conducting fieldwork in Muang Pattani, they awaken my memories but at the same time I am haunted by the fact that I might have forgotten the details, the emotions surrounding discreet contents and contexts, or even the overall feelings of all those summer months I was momentarily there. As with Taussig and others, these uncanny feelings speak loudly about history that lies in the absence, in the traditional cotton Thai shirts I was so fond of wearing during fieldwork that are now completely worn out and see through, and the same with my cotton shorts, linen long pants, and sandals that have since been discarded. As Taussig puts it melancholically, "even more than in the absence, history lies in the adaptation of materials to time, to the exigencies of life, much as a door handle loses its shine or the keys on a keyboard lose their lettering (2003, 135). But most of all, in my absence from their company, have I now managed to capture the meanings and an entire psychology embedded in this one word, *biasa*? Have I managed to illuminate what it "affirmed, indexicalized a certain reality, if not ideology, referentialized or fantasized – and the historical and contemporary assumptions that underlie that reality and ideology" (Crapanzano 1993, 91–2), with an understanding upon which the success of my entire ethnographic project depended? As such, I want to end the book by dwelling, one more time, on *biasa*. I will do so by talking about the bomb explosions at Big C, the biggest supermarket and department store in Thailand's Malay-majority far south. This is what I read in the *Bangkok Post*.

> The bomb explosions at Big C occurred on the afternoon of 9 May 2017, injuring more than 80 people, mostly parents and their children who were shopping for the new school term. Big C was also the target of a bomb blast in 2005 and an arson attack in 2012. On that day, on 9 May 2017 the first bomb exploded at the carpark. About ten minutes later a second bomb, which was planted inside a stolen pickup truck, exploded near the entrance. Video recording shows shoppers walking into the store as the first bomb explodes. As security guards scrambled to seal off the building to prevent people from entering or leaving, the second bomb exploded. Authorities believed a total of 15 people were behind the Big C bombing. Two cooking gas cylinders had been stuffed with explosives weighing about 100 kilograms to make the bomb and were placed inside the stolen pickup truck. The owner of the stolen pickup truck was Nuson Kajornham, a 45-year-old Yala native. According to his wife, her husband made a living installing canvas tents and awnings. He received a phone call from a customer on that disastrous morning to install a canvas awning at a mosque in Pattani. Instead, the assailants took his pickup truck, and Nuson's badly battered body was found in a padi field in Nong Chik district three days after the bomb blasts.[10]

A week after the bombing, and just like the bomb blast at C.S. Pattani Hotel, Big C was back in business. I emailed a local *ajarnn* to update me on the blasts at Big C. This *ajarnn* emailed me back the next day to say that people from the three provinces were queueing up to shop there as if nothing had happened. I am copying and pasting part of the email, which I think pretty much sums up what I have been trying to write, to reflect on, to illuminate the situation in Thailand's far south, especially the Malay Muslims' engagement with the difficulties of their reality, and the multiple meanings of my interlocutors' nonchalant response, *biasa*: "Thank you for your good will and concern. Although so disheartened by the bombing at Big C, we are so resilient you know? I'm not being sarcastic, only a few days after the incident, Big C is back in business and you won't believe the long queue of the cars that waited to get inside the parking space regardless of the strict security check. It was as if there was a festival! That's how we live our lives in Pattani, hei, hei. *Biasa*!!" The email went on to say that life had to go on amid all the mayhem, whether it was Big C or other major and minor incidents of unrest. This *ajarnn* said that parents were more worried about getting their children new shoes and stationery for the new school term. I think the email sums it all: life must go on. After all these years it has become easier for me to stomach the violence there, when those who live there look so normal most of the time, when they just cannot leave.

Fast forward to August 2019. I was having lunch at a Malay food court in Kuala Lumpur, Malaysia. It was one of those food courts with *tom yum* outlets that hire (and exploit) Malay Muslims from Thailand's far south. I was at this food court because I wanted to be *there* (in Pattani). Call it nostalgia, even melancholia. As I chatted with one of the stall's employees, I found out that she was not only from Narathiwat but from Sungai Kolok, one of the most violent sites in Thailand's far south. That naturally spiked my interest to have a conversation. When I asked her why she had left, she gave me the standard response, *cari makan* (to earn a living). I asked her again if the violence was the reason she left. She laughed and, as you can guess, gave me the usual response, *biasa-lah*!

To cite Taussig once again, "we live in two different worlds, and in my effort to communicate between two worlds [in my case, Canada and Thailand's violent far south, although Canada is not that peaceful or innocent]: intellectuals and ordinary civilians; indeed so many kinds of 'two worlds,' such that mostly everything that you write is fractured and incomplete searching for the in-between world, which, in the diary world, is that fragment called yourself. This is another sort of imprisonment, not by love, so much, as by the impossibility of communicating experience ... I wonder what's it like talking of killings day in and day out for so many years? What does it do to you, to your understanding of the things of the world?" (2003, 102).

The "Halalness" of Things

Paradoxically, I think Taussig is saying that this radical limitation on the possibilities of language does not inhibit our elaborate efforts to communicate. We can use a foreign tongue simply because we have to, or try to discover in it linguistic treasures that are unique to it, untranslatable, and which, paradoxically, therefore enrich our mind, not only our technical ability to communicate. Or, during an interview on her novel *The Ministry of Upmost Happiness*, Arundhati Roy gave an assessment of two categories of writers. Here I am paraphrasing: "It would seem to me that as writers we spend a lifetime trying to close or bridge language and thought. But sometimes I wonder if this is a correct assessment if you consider how many writers spend a lifetime trying to derive a language to mask thought." I sincerely hope this ethnography does not fall under Arundhati's second category.

In the end, as I began to see through the epistemic murk of the entire psychology and mythology surrounding my ethnographic project on Thailand's far south, and especially on the word *biasa*, I wondered why I should still be encapsulated by what we call standard language, lexicon, grammar, and so forth, when all along my description and telling of the contents and contexts of how my interlocutors described their "worlds" and their engagement with the difficulties of reality as biasa is good enough for them. In other words, were my descriptions, my words, and my thoughts able to give voice to the lives and livelihoods of my interlocutors? In short, can language bear the violence and carry the weight of illuminating the degree of their precarity, their endurance, their engagement with the difficulties of their reality? At the end of it all, meaning in the present, I want to acknowledge that we need to appreciate the limitation of language and to just allow the words spoken by our interlocutors to illuminate their emotions, their underpinnings, and their experiences; in this way, they *do things with their words*. I shall leave it at that, *biasa*. To my interlocutors: *Jumpa lagi* (See you again).

Notes

Introduction: Ethnographic Beginning, *Biasa*

1 Except for political and public figures, I have substituted pseudonyms for all my interlocutors.
2 Not only is her point significant in a linguistic sense, but also it has political and social ramifications. In most countries in Southeast Asia, which by linguistic and cultural definition are multicultural societies, it is the minorities and not the majority communities that are bilingual or multilingual. This is not the case in Thailand's far south, where it is the Malay Muslims, not the Thai Thais and Sino-Thais, who are bilingual. The Sino-Thais and the Thai Thais are the minorities living in the Malay-majority provinces of Pattani, Yala, and Narathiwat. Around 1.3 million of the 1.8 million people living in the three provinces are Malay Muslims (McCargo 2011). It is important to note that the Malay Muslims in the far south are far from being homogeneous linguistically. Unfortunately they are treated as one, or homogenized, by the Thai government and the media as such (Montesano and Jory 2008). Furthermore, the Malay Muslims in the far south do not associate themselves with the Thai Muslims in other parts of Thailand. They see the Thai Muslims, especially those in Bangkok, as "over-assimilated, less devout, and too willing to embrace or tolerate the negative features of Thai society" (McCargo 2011, 834).

As a Malaysian Chinese and a minority subject experiencing immense structural racial discrimination, especially since the introduction of the National Economic Policy in 1971, I could empathize with the position of many of my Malay Muslim interlocutors as minority subjects in a modern Thai Buddhist nation. Working with these Malay Muslims in Thailand's far south further illustrated to me that race or ethnicity alone should not be conflated with racism if they are not politicized by both the state and the respective race or ethnic brokers.

3 Prince of Songkhla University has two campuses, one in Hatyai and the other in Muang Pattani. The Hatyai campus, which is located in the Buddhist-majority province of Songkhla, is much larger and has more faculties and facilities than the campus at Muang Pattani even though the latter was built earlier, a point of soreness for some of the faculty members and their students at the Pattani campus.
4 *Ajarnn* is a Thai appellative that translates as "professor" or "teacher." It is derived from the Pali word *acariya* and is a term of respect, similar in meaning to the Japanese *sensei*; it is used as a title of address for high school and university teachers and for Buddhist monks who have passed ten *vassa* (three-months annual rainy season retreat). It can also refer to a Buddhist monk performing a traditional Sak Yant tattoo. Even a *farang* (foreigner) teaching English in Thailand is called an *ajarnn*.
5 *Lah* is a slang word used mainly by many Malaysians and Singaporeans to complement almost any sentence in a social conversation. As they would say, it gives more "kick" to the conversation. Even though the origin of this slang word is the Chinese language, it is now used by almost everybody (even among Western expatriates) in the two countries. In fact, those who avoided using the *lah* slang are often considered to be snobs to a certain degree by those who do. The fact that Hanisah had worked in Kuala Lumpur for two years might have attributed to her propensity to use *lah*.
6 As Saroja Dorairajoo (2004, 468) points out, it was primarily the threat of losing more land that forced the Malay elites in the 1960s to appeal to the masses under the pretext that Malay identities were being annihilated by the encroaching state authorities. These movements were appealing to ethnicity rather than religion because Islam was not under threat during that time. As many of these elites have fled overseas, these movements have since lost their appeal among the contemporary Malay Muslim population in the region.
7 A military intelligence officer once told me: "The soldiers have to look 'soft' instead of having a stern image. It goes well with our duties to make friends with the people. The trouble is that not all of our personnel understood that."
8 My journey took place in 2009. When I went back in 2010, there were signs in Malay for "Welcome to the Province of Pattani" (*Selamat Datang ke Wilayah Pattani*). The same was true for the provinces of Narathiwat and Yala.
9 Malay Muslims here refer to the regional majority population of Malay-speaking Muslims who occupy Thailand's southernmost provinces of Narathiwat, Pattani, and Yala. Although Muslims form a sizeable population in other parts of Thailand's south, including the provinces of Songkhla, Nakhon Sri Thammarat, Trang, Phuket, and almost all of Satun,

they are primarily Thai speakers. The Malay Muslims in the far south speak a dialect close to that of Kelantanese Malay. Although scholars and Thai nationalists often refer their language as Patani Malay (to highlight its linguistic and cultural genealogy to the Sultanate of Patani), most locals simply say they are speaking *basor* Islam to distinguish their language loyalty from *basor* Sieh (Siamese).

10 According to Kasian Tejapira, this was a period when a benefit-sharing arrangement between the military, civilian bureaucracy, and local Malay Muslim leaders was brokered by the then prime minister Prem Tinsulanond.

11 I use the term *worked* to describe my interactions (or working relations) with my interlocutors. It has several connotations. It could be a working relationship that was ongoing each time I returned for more fieldwork – sometimes even a confidential relationship. It could comprise sporadic conversations or only greetings. It also underscores the unequal footing between the researcher and his or her interlocutors.

12 See Human Rights Watch (2007); Deep South Watch (2010, 2020); Askew (2010c).

13 These vendors called themselves *mak pasar*. *Mak* is the colloquial word for "mother(s)," and *pasar* for "market(s)," thus, my interpretation, "mothers of markets."

14 For a critique of the Thai state's accusation of the insurgents as a group of bandits, terrorists, or militia, see Askew (2007), McCargo (2009), and Helbardt (2015).

15 For accuracy purposes, the latest insurgency is strictly confined to the Malay Muslim provinces of Yala, Narathiwat, and Pattani and several districts in the Buddhist-majority province of Songkhla. Satun, which is also a Malay Muslim province in Thailand's far south, is not afflicted, at least not yet. It is not uncommon to hear some of my Malay Muslim interlocutors employing such *not yet* expressions because Satun was afflicted by conflicts in the past.

16 The official name for the military (or armed forces) in Thailand is called *tahann*. This is similar to the *tatmadaw* in Myanmar.

17 According to official view, the current insurgency is being carried out by a clandestine group of people who call themselves Runda Kumpulan Kecil (RKK), the military wing of the Barisan Revolusi Nasional – Coordinate (National Revolution Front – Coordinate).

18 For an excellent discussion on the common discrepancies in using the faceless and unsentimental politic of numbers as an indicator of the ebb and flow of violence, see Tate (2007).

19 In making the connection between modern political legitimacy and the rationality of number, in his important book *The Taming of Chance* (1990),

Ian Hacking brilliantly illuminates the emergence of the statistical and probabilistic rationality upon which these assumptions regarding the constitutive privilege of number depended and the importance of this for the governmentalization of the state in the nineteenth and twentieth centuries. Seemingly, as Hacking points out, the ideological neutrality of pure number is after all a tactic of colonial governmental calculus.

1 The Violent Historical Debris

1 Thailand has a history of being extremely cooperative with foreign powers as seen in its series of *sia din daen* (territories-ceding) treaties with Western powers during European colonialism. And during the Second World War Thailand saw Japan as "the light of Asia" and thought that it was to its advantage to align itself with a modern Japan (Anderson 1966). Twenty years later, Thailand was host to the war in Indochina, so much so that American privates (GIs) used to call the kingdom America's landlocked aircraft carrier (Klima, 2002). Immediately after the 2002 Bali bombing, former prime minister Thaksin Shinawatra was the first leader in Southeast Asia to jump onto the bandwagon of George W. Bush's war on terror.
2 For over two decades since its establishment, SBPAC has achieved a degree of trust with the local Malay populations for its role of not only monitoring the work of civilian government agencies but also coordinating with security forces in the far-south troubles (Wheeler 2010).
3 *Al-Fatani* is affixed to the names of scholars in the Middle East from Patani.
4 The labelling the Malay Muslims as *khaek* had a certain historical tradition of manufacturing otherness in Thailand. For instance, as early as 1898, Warrington Smyth, the British director of the Royal Department of Mines in Thailand, called the Chinese in Thailand the "Jews of Siam." Soon anti-Semitism and the "Yellow Peril" doctrines were circulating among the Western-educated Thai elites. In 1914 King Wachirawut launched several Sinophobic discourses, starting with a series of articles called "The Jews of the East" that equated the Chinese with anti-Semitic caricatures of the Jews (Skinner 1957; Soon 1962).
5 It has since been back on YouTube.
6 Plato, "The Apology of Socrates," in *The Trials of Socrates: Six Classic Texts*, edited by C.D.C. Reeve (Cambridge: Hackett, 2002), 26.
7 An illocutionary act is an act of language in which the utterance of words is the action in and of itself (Austin 1962, 102).
8 Since the "disappearance" of Haji Sulong and his entourage, stories of Haji Sulong and his push for reforms cannot be publicly discussed.
9 According to Trouillot (1995), history is an ambiguous blend of "broadcasting" and "silences," whereby some peoples and their times are

left out of history. Broadcasting and silences are thus active, dialectical counterparts through which history is produced and always sustained by silencing.
10 The Sultanate of Kelantan is connected to the former Sultanate of Patani.
11 In his critiques of the conflation of history with progress, Benjamin presents the allegory about the "angel of history" as a critique on the linear conception of progress (1968, 257). He argues that the concept of humanity's historical progress "cannot be sundered from the concept of its progression through *homogenous, empty time*" and that this concept of progression must be the starting point for critiques on the concept of progress itself (261). By contrast, for Benjamin the structure of history is "time filled by the presence of the now [*Jetztzeit*]" (261), the eternal now as standing still in the present. Notably, for Benjamin, "redemption and messianism have an apocalyptic connotation in a dual sense: they symbolize not only a sudden and radical break with the past, but a different temporal (metaphysical) dimension altogether" (Eddon 2006, 264).
12 For an excellent discussion on the emphasis of writing a glorious history of Patani, as one written by court historians, and in essence a moral history written during the decline of the sultanate, see Bradley (2009).
13 Over the years I have made the acquaintance of a few military intelligence officers, and each time that there was a Malay Muslim gathering within Muang Pattani, they would summarily equate them with Wahhabi events. As if that was not bad enough, they would chuckle when calling them Wahhabi events.
14 According to Crapanzano, "though largely ignored, every exchange is accompanied by what I have called shadow dialogues – the silent mentation, the self-conversation, that accompanies all exchanges and is in response, at least tangentially, to those exchanges (1992, 213–15). Crapanzano touches further on the topic: "They affect the course of the exchanges they shadow both dramatically and in terms of content. Put simply: What is my interlocutor really thinking about? What and why am I saying or doing what I am saying or doing? What is he getting at?" (2014, 264).
15 There was another matter that might have led to the increase in violence at Sai Buri, something to do with a development scheme that I will touch upon in chapter 8.

2 Militarized and Islamified

1 The cellphone is one of the devices often used by insurgents to detonate bombs. Consequently, at certain "hot zones" within the three provinces, one had not only to present an identity card to buy a cellphone and

SIM card but also to register it with the military. The jamming of signals prevented the insurgents from using stolen cellphones to detonate improvised explosives devices (IEDs) that were usually placed inside stolen motor vehicles, including motorbikes. Since 2017, IEDs have been found inside bicycle frames.

2 This was not the case during my reconnaissance visit back in 2005 when booze was sold at many booths during the university fair.

3 *Nasi dagae* is a very popular dish consisting of coconut-flavoured rice, fish, hard-boiled egg, and chili wrapped in a banana leaf.

4 On the notion that trauma, under the extreme structural racism in colonial or post-colonial contexts, Fanon writes: "Since the racial drama is played out in the open, the black man has no time to 'make it unconscious' … The Negro's inferiority or superiority complex or his feeling of equality is *conscious*. These feelings forever chill him. They make his drama. In him there is none of the affective amnesia characteristic of the typical neurotic" (1967, 150; emphasis in the original).

5 Many of my interlocutors, regardless of their ethnicities, religions, or age groups, alluded to me that they were sicked and tired, fed up with the conflict, and it was not lost on me that, throughout the far south, ordinary civilians use the adjective *bored* (in Malay, *bosan*, or, in Thai, *beuua naai*) about the latest recurring conflict that has no end in sight. In other words, being sicked and tired, fed up, became a kind of regional emotion, one that was expressed in a variety of contexts. Paradoxically, it was as if their sensibilities towards the latest conflict, just as they were choking with historical memories of the episodes of violence since the late 1940s, had become coexistent with tiredness, boredom, and normalcy. In short, as with the Palestinians and others who had endured endlessly with violence, such banality of violence had become their dominant political ethos. "They can be interpreted as a way of taming violence, or reincorporating the extreme and existential into the ordinary … It is expressed in the capacity to stop noticing, or at least stop noticing all the time" (Allen 2008, 473; see also Taussig 1991 and Jenkins and Valient 1994).

6 See, for example, Taussig (1987), Green (1999), and Nordstrom (1997).

7 Although Das (2014b) uses the verb *embracing* instead of *engaging with* the difficulties of reality, I find *engaging* more appropriate for my interlocutors: they are engaging themselves in all the forms and tactics of precarity in order to create the possibility of life, to live sanely in an unjust reality.

8 In Rancière's (1999) critique of identity politics, the scourge of such politics has ghettoized political resistance as it has undermined the potential solidarity across the struggles of minorities, those who stand at the wrong end of power. Put schematically, the question "Who am I?" or "Who are

we?" has come to replace the question "What are we struggling for?" As such, identity politics demands as much as it enables. In other words, an analysis of the politics of identity will need to include a consideration of local power struggles – unfolding in contexts of chaos, corruption, class, and, hence, religious differences and exploitation – and the role they play in promoting primordial expressions of identity.

9 The detail about the production of *Raja Kuning* is taken from Marc Askew's 2009 conference paper. Some of the materials for this chapter expand on the text of an earlier publication (Yong 2014).

10 Drawing on Nietzsche's "On the Uses and Disadvantages of History for Life" ([1874] 1983), Edward Casey suggests that, like the bovine, people are capable of "forgetting what it is to remember," even to the point of having "forgotten [their] own forgetting" (1987, 1–4). To quote Nietzsche, "Even a happy life is possible without remembrance, as the beast shows; but life in any true sense is absolutely impossible without forgetfulness" ([1874] 1983, 62).

3 The *Mak Pasar*

1 The observation that women are more concerned than men are with livelihoods issues is well documented in parts of Southeast Asia, Africa, and Latin America. See Tsing (1993), Kapchan (1996), Nash (2003), Slyomovics (2005), and Menjívar (2011).

2 Some of the materials for this chapter expand on the text of an earlier publication (Yong 2019).

3 My working relations with these *mak pasar* was confined within the spaces of the open-air markets. I never visited their villages not only because I was never invited but also out of safety concerns for them and myself. Besides, it was not safe to be on the outskirts of Muang Pattani at night. Moreover, many of these *mak pasar* share rented rooms in Muang Pattani, and they almost never took a day off to visit their villages unless for emergency reasons. Needless to say, it would have been inappropriate for me as a non-Muslim and a man to visit them in their shared rented rooms in Muang Pattani.

4 The term *choiceless decision* is taken from Begona Aretxaga (1997) in describing the decision of groups of Irish women protesting at courthouses or police stations. Their decision to protest, as Aretxaga puts it, was not based on the freedom to protest but due to an existential dilemma: "Many women had small children and had enough with raising their families. They would have preferred to go on with their lives as before, but they had no choice because their husbands were arrested and also their older sons. They had to do something" (61).

5 Regarding some of the controversies surrounding the recruitment of civil defence group, see the reports by Amnesty International (2006) and International Crisis Group (2009).
6 According to the Luk Riang group, a peace advocate association for children and youths in the far south, more than 7,300 children had been orphaned as the current violence entered its tenth year, and the number was only going to rise (*Bangkok Post*, 11 January 2014).
7 As a measure to tackle the continuing fall in the price of rubber, Thailand's Agriculture and Cooperative Ministry announced on 5 October 2018 that it was planning to offer 3,000 baht (US$91) per rai (a traditional Thai unit of area, equalling 1,600 metres) to any rubber growers who agreed not to tap their rubber trees for three months. See "Ministry to Compensate Rubber Growers," *The Nation*, 5 October 2018, accessed 12 February 2024, https://www.nationthailand.com/in-focus/30355842.
8 Writing about Lebanese children, Suad Joseph talks about the roles of mothers who engage with their children practically, temporally, and affectively, and how that is pivotal in maintaining a household as well as a marital relationship (1999, 176).
9 *Belacan* is a fermented shrimp paste that is widely used in Southeast Asia. When roasted, it produces a strong smell that can be quite pungent.
10 Since 9/11, many Muslim religious boarding schools – from Kandahar to other designated Muslim sites – have been accused of being "jihad factories" or "terrorist dens" (Noor 2009).
11 *Hanyat* refers not only to the hot weather but also to its extreme humidity.
12 A few Muslims interlocutors told me that the possibility of obtaining foreign scholarships, especially from the Middle East, is one of the reasons many Malay Muslim parents send their children, especially their sons, to the *ponok* schools. The deputy prime minister's office claimed that there were currently more than five thousand Thai Muslim students studying abroad, particularly in Egypt, Pakistan, and Indonesia. Of this figure, the majority of them are using scholarships granted by these countries and pursuing religious studies. There are, however, conflicting opinions regarding the sentiments of these students. The National Security Council claimed that more than one hundred of these students were inclined towards the separatism of the far south from Thailand while the Internal Security Operations Command refuted such claim. The latter even went as far as stating that none of these students backed the separatism of the provinces from Thailand.
13 I mentioned to several *mak pasar* that there were a growing number of Malay Muslim Thai restaurants in Kuala Lumpur and other cities in Malaysia, especially in the Malay neighbourhoods. My sister's apartment is in one of these areas. The eateries are usually called Tom Yum

restaurants, generically named after the famous Thai sour-and-spicy soup. They often hire Malay Muslims from Thailand's far south, in part because they pay less wages to them compared to the local Malaysian Malays.

14 The Bawah Rakyat Balik (Bring People Home) scheme is usually activated during Ramadan. During the fasting month, individuals who faced arrest warrants on security-related charges are allowed to turn themselves in. After surrendering to face charges and entering the criminal-justice process, the participants are enrolled in the scheme where they will receive career training to prepare for their re-entry into society. That is how it is advertised.

15 During my work with these *mak pasar* it was very rare for them to openly name the RKK or BRN-C. If they did, it was usually *referred* to.

16 As in Northern Ireland, Sarawak, and other guerrilla warfare sites, when the state made the mistake of being suspicious of a certain segment of the local population as being guerrillas and/or their sympathizers, this not only served to alienate its security forces but also resulted in a failed counter-insurgency campaign and prolonging the conflict (see, for example, Sluka 1989, 2010, for Northern Ireland and Iraq; Feldman 1991 for Northern Ireland; Mahmood 1996 with the Sikh in India; and Yong 2013 with the Hakkas in Sarawak). Having said that, unlike Northern Ireland and elsewhere, the so-called agents of the insurgency in Thailand's far south did not hold the moral high ground in the current as well as past insurgencies, except perhaps during Haji Sulong's time.

17 *Kak* is a Malay word to refer to someone as an elder sister. *Pi* is a Thai social title given as a sign of respect for someone, in terms of either seniority or other social indicators.

18 Pierre Nora (1996) and several French historians came up with the notion of *lieux de mémoire* (realm of memory). These are basically external props "that help incite our remembering ... tangible reminders of that which no longer exists except *qua* memory" (7–8). Borrowing the term of *loci memoriae* from classical mnemotechnique, Nora labels those places and events – artefacts, monuments, rituals, festivities, funerals, and in this case, the wooden netting needle – as "realms of memory" that are capable of stimulating acts of recollection.

19 As Taussig writes elsewhere, "violence has become a titillating tourist attraction to which, I believe, nobody is immune (including anthropologists, human rights workers, etc.). [As such], can we draw the bizarre conclusion that tourism is a better guardian of the history of violence than the well-meaning efforts of the memory professionals in universities and government? If not a better guardian, then at the least a more successful mode of attracting attention? But then it seems most

unlikely that the real instigators of the violence will be named, either by the professionals or the tourist guides or the internet sites. Not only can that be dangerous, but the histories are complex and not easily translated to outsiders, or translatable. What one is left with is titillation, meaning the outer skin and sensation of the untoward horrible, another mimesis, this time of terror" (2018, 182).

4 Households and Marital Unions, the Subject of Insecure Existence

1 It is common to hear Muslims in Thailand's far south calling those who do not *tudong* (wear headscarves) as "modern" Malay women. All the *mak pasar* I worked with were veiled. An *ajarnn* once told me that the wearing of the *tudong* by the Malay women in Thailand's far south was a recent phenomenon. He did not recall his mother and grandmother wearing one when he was growing up. He believed it had to do with the globalization of a certain Islam that came out from parts of the Middle East whereby we were witnessing the increasing pressure on Muslim women to conform to certain dress codes. See also Al-Ali (2010) for a similar discussion on Iraqi women.
2 I have heard plenty of complaints from these *mak pasar* and other women that their husbands spent too much time grooming their songbirds. Most of these men have more than one songbird. The *mak pasar* also complained that these songbirds were expensive, as was the special kind of bananas they were fed. Furthermore, the cages for each of these songbirds were priced accordingly to the pedigrees of the birds. It was a daily ritual, especially in the morning, to see a congregation of men (Malay Muslims and non–Malay Muslims) hanging out at the *warongs* (coffee shops, tea shops) with their songbirds, grooming and feeding them with these expensive bananas. Besides showing off their songbirds, they would often be showing off their latest pricey commodities: their latest expensive ring with this or that *mystical* stone, gem, or hardened wood on it. I have had my share of observing and listening to their ritualistic, even boastful conversations to the point that I stopped going to these *warongs*, in part because I knew how hard their wives had to work to put food on the tables. This was unfortunate because I would also have liked to hear their take on the latest conflict. I did try my best to get them to talk about it, but they would rather talk about songbirds and their latest rings and gemstones. However, I understood their reluctance to talk about the conflict because it was and is a very sensitive and dangerous topic.
3 As Fadil and Fernando (2015) point out, many anthropologists working within the broadly defined "everyday Islam" as well as on everyday ethics

have demonstrated that the alleged opposition between piety and the everyday – and the concomitant opposition between textual norm and individual practice – is untenable.
4 This is similar to the analysis of Palestinian women. As Buch Segal puts it, "the premise for much of the anthropology of adversity is the violent event and its aftermath, or consequence ... namely the lives lived in the braiding of Palestinian and psychological understandings of suffering, the domestic sphere, lived temporality, kin relations, the conjugal relations, and selfhood-as-motherhood (2016, 170).
5 See for example Abu-Lughod (2002), Mahmoud (2004), Schielke (2010), and Buch Segal (2016).
6 Thai officials estimated that by 2007 the insurgency had recruited some five thousand women, predominantly in the organization of demonstrations. In one particular incident, a CCTV caught a woman in a black *tudung* placing an IED at a Yala open-air market. See "Yala Bomb Planted by Woman, Police Say," *Nation*, 12 March 2007 (cited in Abuza 2009, 83).
7 To my knowledge, none of the NGOs or academics who worked on Aceh in the past has written anything about this misleading fatwa, even as Aceh became the most conservative and religious province in Indonesia.
8 A few years later, in January 2018, an estimated twenty-kilogram bomb exploded at an open-air fresh market in Muang Yala, the capital district of Yala province. This market consisted of stalls operated by Muslim and non-Muslim vendors. The blast occurred at six o'clock in the morning during a busy period, killing three people and seriously injuring thirty-four others. According to the police, a young man was seen parking a motorcycle (stolen) near a stall selling pork before rushing away on foot. Minutes later the bomb went off as the female owner of the pork stall was about to move the motorcycle, killing her instantly. A male customer was also killed. The injured were rushed to Yala Hospital where one later died. (See "Blast at Yala Market Leaves Three Civilians Dead," *Bangkok Post*, 23 January 2018).

5 Hiding the Clouds with the Palms of Your Hands

1 Writing on Argentina's Dirty War, Antonius Robben talks about the paradigm whereby the "industrial war" of armies fighting one other on a physical battlefield is being replaced by a "war amongst the people" in contemporary warfare (2010b, 134). To cite British general Rupert Smith, in contemporary counter-insurgency warfare "military engagements can take place anywhere: in the presence of civilians. Civilians are the targets, objectives to be won, as much as an opposing force" (2005, 3–4). This is

true for Thailand's far south and, as in other counter-insurgency warfare, increases the chances of civilian casualties and human rights violations. See for example Rungrawee Chalermsripinyorat (2009).
2. The *tahann* have announced major arms acquisitions each year since 2006. By 2009 the *tahann* had acquired "six Swedish Grispen jet fighters, Chinese surface-to-surface missiles, Russian antiaircraft missiles, a Singaporean-built amphibious frigate … six Russian-made Mi-17 helicopters, nearly 100 South African-made armored personnel carriers (APCs), 96 Ukrainian BTR-3 APCs, and Israeli Tavor assault rifles" (Abuza 2011, 15).
3. Writing on European colonial violence, Amitav Ghosh cites what Jan Coen, the Dutch exterminator of the Bandas once said: "THERE CAN BE NO trade without war and no war without trade" (2021, 42; emphasis in the original).
4. As Askew (2010c) and McCargo (2010) have pointed out, [the late] King Bhumibol Adulyadej, Thailand's widely revered and longest-serving monarch since 1946, was nearly ninety years old then and had been hospitalized for many years. There are many questions and fears concerning the future of the kingdom without King Bhumibol. Any political demands from the far south would be unwelcome by the government at that critical juncture. King Bhumibol passed away in October 2016, and his son, Wajiralongkorn, is the current king.
5. A UNICEF study on children living in the far south found that they suffered anxiety and stress as a result of ongoing threats and fear of violence due to their proximity to places of attack. See UNICEF (2008).
6. *Khun* is a title given as a sign of respect for someone, in terms of either seniority or other social, economic, and political indicators.
7. Besides being the owners of the luxury C.S. Pattani Hotel and many other businesses, the Suwanmonkol family also hold the franchise for Honda and Isuzu in the far south. They also own a huge hotel up north, in Chiang Mai.
8. *Pi* is a title given as a sign of respect for someone and is lower on the social spectrum than *Khun*.
9. Puea Thai (For Thais Party) is basically a renaming of Thai Rak Thai (Thais Love Thais Party) after the latter was deemed illegal by the constitution. As many analysts have commented, the forming of Puea Thai was politically a genius of a tactical move by Thaksin because a vote for Yingluck and her party was basically a vote for him as he lived then, and still does, in exile.
10. In broad terms, the yellow-shirt demonstrators were those who opposed former prime minister Thaksin and his allies. Most of them are southern based with support from the Bangkok elites. Meanwhile, the red-shirt demonstrators were pro-Thaksin, and most of them came from the north

and northeast rural and working classes but some supporters were democracy activists in Bangkok.

11 Jawi is an Arabic script that is traditionally used for writing the Malay language. It also applies for Acehnese, Minangkabau, and several other languages in Archipelago Southeast Asia. Day-to-day usage of Jawi is maintained in more conservative Malay-populated areas such as Pattani, Narathiwat, and Yala in Thailand's far south as well as in Kelantan and Trengganu in Malaysia, especially at the *ponok*, the religious boarding schools.

12 This is the same position taken by Rungrawee Chalermsripinyorat (2020) who suggested that the current peace talk was a departure from the previous liberal approach of the national elites in Bangkok.

13 Krabi is a resort town located on the west coast of southern Thailand.

14 Even though Songkhla is not a Malay Muslim–majority province in Thailand's far south, the current conflict has afflicted several of its districts and subdistricts.

6 Are We *Kon* Thai?

1 As a strategy to win the 2011 election and lead the Pheu Thai Party, one of Yingluck's election platforms was to guarantee the procurement of rice from farmers at nearly double the global market price. Since almost 40 per cent of Thailand's labour force is in the agricultural sector and the majority are rice farmers, Yingluck easily won the election. The strategy was simplistic, if not unrealistic: buy rice from farmers at inflated prices, stockpile it to drive up global prices, and resell it later at a higher price. At the time, Thailand was the largest rice exporter in the world, and Yingluck thought this was large enough to manipulate global prices. But the scheme backfired as other countries, notably India and Vietnam, promptly filled the Thai void. To be sure, countless governments around the world have invested in much costlier failed projects. The failure of the scheme was not the reason why Yingluck eventually faced impeachment. The political tension in Thailand during Yingluck's time goes back to when Thaksin Shinawatra, Yingluck's older brother and former prime minister, was removed in a military coup and convicted of corruption. Yingluck's opponents claimed that she was a mouthpiece for her exiled brother. The rice pledging scheme also drew the ire of the Bangkok middle class, who felt that their taxes were being squandered on "populist" schemes laden with corruption. The junta government has indicated that it intends to pursue civil damages against her to claw back what it considers as losses from the scheme. If Yingluck were convicted, she could face up to ten years of imprisonment. Yingluck has since escaped Thailand and is now

believed to be living somewhere in England or perhaps Dubai, just like her brother Thaksin.

2 Such knowledge or public secret is not unique to Thailand and perhaps is applicable to most nation-states, especially developing and consequently underdeveloped nations. As Taussig puts it, "Colombians live in the shadows of this public secret, or should I say shame. No need for the literary genre of magical realism when reality itself is thus constructed and lived imitates art. Everyone knows, nobody knows, not just because it is generally unwise to speak but because of what you might call blurred vision or double vision and the magma of fear under the surface of everyday life. You can never be sure of what's going on, who did what, and what's behind what. Secrecy magnifies reality and public secrecy magnifies it even more, encumbered by a brittle silence. [They become] a natural habitat" (2018, 15).

3 As Arendt (1958, 58–9) emphasized, there is always the paradoxical and ethical tension with *forgiveness* in that forgivers can be deservedly criticized for failing to remember the injustices they had endured; and remembrance implies, if not vengeance, at least an unwillingness to let go of the desire for vengeance.

4 Surayud Chulanont was the then prime minister of the interim junta government.

5 One of the main ingredients used to make the popular kratom-based cocktail is cough syrup. It is known as the "4 x 100 formula" cocktail.

6 One of these *barang* is methamphetamine.

7 According to Askew (2007), following the coup in 2006, the military has consolidated its authority and taken charge of all policies encompassing counter-insurgency operations and development of the far south. With it, the military budget has risen dramatically. This expansion in funding has allowed renewed major procurement. In September 2007 the cabinet approved the acquisition of ninety-six Ukrainian armoured vehicles and large quantities of Israeli-made light machine guns and assault rifles. In October of the same year, US$1.1 billion was approved for the procurement of twelve multi-role jet fighters and two aircraft. In June 2007 the army requested a total of US$17.6 billion solely to fund counter-insurgency operations by ISOC in the south over the coming four years. The money is categorized as secret budget, meaning officials can spent it without having to account to the government. "East Asia and Australasia," *The Military Balance* 108, no. 1, 359–416, http://dx.doi.org/10.1080/04597220801912879. See also Abuza (2011) for a similar assessment.

8 Concerning choice, Mary McCarthy states: "What is implied in these nuances of social standing is the respect we pay to choice. The exile

appears to have made a decision, while the refugee is the very image of helplessness, choicelessness, incomprehension, driven from his home by forces outside his understanding and control. We speak of flood refugees, earthquake refugees, persecuted by nature on account of the place they live in, war refugees harried by men for no other reason than that" (1994, 50–1).

9 In his abhorrence of the romanticization of an exile, Breytenbach offers this lengthy diatribe: "I dislike the manner in which the subject of exile has been romanticized, with the exiled ones pitied and slobbered over by voyeurs. I abhor feeding the stereotyped expectations of exile as a state of suffering and deprivation. Those who claim to be exiles themselves only too often reinforce the hackneyed perceptions. 'Do feel sorry for us,' they seem to say. 'Blame us on history. Take on the responsibility for our survival.' And for too many … this condition becomes an easy pretext for milking the sentiments of their hosts. They wallow in self-pity. All experience becomes frozen. On auspicious occasions they bring forth the relics and sing the cracked songs and end up arguing about what 'back home' was really like. They are dead survivors waiting for postcards from the realm of the living. The clock has stopped once and for all, the cuckoo suffocated on some unintelligible Swiss sound, and they will continue forever in terms of an absence that, naturally, is now embalmed and imbued with rosy dreams. They lose the language but refuse to integrate the loss, and accordingly will think less, with fewer words and only morbid references from which to suspend their thoughts. They still assume it is possible to hold back the shifting dunes of time. In the meantime, the condition of exile becomes a privileged status from which to morally and emotionally blackmail the world with special pleading. It becomes an excuse for defeat. A meal ticket" (1994, 183).

10 The question of whether or not the current insurgency is Islamic is dealt with by Rungrawee Chalermsripinyorat (2121), who suggests that it is Islamic, an opinion that was not shared by most of my Malay Muslim interlocutors. While these shadow insurgents might be Muslims, and thus Islamic, and even used religiosity as their cause, I would argue that it was the historical political grievances that lay at the core of their struggles.

11 Our jaded mentalities are not shared by many of those in the academy and beyond. Those *talking task* conferences and workshops were still in vogue in the late 2010s. Numerous articles are still being published on proposals to resolve the conflict. There is even a special series of a particular journal that has proposals to resolve the conflict. See the 2019 *Asian International Studies Review*, with an introduction by Paul Chambers, Srisompob Jitpiromsri, and Napisa Waitoolkiat.

12 Prior to my meeting with Ajarnn Abdullah and Sumree that day, I received an email from a close friend regarding a letter about the neo-Kharijite tradition written by Dr. Imtiyaz Yusuf, an *ajarnn* in the Department of Philosophy and Religion, Assumption University, Bangkok.
13 While Buddhism is not violent in and of itself, as a lived tradition it can be appropriated and lend itself to dark and deadly use especially when it can also function as a marker of state nationalism. Indeed, work by Tambiah (1992), Victoria (1998), Jerryson and Juergensmeyer (2010), and many others has debunked the myth of Buddhism as a moderate moral spiritual force "above" the political and outside the state. I want to suggest that Buddhism is hegemonic in Thailand and that it can somehow be characterized as controlled by incipient or potential fascism. Like others who have pointed it out, such incipient or potential fascism is seen as a novel marriage of capitalism, religion, and totalitarianism. See, for example, Arendt (1958) and Peterson (1969) for Nazi Germany and fascist Italy; Skidmore (2004) for Myanmar.
14 When the current conflict erupted in January 2004, many argued that it was the policies implemented under the Thaksin administration in dissolving the Southern Border Provinces Administration Centre in 2000, viewed by many as the key justice mechanism in the south, coupled with his War on Drugs policy – in which allegedly 2,596 suspected drug dealers were shot and disappeared throughout Thailand – that marked a turning point for the situation in the far south (Kasian 2006; Askew 2007; McCargo 2009). As cited by Askew (2010c), "in the words of Major General Nuntadej Meksawas stated in 2006, '[since many] blacklisted [drug] suspects had no mechanism by which to challenge their inclusion on [the black] list, and with the increasingly intensified climate of fear, many ethnic Malay Muslim villagers turned to separatist militants to seek protection from imminent threats of blacklisting, arbitrary arrest, disappearance, and extrajudicial killing" (Nanthadet Meksawat 2006, 35).
15 An exile is by extension also a person marked by a loss, and it can easily be extended to many categorical others. As Breytenbach puts it, "the exiled person is probably marked by a loss that he or she doesn't want to let go of, especially when occasioned by a political situation. But it goes without saying that one can replace, to all intents and purposes, the word 'exile' with refugee, misfit, outcast, outsider, expatriate, squatter, foreigner, clandestine, heretic, stranger, renegade, drifter, displaced person, marginal one, the new poor, the economically weak, the dropout. The irony is that if we were to add up all these individuals, we would probably find ourselves constituting a new silent majority!" (1994, 181).

16 Writing about dramatic representation of trauma, Feldman (2004) cites Adorno who emphasizes that the "ability to be horrified" – the "shudder" – is an affirmation, ultimately, of the humanity of the audience: "The subject is lifeless except when it is able to shudder in response to the total spell … Without shudder, consciousness is trapped in reification. Shudder is a kind of premonition of subjectivity, a sense of being touched by the other" (Adorno 1984, 455).

17 Talking about loss, when Amina said that, right then and there, it reminded me of what I wrote in the first line of the epigraph of my book about the death of three communist heroes in Borneo: "for we are also what we lost" (Yong 2013, 1). How coincidental it was that Amina would say almost the same exact words.

18 *Innalillah*, short for phrase *Inna lillahi wa inna ilayhi raji'un* (in Arabic), is a part of a verse from the Quran that translates to "We belong to Allah and to Him we shall return." The phrase is usually recited by Muslims to denote a tragic experience.

19 Indeed, and ironically, members of the IRA were invited to Thailand's far south to talk about "lessons" learned from the Northern Ireland experience.

20 This is not violence in an organic sense but a violence to destroy that which it conditions. As Klima put it, "this is not a simple condemnation of what happened, but of [illuminating] the inherent instability of the social order through which [nationalism in Thailand and elsewhere] reaches for both its exercise and its aims … [that] the social order never was not fragmentary, never was not brutal, and was only peaceful and reasonable to the degree by which it was able to obscure its genealogy of violence and so render massacre and other atrocity as exceptional and aberrant" (2002, 228).

21 I am also thinking here of their impossible and necessary demand in a Rancièrian sense, not the kind of the demand for equality within the sense of a liberal distributive justice. As he puts it, "the essence of equality is in fact not so much to unify as to declassify, to undo the supposed naturalness of orders and replace it with the controversial figures of division" (2007, 32–3). In many ways, this impossible and necessary demand is also a project of a real democratic politics. As Rancière puts it, the project of a democratic politics is not the unification of a group of people under a particular label, but their declassification from the identities, the *partage du sensible* (a partition of the sensible) of the police order (2007). He later called this "dissensus" as opposed to "consensus," the callings for a dissent from the given police order which he calls "politics." Politics is not a consensus about a particular partition of the sensible; it is a dissensus from it. Equality, Rancière tells us, does not unify;

it declassifies (2010). As May Todd points out, "there is some affinity of such thought with that of Derrida's reflections on democracy in that they both keep democracy under the banner of a declassification rather than an identity, ... a declassification that serves to preserve an equality that goes missing in traditional liberal theory" (2010, 16; see Derrida 2005).

7 War on Terror?

1 Coming from Carl Schmitt (2010), the very concept of the political is predicated on the existence (or fabrication) of an enemy.
2 For a checklist of how neoliberalism is being defined and its inherent contradictions and rhetorics, see Nonini (2008).
3 For a review of the unprecedented surge in popular and voluntary religious ritual, association, and observation in contemporary Asia and elsewhere, see Hefner (2002). For Africa, see Camaroff and Camaroff (2000). For the rise of religious fundamentalism in the United States and its resemblance in conservative judges, see Crapanzano (2001).
4 The local pronunciation of these Islamic boarding schools in Thailand's far south is *ponok* (and not *pondok* as they are called in other parts of the Malay Archipelago).
5 In the famous "Clash of Civilizations" thesis, Samuel Huntington (1998) declared Islam to be enemy number one of the West. See also Andrew McCarthy (2010) and Dinesh D'Souza (2007). That war and conflict have much more to do with political considerations, self-aggrandizement, greed, and economics than with religion or "civilization" is something that Huntington and his company consciously or unconsciously ignore. To find such level of historical delusion among them is not surprising, but unfortunately this type of thinking is not limited to their tight-knit far-right circles. The clash-of-civilizations narrative is also quite popular among the higher echelons of power across Western and non-Western capitals.
6 In the span of sixteen years that bracket 11 September 2001, one before and the other after the event (the Oklahoma bombing of 1995 and the Norway massacre of 2011), there was an instant knee-jerk of politically motivated racist suspicion by leading American and European news organizations – *The New York Times*, *The Wall Street Journal*, the *Washington Post*, the BBC, *The Financial Times*, and a wide range of television and radio stations, websites, and blogs – that publicized derogatory allegations about Islam before any facts were officially announced. It was as if any heinous crimes had to be committed by a Muslim, when in both cases the culprits – American Christian fundamentalist Timothy James McVeigh and Norwegian Anders Behring

Breivik – were white, blonde, and blue eyed. And US congressman Peter King – on the hearings of the "radicalization" of the American Muslim community – refused to widen the scope of the hearings to include other, non-Muslim terrorism threats.

7 Thinking along with Nietzsche (1978), the centrality of the *gift*, according to Deleuze and Guattari, is not exchange and circulation but rather inscription: "The essential thing seemed to us to be, not exchange and circulation, which closely depend on the requirements of inscription, but inscription itself, with its imprint of fire, its alphabet inscribed in bodies, and on blocks of debts" ([1972] 1983, 188).

8 Some of the materials for this chapter are an expanded version of an earlier publication (Yong 2012).

9 *Sepak takraw* is a very popular sport not only in Thailand but also in Southeast Asia. It uses a rattan ball, but, unlike in volleyball, players are only allowed to use their feet, knee, chest, and head to touch the ball.

10 Nik Aziz's deteriorating health was a source of concern not only within the various religious councils but also within the overall Malay Muslim communities in the far south as well as in Kelantan, Malaysia. He eventually passed away in February 2015 at the age of eighty-four.

11 In Arabic, *nasiha* is a central concept in Islamic moral theology. Among many things, it is a morally corrective discourse, one that signifies giving advice for someone's good, integrity, honesty, and ability to do justice to a situation.

12 *Kuih* is the generic name for "cake," prepared by baking, frying, or steaming, and so on. *Kuih kuih* denotes its plurality.

13 There was a history of communism in Thailand, especially within its far south. It is within this context that the association between water and fishes needs to be understood. In Mao Zedong's often-quoted dictum regarding the relationship between the masses and the guerrillas, the masses were likened to water and the guerrillas to the fishes who inhabit it. See Mao Zedong's "Primer on Guerrilla War," 5–11.

14 Farish Noor points out: "Labelled as 'dens of ossified traditionalism' to 'jihad factories,' the madrasahs [or *ponoks*] of the Muslim world have become the bugbear of Westernized liberals, secularists and the 'chicken hawks' of Washington … [They now] stand like some dark forbidding metaphor for a normative of Islamic religiosity caught in a fateful confrontation with the West and all things Western. The hype and hysteria that grips the world, thanks to the discourse on the "war against terror," has not helped to calm the fears of the public; nor has it helped improve our understanding of the madrasah" (2009, 32).

15 Bang Mann is the owner of a motorcycle and bicycle repair shop and an ardent collector, buyer, and seller of vintage Raleigh bicycles and their

original parts, which was one of the reasons for my frequent visits to his shop. It was also at his shop that I talked with his regulars about the current conflict.

16 *Goreng pisang* is fried banana. Ice-syrup is an iced sweetened and flavoured drink.

17 As I mentioned earlier, my subjects' theme of comparing their situation with Malaysia and Myanmar was quite a constant, especially when they dealt with their own dispositions. As a minority from Malaysia, I would often feel rather awkward when they would tell me about the good things in Malaysia: it once had the tallest buildings in the world, Muslims are the majority, there is less corruption, and, most ironic to me, Malaysia's political parties are race-based. They would also tell me that petrol and other basic necessities were cheaper in Malaysia. When it came to Myanmar, they would talk about the bleak situation there and how it was completely controlled by the *tatmadaw* (military), even with (back then) Aung San Suu Kyi and the National League for Democracy Party winning the elections, something that was almost identical to the situation in Thailand if one considered how powerful the armed forces were in both countries. Thailand has the *tahann*; Myanmar has the *tatmadaw*. It was as if, by making referential claims to the so-called favourable situation in Malaysia and the bleak situation in Myanmar, especially with regard to the Rohinyas, they were placing their own dispositions as being somewhere in between the two. In essence, they were creating excuses to tactically resolve their own powerlessness. I should state that the comparison with Myanmar, and not Malaysia, is often part of Thai state rhetoric to tell its population that they are better off than Myanmar, which is, after all, Thailand's historical enemy. Therefore, to hear my interlocutors making these comparisons was not just a reflection of their specific dispositions but also a use of official rhetoric. In other words, their narratives reflected part of the state narratives.

18 Contrary to the popular imagination in the West, many anthropologists as well as subjects in conflict zones viewed humanitarianism not as benevolent and altruistic endeavours by, most often, First World donors and governments but as an ideal violent gift that is immensely political, if not economical. As Dunn puts it, following Fassin and Pandolfi (2010), "humanitarian aid has become a form of 'mobile sovereignty' in which wealthy First World countries take over the functions of government in weaker 'failed states' as a form of trusteeship" (2018, 64).

19 Despite my attempt at not revealing the name of this *ponok*, it should be obvious to most Malay Muslims in the far south which *ponok* I am referring to.

20 Many ordinary Malays and Chinese I met confided to me that it is not uncommon for *ponoks* to receive contributions from local elites and businessmen, but these transactions could not be "broadcast" for fear of the ponok's getting into trouble, especially under the prevailing paranoia in the far south. In fact, I have come across several *ponoks* in Pattani that do not charge any tuition at all. All the parents need to do is to pay for the books and stationeries for their children. Besides, it is not even a public secret that *ponoks* and many local NGOs in the far south are funded by sources from the Middle East. In fact, Thailand's first Islamic university, the Yala Islamic University, was sponsored by the Saudi ministry of religious affairs, the Saudi-based Islamic Development Bank, the king of Qatar, and the king of Kuwait, as well as private donors from Saudi Arabia, Kuwait, and the United Arab Emirates (see Joll 2011).

21 It is common to see these classic Vespas as well as the Mercedes Benz of the 1950s, 1960s, 1970s, and 1980s in Thailand's far south. The fact that these classics are often second-, third-, fourth-, or fifth-hand points to the political economy of these poverty-rampant frontier provinces. However, as abject as the situation is, at least there is an appreciation and aesthetics for these classics.

22 When the latest conflict escalated in 2004, two major Thai newspapers, the *Bangkok Post* and *The Nation*, had almost daily coverages of Thailand's far south. As of 2016, *Bangkok Post* still reports on the far south but it has been sporadic. There is now almost no coverage by *The Nation* even though killings still occur on a daily, if not weekly, basis. As of 2019, the the *Bangkok Post* no longer even had a "Security" section to report on the crisis in the far south. It is as if the conflict and its violence in Thailand's far south has *disappeared* into indifference. But the violence has not *disappeared*. As recently as 31 December 2021, there was a series of explosions in Yala. See "6 bomb explosions in Yala," *Bangkok Post*, 2 January 2022, https://www.bangkokpost.com/thailand/general/2240995/6-bomb-explosions-in-yala-on-new-years-eve.

8 The "Halalness" of Things

1 There is an endless array of halal food items from Malaysia and Indonesia in the far south – whether they are imported legally or otherwise – at supermarkets, retail shops, or at the three open-air markets. They include sugar, cooking oil, monosodium glutamate (one of the gifts from Japan, besides karaoke), instant noodles, fish, squid, beef, and chicken meatballs, and sausages.

2 Following Georges Dumezil, Deleuze and Guattari came up with the concept of the "war machine" as a loose congeries of beings or a pack

of animals that overlap with the state, a war machine that may be appropriated by the state as well as appropriating the state (1986, see chapter 12).

3 Given that a lot of development projects in many parts of the so-called Third World are enabled and protected by military and paramilitary personnel, it begs the question why so little attention has been paid by so-called human rights experts to their roles and the miseries they manufacture. Instead, those who did pay attention, the real experts, are the victims who were displaced, those who ended up as factory workers inside the development machine, those who lived inside this machine in silence, punctuated by words and phrases, but mostly silence without speech. Now that most factories are automated with little need for unskilled labour, more multinational companies are moving into these state-declared, tax-free trade zones, otherwise called industrial parks. As Taussig heuristically and sarcastically puts it, "history moves fast in today's Third World, and the landscape moves with it" (2003, 21).

4 Just to make a point about the level of poverty in the far south, in 2017 the Malaysian authorities at Johor Bharu, the state capital of the state of Johor, arrested twenty-one elderly women from Thailand's far south. These were senior citizens, one of them eighty-one years old. These women were duped into pretending to be beggars and were even told by their recruiters to put on worn-out clothes so that people would pity them. These elderly women were later released, and the Malaysian authorities sent them home to their families (*Bangkok Post*, 18 January 2017).

5 *Ayam* means "chicken" in Malay but is also the local slang word for sex workers.

6 Thais do not need to apply in advance for a visa to enter Malaysia. It is given for free at the Malaysian immigration checkpoints so long as one has a valid passport (with the expiration date not less than six months from the day of entry and with enough blank pages in the passport for the officer to stamp). However, the free visa is only valid for thirty days, and one has to make a "visa/border run" to Thailand and back to Malaysia before the end of the thirty days. Otherwise, one will have to pay a fine of 30 ringgit for any extra days of overstay and the possibility of being denied future re-entry. With these conditions, many Thais working in Malaysia either make their "visa/border run" just before the end of the thirty days or pay some illegal syndicates who would, in essence, make the "visa/border run" on their behalf. The same is true for non-Thais working or travelling in Thailand without a proper work or research permit. The fine for overstay in Thailand is 500 baht per day, and the possibility of being denied re-entry depends on which immigration

checkpoints one passes through as well as the prevailing mood of the immigration officer on any one day.
7 Sadao and Padang Besar are two of the many immigration checkpoints on the southern border of Thailand and Malaysia.
8 As of July 2018, a litre of diesel fuel cost RM2.18, while a litre of petrol RON 95 and of premium RON 98 cost RM2.20 and R2.58, respectively, in Malaysia. Meanwhile a litre of diesel, gasohol 95, and gasohol 91 commonly used by pickup trucks and cars in Thailand cost 29.19 baht (about RM3.64), 29.65 baht (about RM3.70) and 29.38 baht (about RM3.67), respectively. (Cf. "Local Politicians, 'Influential People' behind Smuggled Oil Business in Southern Thai," *Malaysiakini*, 8 July 2018, https://www.malaysiakini.com/news/433235).
9 *Teh tarik* is a popular hot milk tea beverage commonly found in Malaysia, Indonesia, Singapore, and Thailand's far south. Its name is derived from the pouring process of "pulling" (*tarik*) the drink during preparation.
10 See "Pattani Bomb Blasts Leave Scores Hurt," *Bangkok Post*, 10 May 2017. http://www.bangkokpost.com/print/1246622/; "Local Leaders Arrested in Big C Car Bombing," *Bangkok Post*, 11 May 2017, http://www.bangkokpost.com/print/1247667/; "Vendor Brutally Killed for Truck Used as Car Bomb," *Bangkok Post*, 12 May 2017, http://www.bangkokpost.com/print/1248395/; "Big C Bombing: 2 Suspects Killed in 4 Days," *Bangkok Post*, 14 July 2017, http://www.bangkokpost.com/print/1287267/.

Bibliography

Abraham, Itty, and Sumie Nakaya. 2007. "Uncertainty, Knowledge, and Violence in Southern Thailand." *Economic and Political Weekly* 42 (24): 2304–9.

Abu-Lughod, Lila. 2002. "Do Muslim Women Really Need Saving? Anthropological Reflections on Cultural-Relativism and Its Others." *American Anthropologist* 104 (3): 783–90. https://doi.org/10.1525/aa.2002.104.3.783.

Abuza, Zachary. 2009. *Conspiracy of Silence: The Insurgency in Southern Thailand*. Washington, DC: United State Institute of Peace Press.

– 2011. *The Ongoing Insurgency in Southern Thailand: Trends in Violence, Counterinsurgency Operations, and the Impact of National Politics*. Institute of National Strategic Studies Strategic Perspectives, no. 6. Washington, DC: National Defense University Press. https://ndupress.ndu.edu/Portals/68/Documents/stratperspective/inss/Strategic-Perspectives-6.pdf

Adorno, Theodor. 1984. *Aesthetic theory*. Translated by C. Lendardt. London: Routledge and Kegan Paul.

Agha, Asif. 2005. "Introduction." *Journal of Linguistic Anthropology* 15 (1): 1–5.

Al-Ali, Nadje. 2010. "The War on Terror and Women's Rights in Iraq." In *Iraq at a Distance: What Anthropologists Can Teach Us about the War*, edited by Antonius Robben, 57–79. Philadelphia: University of Pennsylvania Press.

Allen, Lori. 2008. "Getting by the Occupation: How Violence Became Normal during the Second Palestinian Intifada." *Cultural Anthropology* 23 (3): 453–87. https://doi.org/10.1111/j.1548-1360.2008.00015.x.

Allerton, Catherine. 2013. *Potent Landscapes: Place and Mobility in Eastern Indonesia*. Hawaii: University of Hawai'i Press.

Al-Marashi, Ibrahim. 2010. Epilogue to *Iraq at a Distance: What Anthropologists Can Teach Us about the War*. Edited by Antonius Robben, 159–74. Philadelphia: University of Pennsylvania Press.

Amnesty International. 2006. *Thailand: Human Rights Protections Must Be Upheld*. https://www.amnesty.or.jp/en/news/2006/0922_571.html.

Anderson, Benedict. 1966. "Japan: The Light of Asia." In *Southeast Asia in World War II: Four Essays*, edited by J. Silverstein, 13–50. New Haven, CT: Yale University, Southeast Asia Studies.

Anusorn Unno. 2010. "We Love 'Mr. King': Exceptional Sovereignty, Submissive Subjectivity, and Mediated Agency in Islamic Southern Thailand." PhD diss. Department of Anthropology, University of Washington.

Appadurai, Arjun. 2006. *Fear of Small Numbers: An Essay on the Geography on Anger*. Durham, NC: Duke University Press.

Arendt, Hannah. 1958. *The Human Condition*. Chicago: University of Chicago Press.

– 1969. *On Violence*. London: Allen Lane.

Aretxaga, Begona. 1997. *Shattering Silence: Women, Nationalism, and Political Subjectivity in Northern Ireland*. Princeton, NJ: Princeton University Press.

Asad, Talal. 1973. *Anthropology and the Colonial Encounter*. Edited by Talal Asad. New York: Humanity Press.

– 1987. "Are There Histories of Peoples without Europe?" *Comparative Studies* in *Society and History* 29 (3): 594–607. http://doi.org/10.1017/S0010417500014742.

– 1993. *Genealogies of Religion: Discipline and Reasons of Power in Christianity and Islam*. Baltimore, MD: Johns Hopkins University Press.

– 2011. "Thinking about the Secular Body, Pain, and Liberal Politics." *Cultural Anthropology* 26 (4): 657–75. https://doi.org/10.1111/j.1548-1360.2011.01118.x.

– 2012. "Fear and the Ruptured State: Reflections on Egypt after Mubarak." *Social Research: An International Quarterly* 79 (2): 271–98. https://doi.org/10.1353/sor.2012.0035.

Askew, Marc. 2007. "Thailand's Recalcitrant Southern Borderland: Insurgency, Conspiracies and the Disorderly State." *Asian Security* 3 (2): 99–120. https://doi.org/10.1080/14799850701331443.

– 2009. "Landscape of Fear, Horizons of Trust: Villagers Dealing with Danger in Thailand's Insurgent South." *Journal of Southeast Asian Studies* 40 (1): 59–86.

– 2010a. "Fighting with Ghosts: Querying Thailand's 'Southern Fire.'" *Contemporary Southeast Asia* 32 (2): 117–55. https://doi.org/10.1355/cs32-2a.

– 2010b. "Insurgency and the Market for Violence in Southern Thailand: Neither War nor Peace." *Asian Survey* 50 (6): 1107–34. https://doi.org/10.1525/as.2010.50.6.1107.

– 2010c. "The Spectre of the South: Regional Instability as National Crisis." In *Legitimacy Crisis in Thailand*, edited by Marc Eskew, 235–72. Chiang Mai, Thailand: Silkworm Books.

Bibliography

Askew, Marc, and Sasha Helbardt. 2012. "Becoming Patani Warriors: Individuals and the Insurgent Collective in Southern Thailand." *Studies in Conflict and Terrorism* 35:779–809. https://doi.org/10.1080/1057610X.2012.720239.

Austin, John L. 1962. *How to Do Things with Words*. Cambridge, MA: Harvard University Press.

Bajunid, Omar Farouk. 1984. "The Historical and Transnational Dimensions of Malay Muslim Separatism in Southern Thailand." In *Armed Separatism in Southeast Asia*, edited by Lim Joo-Jock and Vani S., 234–57. Singapore: Institute of Southeast Asian Studies.

– 2005. "Islam, Nationalism, and the Thai State." In *Dynamic Diversity in Southern Thailand*, edited by Watanna Sugunnasil, 1–20. Chiang Mai, Thailand: Silkworm Books.

Bakhtin, Mikhal. (1965) 1984. *Rabelais and His World*. Translated by Helene Iswolsky. Bloomington: Indiana University Press.

– 1981. *The Dialogic Imagination: Four Essays*. Edited and translated by Caryl Emerson and Michael Holquist. Austin, TX: University of Texas Press.

Barthes, Roland. (1957) 1972. Mythologies. Selected and translated by Annette Lavers. New York: Hill and Wang.

Bataille, Georges. 1991. *The Accursed Share: An Essay on General Economy*. Vol. 1, *Consumption*. New York: Zone Books.

Bauman, Zygmunt. 1991. "Living without an Alternative." Political Quarterly 62: 35–44. https://doi.org/10.1111/j.1467-923X.1991.tb00842.x.

Benjamin, Walter. 1968. "Theses on the Philosophy of History." In *Illuminations*. New York: Schocken.

– 1977. *The Origin of German Tragic Drama*. Translated by John Osborne. London: New Left Books.

– 1983. *Das passagen werk*. Frankfurt, Germany: Suhrkamp.

Bloch, Ernst. (1954) 1986. *The Principle of Hope*. Cambridge, MA: MIT Press.

Blu, Karen. 2001. *The Lumbee Problem: The Making of an American Indian People*. Lincoln: University of Nebraska Press.

Böckenförde, Ernst-Wolfgang. 1991. *State, Society and Liberty: Studies in Political Theory and Constitutional Law*. Oxford: Berg.

Bolano, Roberto. 2003. *By Night in Chile*. New York: New Directions.

Bradley, Francis. 2009. "Moral Order in a Time of Damnation: The Hikayat Patani in Historical Context." *Journal of Southeast Asian Studies* 40 (2): 267–93. https://doi.org/10.1017/S0022463409000150.

Breytenbach, Breyten. 1994. "The Exile as African." In *Altogether Elsewhere: Writers on Exile*, edited by Marc Robinson, 179–83. Winchester, MA: Faber and Faber.

Brown, David. 1988. "From Peripheral Communities to Ethnic Nations: Separatism in Southeast Asia." *Pacific Affairs* 61 (1): 51–77. https://doi.org/10.2307/2758072.

Buch Segal, Lotte. 2016. *No Place for Grief: Martyrs, Prisoners, and Mourning in Contemporary Palestine*. Philadelphia: University of Pennsylvania Press.

Buse, Peter, Ken Hirschkop, Scott McCracken, and Bertrand Taithe. 2005. *Benjamin's Arcades: An Unguided Tour*. Manchester, UK: Manchester University Press.

Camaroff, Jean, and John Camaroff. 2000. "Millenial Capitalism: First Thoughts on a Second Coming." *Public Culture* 12 (2): 291–343. https://doi.org/10.1215/08992363-12-2-291.

Canetti, Elias. 1984. *Crowds and Power*. Translated by Carol Stewart. New York: Farrar, Straus and Giroux.

Casey, Edward. 1987. *Remembering. A Phenomenological Study*. Bloomington: Indiana University Press.

– 2009. *Getting Back into Place: Towards a Renewed Understanding of Place-World*. 2nd ed. Bloomington: Indiana University Press.

Cavell, Stanley. 1976. *Must We Mean What We Say?* Cambridge: Cambridge University Press.

Certeau, Michel de. 1985. "Practices of Space." In *On Signs*, edited by Marshall Blonsky, 122–45. Baltimore, MD: Johns Hopkins University Press.

Chaiwat Satha-Anand. 2004. *Khwam ngiap khong anusawari luk puen: Dusong yo narathiwat 2491* [The silence of the bullet monument]. Dusun Nyior, Narathiwat, 1948.

– 2006. *The Life of This World: Negotiated Muslim Lives in Thai Society*. Singapore: Marshall Cavendish Academic.

– 2007. "The Silence of the Bullet Monument: Violence and 'Truth' Management, Dusun-nyor 1948, and Kru-Ze 2004." In *Rethinking Thailand's Southern Violence*, edited by Duncan McCargo, 11–34. Singapore: National University of Singapore Press.

Chaloemkiat Khunthongphet. 1986. "Kontotan naiyobai rattaban nai si jangwat phak tai khong prathet Thai doi kan nam khong Hayi Sulong Abdunkadae" [Resistance to government policy in the four southern provinces of Thailand under the leadership of Haji Sulong Abdulqadir]. MA thesis, Silapakon University, Bangkok.

Chambers, Paul, Srisompob Jitpiromsri, and Napisa Waitoolkiat. 2019. "Introduction: Conflict in the Deep South of Thailand: Never-Ending Stalemate?" Special issue, *Asian International Studies Review* 20, 1–23. https://doi.org/10.1163/2667078X-02001001.

Che Man, Wan Kadir. 1990. *Muslim Separatism: The Moros of Southern Philippines and the Malays of Southern Thailand*. Singapore: Oxford University Press.

Christie, Clive. 1996. *A Modern History of Southeast Asia: Decolonization, Nationalism and Separatism*. London: Tauris Academic Studies.

Clifford, James. 1992. "Traveling Cultures." In *Cultural Studies*, edited by Lawrence Grossberg, Cary Nelson, and Paula Treichler, 96–116. New York: Routledge.

Cohen, Lawrence. 1998. *No Aging in India: Alzheimer's, the Bad Family, and Other Modern Things*. Berkeley: University of California Press.

Collingwood. R.G. (1946) 1993. *The Idea of History*. Rev. ed. Edited by Jan Van Der Dussen. Oxford: Oxford University Press.

Connors, Michael. 2006. "War on Terror and the Southern Fire: How Terrorism Analysts Get It Wrong." *Critical Asian Studies* 38 (1): 151–75. https://doi.org/10.1080/14672710600556528.

– 2009. "Another Country: Reflections on the Politics and Culture of the Muslim South." In *Divided Over Thaksin: Thailand's Coup and Problematic Transition*, edited by John Funston, 110–23. Singapore: Institute of Southeast Asian Studies.

Cooper, Frederick, and Randall Packard. 2005. "The History and Politics of Development Knowledge." In *The Anthropology of Development and Globalization*, edited by Marc Edelman and Angelique Haugerud, 126–39. Oxford: Blackwell Publishing.

Cortazar, Julio. 1994. "The Fellowship of Exile." In *Altogether Elsewhere: Writers on Exile*, edited by Marc Robinson, 171–78. Winchester, MA: Faber and Faber.

Crapanzano, Vincent. 1992. *Hermes' Dilemma and Hamlet's Desire: On the Epistemology of Interpretation*. Cambridge, MA: Harvard University Press.

– 1993. "Speaking with Names." In *Lothar Baumgarten: America Invention*, 91–100. New York: Guggenheim Museum.

– 2001. *Serving the Word: Literalism in American from the Pulpit to the Bench*. New York: New Press.

– 2011. *The Harkis: The Wound That Never Healed*. Chicago: University of Chicago Press.

– 2014. "Must We Be Bad Epistemologists? Illusions of Transparency, the Opaque Other, and Interpretive Foibles." In The *Ground Between*: *Anthropologists Engaging Philosophy*, edited by Veena Das, Michael Jackson, Arthur Kleinman, and Bhrigupati Singh, 254–78. Durham, NC: Duke University Press.

Das, Veena. 2007. *Life and Words: Violence and the Descent into the Ordinary*. Berkeley: University of California Press.

– 2012. "Ordinary Ethics." In *A Companion to Moral Anthropology*, edited by Didier Fassin, 133–49. Oxford: Wiley-Blackwell.

– 2014a. "Action, Expression, and Everyday Life: Recounting Household Events." In *The Ground Between: Anthropologists Engaging Philosophy*, edited by Veena Das, Michael Jackson, Arthur Kleinman, and Bhrigupati Singh, 279–306. Durham, NC: Duke University Press.

- 2014b. "Ethics, the Householder's Dilemma, and the Difficulty of Reality." *HAU: Journal of Ethnographic Theory* 4 (1): 487–95.
- 2015. *Affliction: Health, Disease, Poverty*. New Delhi, India: Orient Blackswan.

Das, Veena, Michael Jackson, Arthur Kleinman, and Bhrigupati Singh. 2014. "Experiments between Anthropology and Philosophy: Affinities and Antagonism." In *The Ground Between: Anthropologists Engaging Philosophy*, edited by Veena Das, Michael Jackson, Arthur Kleinman, and Bhrigupati Singh, 1–26. Durham, NC: Duke University Press.

Das, Veena, and Deborah Poole, eds. 2004. *Anthropology in the Margins of the State*. Santa Fe, NM: School of American Research Press.

Davisakd Puaksom. 2008. "Of a Lesser Brilliance: Patani Historiography in Contention." In *Thai South and Malay North: Ethnic Interactions on a Plural Peninsula*, edited by Michael Montesano and Patrick Jory, 71–88. Singapore: National University of Singapore Press.

Day, Sophie, Akis Papataxiarchis, and Michael Stewart, eds. 1999. *Lilies of the Field: Marginal people Who Live for the Moment*. Boulder, CO: Westview Press.

Deep South Watch. 2010. "Sixth Year on the Southern Fire: Dynamics of Insurgency and Formation of the New Imagined Violence." http://www.deepsouthwatch.org/node/730
- 2020. "Summary of Incidents in Southern Thailand." https://deepsouthwatch.org/en/node/11971

Deleuze, Gilles. 1994. *Difference and Repetition*. London: Continuum Books.

Deleuze, Gilles, and Felix Guattari. (1972) 1983. *Anti-Oedipus: Capitalism and Schizophrenia*. Translated by Brian Massumi. Minneapolis: University of Minnesota Press.
- 1986. *Nomadology: The War Machine*. Translated by Brian Massumi. New York: Semiotext(e).

Derrida, Jacques. 1994. *Specters of Marx: The State of the Debt, the Work of Mourning, and the New International*. Translated by Peggy Kamuf. New York: Routledge.
- 2005. *Rogues: Two Essays on Reason*. Translated by Pascale-Anne Brault and Michael Nass. Palo Alto, CA: Stanford University Press.

Desjarlais, Robert. 1992. *Body and Emotion: The Aesthetics of Illness and Healing in the Nepal Himalayas*. Philadelphia: University of Pennsylvania Press.
- 1997. *Shelter Blues: Sanity and Selfhood among the Homeless*. Philadelphia: University of Pennsylvania Press.

Dorairajoo, Saroja. 2004. "Violence in the South of Thailand." *Inter-Asia Cultural Studies* 5 (3): 465–71. https://doi.org/10.1080/1464937042000288741.

Dostoyevsky, Fyodor. (1834) 1980. *Notes from Underground; White Nights; The Dream of a Ridiculous Man; and Selections from the House of the Dead*. Translated by Andrew R. MacAndrew. New York: New American Library.

D'Souza, Dinesh. 2007. *The Enemy at Home: The Cultural Left and Its Responsibility for 9/11*. New York: Broadway.

Dunn, Elizabeth Cullen. 2018. *No Path Home: Humanitarian Camps and the Grief of Displacement*. Ithaca, NY: Cornell University Press.

Eddon, Raluca. 2006. "Arendt, Scholem, and Benjamin: Between Revolution and Messianism." *European Journal of Political Theory* 5 (3): 261–79. https://doi.org/10.1177/1474885106064661.

Elias, Norbert. (1969) 1983. *The Court Society*. Translated by Edmund Jephcott. New York: Pantheon Books.

Escobar, Arturo. 1995. *Encountering Development: The Making and Unmaking of the Third World*. Princeton, NJ: Princeton University Press.

Fabian, Johannes. 1983. *Time and the Other: How Anthropology Makes Its Object*. New York: Columbia University Press.

Fadil, Nadia, and Mayanthi Fernando. 2015. "Rediscovering the "Everyday" Muslim: Notes on an Anthropological Divide." *HAU: Journal on Ethnographic Theory* 5 (2): 59–88. https://doi.org/10.14318/hau5.2.005.

Fanon, Frantz. 1967. *Black Skin, White Masks*. Translated by Charles Lam Markmann. New York: Grove Press.

Fassin, Didier, and Mariella Pandolfi, eds. 2010. *Contemporary States of Emergency: The Politics of Military and Humanitarian Interventions*. New York: Zone Books.

Feld, Steven, and Keith Basso. 1996. *Senses of Place*. Advance Seminar Series. Sante Fe, NM: School of American Research Press.

Feldman, Allen. 1991. *Formations of Violence: The Narrative of the Body and Political Terror in Northern Ireland*. Chicago: University of Chicago Press.

– 2004. "Memory Theatres, Virtual Witnessing, and the Trauma-Aesthetic." *Biography* 27 (1): 163–202. https://doi.org/10.1353/bio.2004.0030.

Foucault, Michel. 1980. "Truth and Power." In *Power/Knowledge: Selected Interviews and Other Writings, 1972–1977*. New York: Pantheon.

Freedman, Maurice. 1975. "An Epicycle of Cathay or the Southward Expansion of the Sinologists." In *Social Organization and the Applications of Anthropology*, edited by R.J. Smith, 302–32. Ithaca, NY: Cornell University Press.

Gellner, Ernest. 1988. "Trust, Cohesion, and Social Order." In *Trust: Making and Breaking Cooperative Relations*, edited by Diego Gambetta, 142–57. New York: Basil Blackwell.

Genet, Jean. (1986) 1992. *Prisoner of Love*. Hanover, NH: University Press of New England / Wesleyan University Press.

Ghosh, Amitav. 2021. *The Nutmeg's Curse: Parables for a Planet in Crisis*. London: John Murray.

Goffman, Erwing. 1969. *Stigma: Notes on the Management of Spoiled Identity*. Englewood Cliffs, NJ: Prentice-Hall.

Green, Linda. 1999. *Fear as a Way of Life: Mayan Widows in Rural Guatemala*. New York: Columbia University Press.

Gupta, Akhil, and James Ferguson. 1992. "Beyond 'Culture': Space, Identity, and the Politics of Difference." *Cultural Anthropology* 7 (1): 6–23. https://doi.org/10.1515/9780822382089-003.

Hacking, Ian. 1990. *The Taming of Chance*. Cambridge: Cambridge University Press.

Hankins, Joseph. 2012. "Maneuvers of Multiculturalism: International Representations of Minority Politics in Japan." *Japanese Studies* 32 (1): 1–19. https://doi.org/10.1080/10371397.2012.669730.

Hastrup, Kirsten. 2002. "Anthropology's Comparative Consciousness: The Case of Human Rights." In *Anthropology, by Comparison*, edited by Andre Gingrich and Richard Fox, 27–43. London: Routledge.

Heaney, Seamus. 1995. "Nobel Lecture." The Nobel Prize in Literature. https://www.nobelprize.org/prizes/literature/1995/heaney/lecture/.

Hefner, Robert. 2002. "Global Violence and Indonesian Muslim Politics." *American Anthropologist* 104 (3): 754–65. https://doi.org/10.1525/aa.2002.104.3.754.

Helbardt, Sascha. 2011. "Deciphering Southern Thailand's Violence: Organization and Insurgent Practices of BRN Coordinate. PhD diss., Department for Southeast Asian Studies II, Faculty of Philosophy, University of Passau.

– 2015. *Deciphering Southern Thailand's Violence: Organization and insurgent practices of BRN-Coordinate*. Singapore; Institute of Southeast Asian Studies, Yusof Ishak Institute.

Herring, Eric, and Glen Rangwala. 2006. *Iraq in Fragments: The Occupation and Its Legacy*. Ithaca, NY: Cornell University Press.

Hinton, Alexander. 2010. "'Night Fell on a Different World': Dangerous Visions and the War on Terror, a Lesson from Cambodia. In *Iraq at a Distance: What Anthropologists Can Teach Us about the War*, edited by Antonius Robben, 24–56. Philadelphia: University of Pennsylvania Press.

Ho, Engseng. 2004. "Empire through Diasporic Eyes: A View from the Other Boat." Comparative Study of Society and History 46 (2): 210–46. https://doi.org/10.1017/S001041750400012X.

Hobbes, Thomas. 1962. *Leviathan: Or the Matter, Forme and Power of a Commonwealth Ecclesiasticall and Civil*. London: Collier Books.

Human Rights Watch. 2007. *No One Is Safe: Insurgent Attacks against Civilians in Thailand's Southern Border Provinces*. 27 August. https://www.hrw.org/report/2007/08/27/no-one-safe/insurgent-attacks-civilians-thailands-southern-border-provinces.

Huntington, Samuel. 1998. *The Clash of Civilizations and the Remaking of World Order*. New York: Simon & Shuster.

International Crisis Group. 2009. *Recruiting Militants in Southern Thailand.* https://www.crisisgroup.org/asia/south-east-asia/thailand/recruiting-militants-southern-thailand.

Jenkins, Janis, and Martha Valient. 1994. "Bodily Transactions of the Passions: El Calor among Salvadoran Women Refugees." In *Embodiment and Experience: The Existential Ground of Culture and Self,* edited by Thomas Csordas, 163–82. Berkeley: University of California Press.

Jerryson, Michael. 2009. "Appropriating a Space for Violence: State Buddhism in Southern Thailand." *Journal of Southeast Asian Studies* 40 (1): 33–57. https://doi.org/10.1017/S0022463409000034.

– 2011. *Buddhist Fury: Religion and Violence in Southern Thailand.* New York: Oxford University Press.

Jerryson, Michael, and Mark Juergensmeyer, eds. 2010. *Buddhist Warfare.* New York: Oxford University Press.

Johnson, Andrew Alan. 2020. *Mekong Dreaming: Life and Death along a Changing River.* Durham, NC, and London: Duke University Press.

Joll, Christopher. 2011. *Muslim Merit-Making in Thailand's Far South.* London: Springer.

Jory, Patrick. 2006. "From 'Patani Melayu' to 'Thai Muslim.'" ISIM (*International Institute for the Study of Islam in the Modern World*) *Review* 18 (Autumn): 42–3.

Joseph, Suad. 1999. *Intimate Selving in Arab Families: Gender, Self, and Identity.* Syracuse, NY: Syracuse University Press.

Kachatpai Burupat. 1976. *Thai Muslims.* Bangkok, Thailand: Phrae Pitaya.

Kapchan, Deborah. 1996. *Gender on the Market: Moroccan Women and the Revoicing of Tradition.* Philadelphia: University of Pennsylvania Press.

Kasian Tejapira. 2006. "Toppling Thaksin." *New Left Review* 39 (5): 5–37. https://doi.org/10.4324/9781315240756-14.

Kelly, Tobias. 2009. "The U.N. Committee against Torture: Human Rights Monitoring and the Legal Recognition of Torture." *Human Rights Quarterly* 31 (3): 777–800. https://doi.org/10.1353/hrq.0.0094.

– 2013. "A Life Less Miserable?" *HAU: Journal of Ethnographic Theory* 3 (1): 213–16.

Keyes, Charles. 2010. "Muslims 'Others' in Buddhist Thailand." *Thammasat Review* 13:19–42. https://sc01.tci-thaijo.org/index.php/tureview/article/view/40819/33803.

Khalidi, Rashid. 2005. *Resurrecting Empire: Western Footprints and America's Perilous Path in the Middle East.* Reprint. Boston: Beacon Press.

– 2010. *Sowing Crisis: The Cold War and American Dominance in the Middle East.* Boston: Beacon Press.

Kilcullen, David. 2009. *The Accidental Guerrilla: Fighting Small Wars in the Midst of a Big One*. New York: Oxford University Press.

King, Phil. 2005. "The Indonesia-Malaysia-Thailand Growth Triangle: How the South Was Won … and Then Lost Again." In *Dynamic Diversity in Southern Thailand*, edited by Wattana Sugunnasil, 93–108. Chiang Mai, Thailand: Silkworm Books.

Kleinman, Arthur, Veena Das, and Margaret Lock. 1997. *Social Suffering*. Edited by Arthur Kleinman, Veena Das, and Margaret Lock. Berkeley: University of California Press.

Klima, Alan, 2002. *The Funeral Kasino: Meditation, Massacre, and Exchange with the Dead in Thailand*. Princeton, NJ: Princeton University Press.

Kobkua Suwannathat-Pian. 1988. *Thai-Malay Relations: Traditional Intra-regional Relations from the 17th to the Early 20th Centuries*. Singapore: Oxford University Press.

Koselleck, Reinhart. 2002. *The Practice of Conceptual History: Timing History, Spacing Concepts*. Translated by Todd Samuel Presner, Kerstin Behnke, and Jobst Welge. Stanford, CA: Stanford University Press.

– 2004. *Futures Past: On the Semantics of Historical Time*. Translated by Keith Tribe. New York: Columbia University Press.

Kublitz, Anja. 2013. "Seizing Catastrophes: The Temporality of Nakba among Palestinians in Denmark." In *Times of Securities: Ethnographies of Fear, Protest and the Future*, edited by Martin Holbraad and Morten Axel Pedersen, 103–21. Milton Park, UK: Routledge.

Liow, Joseph. 2009. *Islam, Education and Reform* in *Southern Thailand: Tradition and Transformation*. Singapore: Institute of Southeast Asian Studies.

Liow, Joseph, and Don Pathan, 2010. *Confronting Ghosts: Thailand's Shapeless Southern Insurgency*. Sydney, Australia: Lowy Institute for International Policy.

Loos, Tamara. 2006. *Subject Siam: Family, Law, and Colonial Modernity in Thailand*. Ithaca, NY: Cornell University Press.

Lowenthal, David. 1985. *The Past Is a Foreign Country*. Cambridge: Cambridge University Press.

– 1996. *Possessed by the Past: The Heritage Crusade and the Spoils of History*. New York: Free Press.

MacIntyre, Alasdair. 1984. *After Virtue: A Study of Moral Theory*. 2nd ed. Notre Dame, IN: University of Notre Dame Press.

Madmarn, Hassan. 1989. "Pondok and Change in South Thailand." In *Aspects of Developments: Islamic Education in Thailand and Malaysia*, edited by R. Scupin, 47–92. Bangi: ATMA, University Kebangsaan Malaysia.

– 2003. "Secular Education, Values and Development in the Context of Islam in Thailand: An Outlook on Muslim Attitudes towards Thai Educational Policy." In *Asian Interfaith dialogue: Perspectives on Religion, Education and*

Social Cohesion, edited by S.F. Alatas, L. Teek Ghee, and K. Kuroda, 66–77. Singapore: Centre for Research on Islamic and Malay Affairs (RIMA).

Mahmood, Cynthia Keppley. 1996. *Fighting for Faith and Nation: Dialogues with Sikh Militants*. Philadelphia: University of Pennsylvania Press.

Mahmoud, Saba. 2004. *Politics of Piety. The Islamic Revival and the Feminist Subject*. Princeton, NJ: Princeton University Press.

Mamdani, Mahmood. 2002. "Good Muslim, Bad Muslim: A Political Perspective on Culture and Terrorism." *American Anthropologist* 104 (3): 766–75. https://doi.org/10.1525/aa.2002.104.3.766.

Mao Zedong. 1962. "Primer on Guerrilla War." In *The Guerrilla and How to Fight Him*, edited by T.N. Greene and translated by S.B. Griffith II, 5–10. New York: Frederick A. Praeger.

Massumi, Brian. 2010. "The Future Birth of the Affect Fact: The Political Ontology of Threat." In *The Affect Theory Reader*, edited by Melissa Gregg and Gregory Seigworth, 52–70. Durham, NC: Duke University Press.

Matheson, V., and M.B. Hooker. 1988. "Jawi Literature in Pattani: The Maintenance of an Islamic Tradition." *Journal of Malaysian Branch of the Royal Asiatic Society* 61 (1): 14–15.

Mauss, Marcel. (1950) 1990. *The Gift: The Form and Reason for Exchange in Archaic Societies*. Translated by W.D. Halls. New York: W.W. Norton.

– 1973. "Techniques of the Body." *Economy and Society* 2 (1): 70–88. https://doi.org/10.1080/03085147300000003.

May, Todd. 2010. *Contemporary Political Movements and the Thought of Jacques Rancière: Equality in Action*. Edinburgh, Scotland: Edinburgh University Press.

Mbembe, Achille. 2001. *On the Postcolony*. Berkeley: University of California Press.

– 2019. *Necro-politics*. Durham, NC: Duke University Press.

McCargo, Duncan. 2009. *Tearing Apart the Land: Islam and Legitimacy in Southern Thailand*. Singapore: National University of Singapore Press.

– 2010. "Autonomy for Southern Thailand: Thinking the Unthinkable?" *Pacific Affairs* 83 (2): 261–81. https://doi.org/10.5509/2010832261.

– 2011. "Informal Citizens: Graduated Citizenship in Southern Thailand." *Ethnic and Racial Studies* 34 (5): 833–49. https://doi.org/10.1080/01419870.2010.537360.

– 2012. *Mapping National Anxieties: Thailand's Southern Conflict*. Copenhagen, Denmark: Nordic Institute of Asian Studies.

McCarthy, Andrew. 2010. *The Grand Jihad: How Islam and the Left Sabotage America*. New York: Encounter Books.

McCarthy, Mary. 1994. "A Guide to Exile, Expatriates, and Inner Emigres." In *Altogether Elsewhere: Writers on Exile*, edited by Marc Robinson, 49–58. Winchester, MA: Faber and Faber.

McDowell, John Henry. 1998. *Meaning, Knowledge, and Reality*. Cambridge, MA: Harvard University Press.

Menjívar, Cecilia. 2011. *Enduring Violence: Ladina Women's Lives in Guatemala*. Berkeley: University of California Press.

Merleau-Ponty, Maurice. 1962. *Phenomenology of Perception*. New York: Routledge.

Montesano, Michael, and Patrick Jory, eds. 2008. *Thai South and Malay North: Ethnic Interactions on a Plural Peninsula*. Singapore: National University of Singapore Press.

Morris, Rosalind. 2002. "Crises of the Modern in Northern Thailand." In *Cultural Crisis and Social Memory: Modernity and Identity in Thailand and Laos*, edited by Shigeharo Tanabe and Charles F. Keyes, 68–94. Honolulu: University of Hawai'i Press.

— 2010. "Remembering Asian Anticolonialism, Again." *Journal of Asian Studies* 69 (2): 347–69. https://doi.org/10.1017/S0021911810000082.

Nanthadet Meksawat. 2006. *Secret Action to Quench the Fire in the South*. Bangkok, Thailand: Ruamduai Chuaikan Publisher.

Narongraksakhet, Ibrahim. 2005. "Pondoks and Their Roles in Preserving Muslim Identity in Southern Border Provinces of Thailand." In *Knowledge and Conflict Resolution: The Crisis of the Border Region of Southern Thailand*, edited by U. Dulyakasem and L. Sirichai, 70–128. Nakhon Sri Thammarat, Thailand: Walailak University.

Nash, June. 2003. "The War of the Peace in Chiapas: Indigenous Women's Struggles for Peace and Justice." In *What Justice? Whose Justice? Fighting for Fairness in Latin America*, edited by Susan Eckstein and Timothy Wickham-Crowley, 285–312. Berkeley: University of California Press.

Navaro-Yashin, Yael. 2002. *Faces of the State: Secularism and Public Life in Turkey*. Princeton, NJ: Princeton University Press.

Nietzsche, Friedrich. (1874) 1983. "On the Uses and Disadvantages of History for Life." In *Untimely Meditations*, translated by R.J. Hollingdale, 57–124. Cambridge: Cambridge University Press.

— 1978. *Thus Spoke Zarathustra: A Book for All and None*. Translated by Walter Kaufmann. Harmondsworth, UK: Penguin.

Nik Mahmud, Nik Anuar. 1999. *Sejarah perjuangan Melayu Patani 1785–1954* [The history of Patani Malay rebellion 1785–1954]. Bangi: Universiti Kebangsaan Malaysia.

Nonini, Donald M. 2008. "Is China Becoming Neoliberal?" *Critique of Anthropology* 28 (2): 145–76. https://doi.org/10.1177/0308275X08091364.

Noor, Farish. 2007. "Pathans to the East! The Development of the Tablighi Jama'at Movement in Northern Malaysia and Southern Thailand." *Comparative Studies of South Asia, Africa and the Middle East* 27 (1): 7–25. https://doi.org/10.1215/1089201x-2006-040.

– 2009. *Qur'an and Cricket: Travels through the Madrasahs of Asia and Other Stories*. Kuala Lumpur, Malaysia: Silverfish Books.
Nora, Pierre. 1996. *Conflicts and Divisions*. Vol. 1, *Realms of Memory: Rethinking the French Past*. Translated by Arthur Goldhammer. New York: Columbia University Press.
Nordstrom, Carolyn. 1997. *A Different Kind of War Story*. Philadelphia: University of Pennsylvania Press.
– 2004. *Shadows of War: Violence, Power, and International Profiteering in the Twenty-First Century*. Berkeley: University of California Press.
– 2007. *Global Outlaws: Crime, Money, and Power in the Contemporary World*. Berkeley: University of California Press.
North, Chris. 2008. "Redefining Insurgency." *Military Review*, January–February, 117.
Ockey, James. 2011. "Individual Imaginings: The Religio-Nationalist Pilgrimages of Haji Sulong Abdulkadir al-Fatani." *Journal of Southeast Asian Studies* 42 (1): 89–119. https://doi.org/10.1017/S002246341000055X.
Orwell, George. 1986. *The Complete Works of George Orwell*. Vol. 1, *Down and Out in Paris and London*. London: Martin Serker and Warburg.
Pandey, Gyanendra. 2005. *Routine Violence: Nations, Fragments, Histories*. Stanford, CA: Stanford University Press.
Pandolfi, Mariella. 2010. "From Paradox to Paradigm: The Permanent State of Emergency in the Balkans." In *Contemporary States of Emergency: The Politics of Military and Humanitarian Interventions*, edited by Didier Fassin and Mariella Pandolfi, 153–72. New York: Zone Books.
Peteet, Julie. 2010. "The War on Terror, Dismantling, and the Construction of Place: An Ethnographic Perspective from Palestine." In *Iraq at a Distance: What Anthropologists Can Teach Us about the War*, edited by Antonius Robben, 80–105. Philadelphia: University of Pennsylvania Press.
Peterson, Edwards. 1969. *The Limits of Hitler's Power*. Princeton, NJ: Princeton University Press.
Povinelli, Elizabeth. 2011. *Economies of Abandonment: Social Belonging and Endurance in Late Liberalism*. Durham, NC: Duke University Press.
– 2012. "After the Last Man: Images and Ethics of Becoming Otherwise." *E-flux* 35 (5). https://www.e-flux.com/journal/35/68380/after-the-last-man-images-and-ethics-of-becoming-otherwise/.
Rancière, Jacques. 1999. *Disagreement: Politics and Philosophy*. Translated by Julie Rose. Minneapolis: University of Minnesota Press.
– 2007. *On the Shores of Politics*. London: Verso.
– 2010. *Dissensus: On Politics and Aesthetics*. Edited and translated by Steven Corcoran. London: Bloomsbury Academic.
Record, Jeffrey. 2007. *Beating Goliath. Why Insurgencies Win*. Washington, DC: Potomac Books.

Reed, Adam. 2003. *Papua New Guinea's "Last Place": Experiences of Constraint in a Postcolonial Prison*. Oxford: Berghahn Books.

Reeve, C.D.C. 2002. "The Apology of Socrates." In *The Trials of Socrates: Six Classic Texts*, edited by C.D.C. Reeve, 26–61. Cambridge: Hackett.

Reeves, Madeline. 2014. *Border Work: Spatial Lives of the State in Rural Central Asia*. Ithaca, NY: Cornell University Press.

Report of the National Reconciliation Commission. 2006. *Overcoming Violence through the Power of Reconciliation*. Bangkok, Thailand.

Robben, Antonius. 2010a. "Ethnographic Imagination at a Distance: An Introduction to the Anthropological Study of the Iraq War." In *Iraq at a Distance: What Anthropologists Can Teach Us about the War*, edited by Antonius Robben, 1–23. Philadelphia: University of Pennsylvania Press.

— 2010b. "Mimesis in a War among the People: What Argentina's Dirty War Reveals about Counterinsurgency in Iraq." In *Iraq at a Distance: What Anthropologists Can Teach Us about the War*, edited by Antonius Robben, 133–58. Philadelphia: University of Pennsylvania Press.

Robbins, Richard. 2006. "The Construction of the Nation-State." In *Cultural Anthropology: A Problem-Based Approach*, 81–111. Belmont. CA: Thomsom Wadsworth.

Ross, Kristin. 1991. Translator's introduction to *The Ignorant Schoolmaster: Five Lessons in Intellectual Emancipation*, by Jacques Rancière, vii–xxiii. Stanford, CA: Stanford University Press.

Rungrawee Chalermsripinyorat. 2009. "The Security Forces and Human Rights Violations in Thailand's Insurgency-Wracked South." In *Imagined Land? The State and Southern Violence in Thailand*, edited by C. Satha-Anand, 73–92. Fuchu, Japan: Research Institute for Languages and Cultures of Asia and Africa.

— 2020. "Dialogue without Negotiation: Illiberal Peace-Building in Southern Thailand." *Conflict, Security & Development* 20 (1): 71–95. https://doi.org/10.1080/14678802.2019.1705069.

— 2021. "Islam and the BRN's Armed Separatist Movement in Southern Thailand." *Small Wars & Insurgencies* 32 (6): 945–76. https://doi.org/10.1080/09592318.2021.1915679.

Sartre, Jean-Paul. 1977. *Elections, piége á cons* [Elections, trap for fools]. Situations, X. Paris: Gallimard.

Scarry, Elaine. 1985. *The Body in Pain: The Making and Unmaking of the World*. Oxford: Oxford University Press.

Scheper-Hughes, Nancy. 1995. "The Primacy of the Ethical: Propositions for a Militant Anthropology." *Current Anthropology* 36 (3): 409–40.

Schielke, Samuli. 2010. "Second Thoughts about the Anthropology of Islam, or How to Make Sense of Grand Schemes in Everyday Life." *ZMO Working Papers* 2: 1–16.

Schmitt, Carl. (1932) 1996. *The Concept of the Political*. Expanded ed. Translated by George Schwab. Chicago: University of Chicago Press.
– 2004. *Legality and Legitimacy*. Translated and edited by Jeffrey Seitzer. Durham, NC: Duke University Press.
– 2010. *Political Theology: Four Chapters on the Concept of Sovereignty*. Chicago: University of Chicago Press.
Schwarz, Adam. 1994. *A Nation in Waiting: Indonesia in the 1990s*. Boulder, CO: Westview Press.
Scott, David. 1999. *Refashioning Futures: Criticism after Postcoloniality*. Princeton, NJ: Princeton University Press.
– 2004. *Conscripts of Modernity: The Tragedy of Colonial Enlightenment*. Durham, NC: Duke University Press.
Scott, David, and Charles Hirschkind. 2006. *Powers of the Secular Modern: Talal Asad and His Interlocutors*. Stanford, CA: Stanford University Press.
Scott, James. 1985. *Weapons of the Weak: Everyday Forms of Peasant Resistance*. New Haven, CT: Yale University Press.
– 1992. Domination and the Arts of Resistance: Hidden Transcripts. Rev. ed. New Haven, CT: Yale University Press.
Scupin, Raymond. 2013. "Review: South Thailand, Politics, Identity and Culture." *Journal of Asian Studies* 72 (2): 423–32. https://doi.org/10.1017/S0021911813000065.
Shattuck, Roger. 1965. "Introduction: Love and Laughter; Surrealism Reappraised." In *The History of Surrealism*, edited by M. Nadeau, 11–34. New York: Palgrave Macmillan.
Sinlapa Watthanatham [Arts and culture magazine] 25 (9): 98–105.
Skidmore, Monique. 2004. *Karaoke Fascism: Burma and the Politics of Fear*. Philadelphia: University of Pennsylvania Press.
Skinner, William. 1957. Chinese Society in Thailand: An Analytical History. Ithaca, NY: Cornell University Press.
Sluka, Jeffrey. 1989. *Hearts and Minds, Water and Fish: Support for the IRA ad INLA in a Northern Irish Ghetto*. Greenwich, CT: Jai Press.
– 2010. "Losing Hearts and Minds in the 'War on Terrorism.'" In *Iraq at a Distance: What Anthropologists Can Teach Us about the War*, edited by Antonius Robben, 106–32. Philadelphia: University of Pennsylvania Press.
Sluka, Jeffrey, and Antonius Robben. 2007. "Fieldwork in Cultural Anthropology: An Introduction." In *Ethnographic Fieldwork: An Anthropological Reader*, edited by Antonius Robben and Jeffrey Sluka, 1–28. Malden, MA: Blackwell.
Slyomovics, Susan. 2005. *The Performance of Human Rights in Morocco*. Philadelphia: University of Pennsylvania Press.
Smith, Catherine. 2015. "A Stranger in One's Own Home: Surveillance, Space, Place and Emotion during the GAM Confict in Aceh." *Indonesia* 100:53–76. https://doi.org/10.1353/ind.2015.0011.

Smith, Rupert. 2005. *The Utility of Force: The Art of War in the Modern World*. London: Penguin / Allen Lane.
Sontag, Susan. 2003. *Regarding the Pain of Others*. Farrar, Straus, and Giroux.
Soon, Alice Tay Erh. 1962. Chinese in Southeast Asia. *Race* 4 (1): 34–48.
Steedly, Mary Margaret. 1993. *Hanging without a Rope: Narrative Experience in Colonial and Postcolonial Karoland*. Princeton, NJ: Princeton University Press.
Suhrke, Ahmed. 1975. "Irredentism Contained: the Malay Muslim Case." *Comparative Politics* 7 (2): 196–7. https://doi.org/10.1017/9781108868082.008.
Surin Pitsuwan. 1985. *Islam and Malay Nationalism: A Case Study of the Malay Muslims of Southern Thailand*. Bangkok, Thailand: Thai Khadi Research Institute, Thammasat University.
– 1988. "The Lotus and the Crescent: Clashes of Religious Symbolism in Southern Thailand." In *Ethnic Conflict in Buddhist Societies: Sri Lanka, Thailand, and Burma*, edited by K.M. de Silva, Pensri Duke, Ellen S. Goldberg, and Nathan Katz, 187–201. Boulder, CO: Westview Press.
Syukri, Ibrahim. 1985. *Sejarah kerajaan Melayu Patani* [History of the Malay Kingdom of Patani]. Translated by C. Bailey and J. Miksic. Athens: Ohio University, Southeast Asia Series 68(86).
Talebi, Shahla. 2011. *Ghosts of Revolution: Rekindled Memories of Imprisonment in Iran*. Stanford, CA: Stanford University Press.
Tambiah, Stanley. 1992. *Buddhism Betrayed? Politics and Violence in Sri Lanka*. Chicago: University of Chicago Press.
– 1996. *Leveling Crowds: Ethnonationalist Conflicts and Collective Violence in South Asia*. Berkeley: University of California Press.
Tate, Winnifred. 2007. *Counting the Dead: The Culture and Politics of Human Rights Activism in Colombia*. Berkeley: University of California Press.
Taussig, Michael. 1987. *Shamanism, Colonialism, and the Wild Man: A Study in Terror and Healing*. Chicago: University of Chicago Press.
– 1991. "Tactility and Distraction." *Cultural Anthropology* 6 (2): 147–53. https://doi.org/10.1525/can.1991.6.2.02a00020.
– 1992. *The Nervous System*. London: Routledge.
– 1997. *The Magic of the State*. New York: Routledge.
– 1999. *Defacement: Public Secret and the Labor of the Negative*. Stanford, CA: Stanford University Press.
– 2003. *Law in a Lawless Land: Diary of a Limpieza in Colombia*. Chicago: University of Chicago Press.
– 2018. *Palma Africana*. Chicago: University of Chicago Press.
Teeuw, Andries, and David Wyatt. 1970. *Hikayat Patani: The Story of Patani*. Bibliotecha Indonesica, no. 5, The Hague: Martinus Nijhoff.

Thanet Aphornsuvan. 2004. "Origins of Malay Muslim 'Separatism' in Southern Thailand." Asia Research Institute Working Paper Series, no. 32: 1–50. National University of Singapore.
– 2008. "Origins of Malay Muslim 'Separatism' in Southern Thailand." In *Thai South and Malay North: Ethnic Interactions on a Plural Peninsula*, edited by Michael Montesano and Patrick Jory, 91–123. Singapore: National University of Singapore Press.
Thiranagama, Sharika. 2011. *In My Mother's House: Civil War in Sri Lanka*. Philadelphia: University of Pennsylvania Press.
Thongchai Winichakul. 1994. *Siam Mapped: A History of the Geo-body of a Nation*. Honolulu: University of Hawai'i Press.
– 2002. "Remembering/Silencing the Traumatic Past." In *Cultural Crisis and Social Memory*, edited by Shigeharo Tanabe and Charles F. Keyes, 243–83. Honolulu: University of Hawai'i Press.
Trouillot, Michel-Ralph. 1995. *Silencing the Past: Power and the Production of History*. Boston: Beacon Press.
Tsing, Anna Lowenhaupt. 1993. *In the Realm of the Diamond Queen: Marginality in an Out-of-the-Way Place*. Princeton, NJ: Princeton University Press.
– 2015. *The Mushroom at the End of the World: On the Possibility of Life in Capitalist Ruins*. Princeton, NJ: Princeton University Press.
UNICEF. 2008. *Everyday Fears: A Study of Children's Perceptions of Living in the Southern Border Area of Thailand*. Bangkok, Thailand. www.http://www.unicef.org/thailand/Everydabings:theusualpattern.Byaclevertrick.yfears.pdf.
Victoria, Brian Dizen. 1998. *Zen at War*. New York: Weatherhilt.
Vine, David. 2021. *The United States of War: A Global History of America's Endless Conflict, from Columbus to the Islamic State*. Berkeley: University of California Press.
Wheeler, Matt. 2010. "People's Patron or Patronizing the People? Southern Border Provinces Administrative Centre in Perspective." *Contemporary Southeast Asia* 2 (1): 208–33.
Wittgenstein, Ludwig. (1953) 2009. *Philosophical Investigations*. Oxford: Wiley-Blackwell.
Yong, Kee Howe. 2006. "Silences in History and Nation-State: Reluctant Accounts of the Cold War in Sarawak." *American Ethnologist* 33 (3): 462–73. https://doi.org/10.1525/ae.2006.33.3.462.
– 2012. "There Are *Ponoks*, and There Are *Ponoks*: Traditional Religious Boarding Schools in Thailand's Far South." *Advances* in *Anthropology* 2 (3): 161–68. https://doi.org/10.4236/aa.2012.23019.
– 2013. *The Hakkas of Sarawak: Sacrificial Gifts of Cold War Era Malaysia*. Toronto: University of Toronto Press.

- 2014. "Staging History for Thailand's Far South: Fantasy for a Supposedly Pliant Muslim Community." *Social Identities: Journal for the Study of Race, Nation and Culture* 20 (2–3): 171–85. https://doi.org/10.1080/13504630.2013.878093.
- 2019. "The *Mak Pasar*: Engaging with the Difficulty of Reality in a Recurring Conflict-Ridden Thailand's Far South." *Public Anthropologist* 1:246–64.

Zemon, Rubin. 2018. "'Us,' 'Them,' and the Problem with 'Balkanization.'" *Global-e* 11 (16).

Zubaida, Sami. 2011. *Beyond Islam: A New Understanding of the Middle East*. London: I.B. Tauris.

Zurbuchen, Mary. 2005. "Historical Memory in Contemporary Indonesia." In *Beginning to Remember: The Past in the Indonesian Present*, edited by M. Zurbuchen, 3–32. Singapore: Singapore University Press.

Index

Abhisit Vejjajiva, 126
Abraham, Itty, 9, 137
Aceh, Indonesia, 68, 104, 107, 133, 134
aesthetics of vulgarity, 179
Algerian Harkis, 153
alienation, 110–11, 148–9
Allen, Lori, 64
Allerton, Catherine, 73
Al-Marashi, Ibrahim, 154
Anant Wattananikorn, 31
Anglo-Siamese treaty (1909), 22–3, 48, 165, 199
anti-Hobbesian spaces, 108–12
anti-terror industry, 164–5
Anusas Suwannamongkol, 19, 121
apologia and politics of regret, 36–7
Apology of Socrates (Plato), 36
Appadurai, Arjun, 170
"Arabicization," 164
Arab Spring, 34
Arendt, Hannah, 137, 218n3
Aretxaga, Begona, 211n4
arms supply to civilians, 68
Asad, Talal, 25–6, 125, 158, 199
ASEAN Economic Community (AEC), 195–7
Asia, United States foreign policy and, 160
Asian Infrastructure Investment Bank, 160

Askew, Marc: on "ghost" insurgents, 16; on homogenization, 69; on insurgency, 17, 18; military budget increases, 218n7; on *Raja Kuning* series, 55, 57; on state ineffectiveness, 126; on unattributable shootings, 19
Association of Southeast Asian Nations (ASEAN), 53
Austin, John L., 23, 102–3
Australia, 161, 162
autonomy, paradoxical expressions of, 5–6, 7

bagzi dongeng (fantasy stories), 56–7
Bakhtin, Mikhal, 50, 62, 196
Baldwin, James, 37, 39
"banality of terrorology," 154
Barthes, Roland, 26–7
Basso, Keith, 13
Bauman, Zygmunt, 50
Belt and Road Initiative (BRI), 160
Benjamin, Walter, 13, 22, 35, 39, 58, 124, 209n11
Bercht, Bertolt, 140
Berkeley Mafias, 162
Bhumibol Adulyadej, King of Thailand, 116, 216n4
biasa (normal): alternative histories, 53–9; characterizing, 3–8, 50,

biasa (normal) (*continued*)
63–6, 156; fear as form of control, 47; forms of life and, 49–53; limitations of language and, 200–3; quotidian experiences of militarization, 46–7; resourcefulness in humour, 64; routineness of things, 121–4; "sick and tired," as regional emotion, 210n5; speed of normalcy, 118–21
Big C supermarket bomb explosion (2017), 201–2
Bloch, Ernst, *The Principle of Hope*, 148
"bodily techniques" of resourcefulness, 74
"body-as-commodity," 196
Bolano, Robert, *By Night in Chile*, 121
Breytenbach, Breyten, 142, 219n9, 220n15
BRN (Barisan Revolusi Nasional), 141, 146, 169
Brunei, 161
Buch Segal, Lotte, 64, 65, 92
Buddhism: Buddhist victims of insurgency, 18, 116; civilian recruitment of Buddhists, 68; Islamification amid, 48; as marker of state nationalism, 145, 220n13; Thai identity and, 32, 132, 179
burdened agency, 71
Burma, 22
Bush, George W., administration of, 154–5, 158, 161
business rivalries, 108, 119
By Night in Chile (Bolano), 121

Cambodia, 127, 152, 160
capitalism, 98, 110–11, 194, 200, 220n13. *See also* development; neoliberalism
"carnivalesque," phenomenon of, 62, 196
Casey, Edward, 72, 211n10

Cavell, Stanley, 51, 65
Central Islamic Committee of Thailand, 165–6
Certeau, Michel de, 117
Chaiwat Satha-Anand, 30
children: attacks on schools, 18, 49, 116; civilian death rates, 9; family separation, 70, 71–2, 73; insurgent recruitment of, 44; kratom leaf consumption, 137–40, 172–3; orphaned, 18, 69, 79, 80; state narratives targeted at, 84–5, 87; as Tai Bai protesters, 35. *See also* ponoks (Muslim boarding schools)
China, 160
choiceless decisions, 66–71, 211n4
Chor Ror Bor (Village Defense Volunteers), 67, 68, 69
Chulalongkorn, King of Siam, 165
citizenship, 132–4, 146, 198. *See also* Thainess (*khwampen* Thai)
civilian-based self-defence forces, 68
civilian experiences of war, 9–10
civilians as targets, 115, 215n1
Clash of Civilizations (Huntington), 164, 222n5
coevalness, denial of, 182, 199
Cohen, Lawrence, 196
Cold War, 158, 159, 165
Collingwood, Robin C., 23
Colombia, 7, 18, 52, 218n2
colonialism: assimilation and, 23–4; imperialism vs., 158; Islamic reform and, 43; post-colonial notions of culture, 94–5; post-colonial perceptions of the future, 97; territory-ceding treaties, 22–3, 48, 165, 199
communism, 158, 165, 174, 223n13
Cooper, Frederick, 185
corruption, 136, 217n1
Crapanzano, Vincent, 65, 153, 209n14

C.S. Pattani Hotel bomb explosion (2012), 19, 118–21, 122, 201
cultural spectacles, 195–7, 199–200
"culture talk," 163

Das, Veena: civilian experiences of violence, 10; difficulty of reality, 52; pain and language, 80; on performances of the state, 199–200; on performative language, 103; "poisonous knowledge" metaphor, 90; on role of anthropologists, 8; on rumour, 119; social violence, 94; on violence within the ordinary, 60–1, 155
dek ponoks (ponok students), 166–76. *See also* ponoks (Muslim boarding schools)
Deleuze, Gilles, 105
denial of coevalness, 182, 199
Den Tohmena, 124
Derrida, Jacques, 94, 155
development: as discourse, 185–6; Growth Triangle development projects, 184–5; Halal Industrial Park, 186–9, 226n3; loss of local livelihoods, 189–95. *See also* economics; modernism; talking task industry
dialogical social utterances, 14–15
displacement, 71–4
divorce, 91–3
Dorairajoo, Saroja, 206n6
Down and Out in Paris and London (Orwell), 156
drug-related violence, 19, 138–9
Dunn, Elizabeth, 71, 73–4
Dusun Nyior Awakening, 30–5, 38–42, 123–4

East Timor, 162
ecological damage, 189–90

economic imperialism, 158–60
economics: capitalism, 98, 110–11, 194, 200, 220n13; internationalization and spectacle, 195–7; loss of local livelihoods, 189–95; neoliberalism, 54, 55, 87–8, 125, 150, 159, 164. *See also* talking task industry
economy of fear and terror, 53–4
education, 18, 49, 116. *See also* ponoks (Muslim boarding schools)
Eid ul-Fitr (Festivity of breaking the fast), 109–10
Elias, Norbert, 136
embodiment and emplacement, 72
enemy, concept of, 140, 159–60
Escobar, Arturo, 185–6
essentialism, 69, 134–7, 144–5, 147
ethnicity and identity politics, 31–2, 54, 210n8
ethnonationalism, 26–7
Evans-Pritchard, Evan, 65
exile, 140–2, 145, 151, 152, 219n9, 220n15
expectation, 99

Fanon, Frantz, 51, 210n4
fear: economy of terror and, 53–4; erosion of law and order, 124–5; as form of state control, 47; *mak pasar* (mothers of markets) and, 74–8; modern European law and, 25–6; perpetuated by rumour, 117; silence as response to, 63, 75, 78, 81, 104; threat, temporal dimension of, 103; topographies of, 49; *waktu geriya* (hours of the guerrillas), 66–7
Feld, Steven, 13
Feldman, Allen, 49
feminist organizations, 163
"fighting with ghosts," 16, 143, 175
fishing industry, 189–91
forms of life, 49–53, 65

Foucault, Michel, 23–4
France, 22, 153, 165
Freedman, Maurice, 181
freedom, 148–54, 160
Free Trade Area of the Asia-Pacific, 160

Gellner, Ernest, 108–9
Genet, Jean, *Prisoner of Love*, 52
Gerakan Aceh Merdeka (Free Aceh Movement), 107
Goffman, Erving, 54, 161
Great Britain, 22–3, 48, 165, 199
Guatemala, 94
guns supply to civilians, 68

Hacking, Ian, *The Taming of Chance*, 207n19
Haji Sulong: accusations of Wahhabism, 43; death of, 34, 151–2; Dusun Nyior Awakening and, 30–5, 38–42, 124; expressions of autonomy and, 5–6, 7; legacy of, 124, 151–2, 156, 170–1
Halal Industrial Park: construction of, 186–8; described, 189; impact on local livelihoods, 189–95
Hankins, Joseph, 54
Hari Rayo, 109–10
Heaney, Seamus, 133, 155
Hegel, Georg Wilhelm Friedrich, 12
Helbardt, Sascha, 83
historical context: formulation of "minority/majority," 23–6; glorification of the past, 37–42; Haji Sulong and Islamic Awakening, 30–5; Krue Se massacre, 28–30; language of separatism, 26–7; Tak Bai tragedies, 35–7; Wahhabism, accusations of, 42–5
history: act of naming and labeling, 32; as "adaptation of materials to time," 201; alternative histories, 53–9; and conditions of possible action, 199; conflation of progress with, 35, 209n11; glorification of, 37–42, 84–5; impact on the present, 6; obfuscation by "culture talk," 163; as series of broken promises, 200; social utterances, in understanding of, 14; tradition as obstacle, 148–50
Ho, Engseng, 158
Hobbes, Thomas, 108–9, 160
home and family, displacement from, 71–4
homogenization, 69, 134–5, 152–3, 169–72, 205n2
"horizon of expectation," 99
households and marital unions: doing things with words, 102–7; futures past, 96–9; hesitancy and argument, 89–93; misrecognized violence, 94; Phayta Tani replica cannon, 99–102; power dynamics, 94–6; responses to violence, 107–8; social cohesion and trust, 108–12
How to Do Things with Words (Austin), 102–3
humanity, as ideological instrument, 159–60
Huntington, Samuel, *Clash of Civilizations*, 164, 222n5

identity: beyond ethnicity, 157; ethnic Thai nationalism and, 31–2; homogenization, 69, 134–7, 152–3, 169–72, 205n2; within modern nation-states, 198–200; Muslimness and, 11, 132; politics of, 54–5, 185, 210n8; rage and, 137; religion as determinant of, 134–5, 144–5; social utterances and, 14. *See also* Muslimness; Thainess (*khwampen* Thai)
imperialism, 158–60

Indonesia, 43, 68, 73, 104, 107, 133, 134, 161–2
Indonesia-Malaysia-Thailand Growth Triangle (IMT-GT), 184–6, 200
insurgency: civilian-based defense forces, 68; civilian impacts, 49, 135; civilian support for, 67–8; cooperation with local mafias, 173–4; defined, 16–17; investment in continued conflict, 115–16, 119, 128, 170, 175; as Islamic, 219n10; kratom leaf consumption and, 139; as ongoing violence, 49–53; politics of numbers, 17–20; presumed allegiances, 101–2; recruitment of women, 215n6; shadow insurgency, 15–17, 63, 82–3, 104; silence as response to, 63, 75, 78, 81, 104; social identity and, 134, 136, 137; state ineffectiveness and, 125–8; state reparations for, 129–31; *waktu geriya* (hours of the guerrillas), 66–7, 179, 181
internationalization, 195–7
Islam: alternative histories of Patani, 55–9; as determinant of identity, 134–5, 144–5; essentialization of, 163–4; establishment of Islamic courts, 23–4; Haji Sulong and Islamic Awakening, 30–5, 39; insecurity, social violence and, 93–4; "moderate Muslim" states, 161–3; proposed Fridays as holidays policy, 105–7; separatism and, 140–7, 219n10; Wahhabism and, 33, 41, 42–5, 143, 144, 164, 166. *See also* Malay Muslims; militarization and Islamification; Muslimness; war on terror

Jarry, Alfred, 113
jihadism, 143

Jory, Patrick, 132
Joyce, James, *Ulysses*, 6
justice, legitimizing political ambitions, 160

Kabot Dusong Yo (Dusong Yo Disturbance), 30
kampung (villages), 71
Kapchan, Deborah, 62
Kasian Tejapira, 9
Kaum Muda (Youth Movement), 42, 43
Kelly, Tobias, 154
keluarga (families), 71
Kentucky Fried Chicken, 76, 117
khaek (darker-skinned people), 31–2, 133, 139–40, 208n4
King, Philip, 182, 185
Kleinman, Arthur, 10, 94
Klima, Alan, 153, 191, 200, 221n20
Koselleck, Reinhart, 39, 98–9
kratom leaf consumption, 137–40, 172–3
Krue Se mosque, 28–31, 38–9, 84–8, 94, 95, 99–102

language: appreciating limitations of, 201–3; bilingualism, 205n2; characterizing *biasa*, 5–6, 50, 63–6, 156; concepts, semantic function of, 98–9; of divorce, 91–2; exceeding its signification, 196; Malay language, 3, 8, 206n9; mythology within, 65; pain and, 80; performative language, 102–7; of separatism, 26–7, 134, 175; shadow dialogues, 209n14; silence as response to fear, 63, 75, 78, 81, 104; social utterances, 14; Thai as language of Islam, 165; Thai vocabulary for "insurgency," 16–17; of war on terror, 154–5, 159. See also *biasa* (normal)

Laos, 22
latex, tapping, 69–70, 101, 111, 117, 179, 191
laughter and cynicism: arbitrary reparation, 129–31; defiance through, 113–15; erosion of law and order, 124–8; perpetual conflict, 115–16; routineness of things, 121–4; rumour and fear, 117; speed of normalcy, 118–21
law: erosion of order and, 124–8; interweaving of arms and, 189; legality vs. legitimacy, 47–8; in legitimizing political ambitions, 160
Lenin, Vladimir, 15
"leveling crowds," 163
lieu de mémoire (realm of memory), 81, 84, 213n18
livelihood, loss of, 189–95
liveliness, as protective, 73
Lock, Margaret, 94
Loos, Tamara, 23
loss: of ability to hope, 148; exile and, 220n15; failure of reparations to address, 80; of local livelihoods, 189–95; through displacement, 72–3; "we are what we have lost," 151, 221n17
Lowenthal, David, 41, 59

MacIntyre, Alasdair, 14, 149
madrasah. *See* ponoks (Muslim boarding schools)
Majlis Syura Patanai (separatist organizations), 127
majoritarianism, 95
mak pasar (mothers of markets): author's approach, 10–11, 60–2, 211n3; characterizing *biasa* and, 63–6; choiceless decisions, 66–71, 211n4; on cultural spectacle, 197, 199; cynicism and defiance, 113–15, 127–8; facing fear and trouble, 74–8; on fear and piousness, 123; imagined futures of, 96–8; on kratom leaf consumption, 137–9; marriage insecurity and divorce, 89–94; on mega-development projects, 184, 185; proximate displacement, 71–4; on *Raja Kuning* series, 56–7, 59; as recipients of performative speech, 102–7; reparations, 78–84; responding to IED attack, 107–8; silence and uncertainty, 63; social cohesion and trust, 108–12, 135; staging of Krue Se anniversary, 84–8; on *tahann* (armed forces), 95–6. *See also* households and marital unions; laughter and cynicism
Malaya, 22, 34
Malay language, 3, 8, 206n9
Malay Muslims: author's approach, 10–12, 20–1, 207n11; as challenge to Thai nationalism, 12, 24, 94–5; characterizing *biasa* and, 3–8, 50, 63–6, 156; charges of separatism, 26–7; cultural spectacles and, 196–7; establishment of Islamic courts, 23–4; Haji Sulong and Islamic Awakening, 30–5; history of conflict, 8–9; homogenization of, 69, 134–5, 152–3, 169–72, 205n2; identity politics, 54–5, 185, 210n8; identity structures and *Muslimness*, 11, 132; identity within modern nation-state, 198–200; as *khaek* ("dark-skinned"), 31–2, 133, 139–40, 208n4; lack of agency, 169; "modern" Malay women, 90, 214n1; position on insurgency, 67; recruitment to civilian defence forces, 68–9; as state-created category, 13, 94–5; term usage

herein, 206n9. *See also* historical context; households and marital unions; laughter and cynicism; *mak pasar* (mothers of markets); militarization and Islamification; talking task industry; Thainess (*khwampen* Thai); war on terror

Malaysia: comparisons made with, 134, 224, 224n17; identity formation and, 198; illicit trade, 192–4; insurgents' alignment with, 83; as "moderate Muslim" state, 161, 162–3; Phayta Tani replica cannon and, 100, 101; policy on Fridays as holidays, 106; race-based political policy, 133–4; separatist movement and, 141; Thai employment in, 182, 191–2, 200, 226n6

Mamdani, Mahmood, 163

Manggarai people, 73

Maritime Silk Road plan, 160

marriage insecurity, 89–94, 109. *See also* households and marital unions

Massumi, Brian, 103

Mauss, Marcel, 14

Mbembe, Achille, 101, 179

McCargo, Duncan, 69, 132

McDowell, John Henry, 102–3

memory: author's approach, 15; "forgetting to remember," 211n10; historical memory making, 37–42; *lieu de mémoire* (realm of memory), 81, 213n18; remembering as agency-making, 58–9; state narratives of Krue Se massacre, 29–30; willingness to remember, 84

Menjívar, Cecilia, 94

Merleau-Ponty, Maurice, 72

militarization and Islamification: alternative histories, 53–9; forms of life, 49–53; legality and legitimacy, 47–8; militarization of urban space, 121–2; quotidian experiences of, 46–7; topographies of fear, 49

military (armed forces). See *tahann* (armed forces)

Ministry of Culture, 195

Ministry of Social Development and Human Security, 55, 56–7

Ministry of Upmost Happiness, The (Roy), 203

"minority/majority" dynamic, 23–6, 198–9

minority perspective, 133, 153

Minu Makaue, 105–6

"moderate Islamic" states, 161–2

modernism: in alleviating poverty, 185; denial of coevalness, 182; development as discourse, 185–6; fear and modern European law, 25–6; identity within modern nation-state, 198–200; Islamic courts, establishment of, 23–4. *See also* talking task industry

Morris, Rosalind, 196

muafakat (agreement), 3

Muang Pattani: author's approach, 3–5, 8, 10; cultural festivals, 195; fear associated with guerrillas, 66–7; as location of Tak Bai apology, 36–7; military presence and Islamification, 46–9; open-air markets, 61. *See also* historical context; households and marital unions; laughter and cynicism; *mak pasar* (mothers of markets); militarization and Islamification; talking task industry; Thainess (*khwampen* Thai); war on terror

Muhammad Abduh, 42–3

Muḥammad Rashīd Riḍā, 42–3

multiculturalism: ethnicity and identity politics, 31–2, 54–5, 210n8; neoliberal anxieties and, 87–8;

multiculturalism (*continued*)
    production of otherness, 23–6,
    208n4; race-based political policy,
    133–4
Muslimness: author's approach, 11; as
    form of identity politics, 54–5, 185,
    210n8; identity structures and, 11,
    132; "moderate Muslim" states,
    161–3; reductionist characterizations,
    69, 134–7, 144–5, 147; United States
    foreign policy and, 161. *See also*
    Islam; Malay Muslims
Myanmar, 63, 83, 121, 135, 145, 175,
    224n17

Nahdatul Ulama (Islamic
    organization), 162
Najib Razak, 161
Nakaya, Sumie, 9, 137
naming, act of, 32
Narathiwat province: 2004 conflict
    escalation, 15; calls for UN
    involvement, 34; cultural festivals,
    195; ongoing conflict, 8–9; ponok
    (Muslim boarding schools) in,
    176–81; Tak Bai incident, 9, 35–7;
    territory-ceding treaties, 22–3, 48,
    165, 199
National Economic Policy
    (Malaysia), 133
nationalism: Buddhism as marker of,
    145, 220n13; creation of "Thainess,"
    25, 31–2; ethnonationalism, 26–7;
    Malay Muslims as challenge to, 12,
    24, 94–5; production of otherness,
    23–6, 208n4
Navaro-Yashin, Yael, 73
necropolitics, 101–2
neoliberalism, 54, 55, 87–8, 125, 150,
    159, 164
NGOs (non-governmental
    organizations), 53–4, 107, 114

Nietzsche, Friedrich, 200, 211n10
Nik Aziz, 166
9/11 attacks. *See* September 11th
    attacks
Noor, Farish, 42
Nora, Pierre, 213n18
Nordstrom, Carolyn, 10, 47, 111
North, Chris, 16
Northern Ireland, 49, 83, 104, 155
nostalgia, 40

Obama, Barack, administration of,
    160–1
Obeyesekere, Gananath, 28
oil smuggling, 192–4
O'Neill, Eugene, 6
1Malaysia Development Berhad
    scandal, 134
ongoing imperialism, 158–60
open-air markets, described, 61–2.
    See also *mak pasar* (mothers of
    markets)
orang Melayu, 198
orang Patani (Patani people), 42, 139,
    198
Orwell, George, *Down and Out in
    Paris and London*, 156
otherness, production of, 23–6, 208n4

Packard, Randall, 185
Palestine, 51, 52, 64, 65, 154, 210n5
Pandolfi, Mariella, 125
Pan Malaysian Islamic Party (PAS),
    166
Papua New Guinea, 154
"paradox of contemporaneity," 105
paramilitarism, 180, 186–9, 191
paranoia, 49, 104, 180
Parti Komunis Indonesia, 162
"past futures," 99
paternalism, 53–4
patriarchal hierarchies, 90–4

Pattani province: calls for UN involvement, 34; government apology for Tak Bai incident, 36; ongoing conflict, 8–9; territory-ceding treaties, 22–3, 48, 165, 199
"peace industry," 54
performative language, 102–7
pesantren. See ponoks (Muslim boarding schools)
Peteet, Julie, 154
Phayta Tani replica cannon, 99–102
Phibul Songkhram, 24–5, 31, 34
PLA (Patani Liberation Army), 141
place and home, 72
Plato, *Apology of Socrates,* 36
"plurilinguistic poetics," 50
politics: cultural spectacles, 195–7; of identity, 54–5, 185, 210n8; IMT development projects, 187; lack of party cooperation, 126; "minority/majority" dynamics, 25–6, 198–9; necropolitics, 101–2; of numbers and statistics, 17–20, 130, 207n19; producing exclusion, 23–4; of regret, 36–7; stigma, political agency through, 54–5. *See also* state powers
polygamy, 90, 92, 93, 109
ponoks (Muslim boarding schools): denial of coevalness, 182–3; homogenization, 169–72, 181; humanity as ideological instrument, 159–60; as metaphors for extremism, 163–6; "moderate Muslim" states, 161–3; in Narathiwat, 176–81; ongoing imperialism, 158–60; students *(dek ponoks),* 166–76; sustained conflict, 170, 173–6
poverty, as tool of the state, 45
Prayud Chan-o-cha, 96, 127
precarity, tactics of, 70
Prem Tinsulanonda, 27

Prince of Songkhla University (PSU), 4, 40, 46, 206n3
Principle of Hope, The (Bloch), 148
Prisoner of Love (Genet), 52
progress, conflation of history with, 35, 209n11
propaganda, 37–42, 43, 55–8
Proust, Marcel, 131
proximate displacement, 71–4
public secret, 136, 180, 197, 218n2
PULO (Patani United Liberation Organization), 141, 169

race-based political policy, 133–4
racism, 31–2, 88, 115, 139–40, 208n4, 210n4
rage and identity, 137
Raja Kuning television series, 55–8
Ramadan, 107, 109
Rancière, Jacques, 137, 210n8
realm of memory *(lieu de mémoire),* 81, 84, 213n18
reductionism, 69, 134–7, 144–5, 147
Reed, Adam, 154
Regional Comprehensive Economic Partnership, 160
religion: class politics and, 133–4; commodification of, 188–9; as determinant of identity, 134–5, 144–5; "moderate Muslim" states, 161–3; terrorism and, 159
reparations, 78–84, 129–31
repetitive temporality, 154–7
"retroactive expectation," 99
rice pledging scheme, 136, 217n1
Robben, Antonius, 50, 215n1
Rohingyas, 101, 152, 174–5
Roy, Arundhati, *The Ministry of Upmost Happiness,* 203
rubber tapping, 69–70, 101, 111, 117, 179, 191
rumah (homes), 71

rumour, 117, 119, 120–1
Runda Kumpulan Kecil (RKK), 45, 102–5, 107, 108, 135, 146, 179–80
Rungrawee Chalermsripinyorat, 219n10

sangop (calmness, tranquility), 56
Sartre, Jean-Paul, 126
Satun territory, 22–3, 34, 48, 165, 199
scandal, 200
Schielke, Samuli, 93
Schmitt, Carl, 48, 159, 198
schools, attacks on, 18, 49, 116. *See also* ponoks (Muslim boarding schools)
Schwarz, Adam, 6
Scott, David, 23–4, 95, 97, 149
Scott, James, 101, 185
secrecy, 29, 136, 180, 197, 218n2
security: civilian-based self-defence forces, 68; minority population as threat to, 95; paramilitarism, 180, 186–9, 191; paternalism in, 53–4; terror as form of control, 47, 48–9. *See also tahann* (armed forces)
separatism *(baeng yaek dindaen)*: battles for Islam and, 140–7; homogenization of Muslims and, 169–72; language of, 26–7, 134, 175; Majlis Syura Patanai (separatist organizations), 127. *See also* insurgency
September 11th attacks: "banality of terrorology," 154; closing of Muslim schools and, 178, 181; definitions "insurgency" following, 16; Islamic cause and, 11, 142; re-creation of terror, 124; "we" vs. "them" divisions and, 105. *See also* war on terror
shadow dialogues, 209n14
Shafi'i Sunni Islam, 163
sharia law, 161

sia din daen (territory-ceding) treaties, 22–3, 48, 165, 199
Siam: establishment of Islamic courts, 23–4; fantasies of harmonious past, 55–8; nationalist military takeover, 24–5; Phayta Tani cannon, 100; territory-ceding treaties, 22–3, 48, 165, 199. *See also* Thailand
Siam Mapped (Thongchai), 140
sick and tired, as regional emotion, 210n5
silence, as response, 63, 75, 78, 81, 94, 104
Singapore, 185
Sino-Thais, 48, 87, 88, 128, 132, 205n2
Skidmore, Monique, 63, 121, 135
Smith, Catherine, 68
Smith, Rupert, 215n1
social cohesion and trust, 108–12, 135
social violence, 94
Somchai Neelaphaijit, 9
Sonthi Boonyaratglin, 137
Southern Border Provinces Administrative Centre (SBPAC), 27, 145
southern Thailand: author's approach, 10–12, 20–1, 50–3, 207n11; bilingualism in, 205n2; characterizing *biasa* and, 3–8; civilian experiences of violence, 9–10; frontier provinces as sites of contestation, 12–13; Growth Triangle development projects, 185; identity within modern nation-state, 198–200; politics of numbers, 17–20; shadow insurgency, 15–17, 63, 82–3; theoretical frameworks, 13–15; violence as part of the ordinary, 51–3. *See also* historical context; households and marital unions; laughter and cynicism; *mak*

pasar (mothers of markets); militarization and Islamification; talking task industry; Thainess (*khwampen* Thai); war on terror
"space of experience," 99
Sri Lanka, 10, 28, 61, 72, 83, 145
state of exception, 125
state powers: arbitrary reparation, 129–31; civilian-based self-defence forces, 68; corruption, 136, 217n1; crafting alternative histories, 53–9, 84–5; definitions of insurgency and, 16; erosion of law and order, 124–8; fear as form of control, 47; Halal Industrial Park and, 194; identity within modern nation-state, 198–200; illicit trading, 192–4; investment in continued conflict, 115–16, 128, 170, 215n1; language of separatism, 26–7; legality vs. legitimacy, 47–8; majoritarianism as democracy, 94–5; Phayta Tani replica cannon and, 99–102; politics of numbers, 17–20, 130, 207n19; politics of regret, 36–7; poverty as tool of, 45; privileging of nation-state, 12; production of otherness, 23–6, 208n4; staging of Krue Se anniversary, 84–8; state-sponsored cultural spectacles, 195–7; Tak Bai reparations, 78–84; violent dimensions of, 13–14. *See also* historical context; nationalism; politics; *tahann* (armed forces)
Steedly, Margaret, 29
stigma, political agency through, 54–5
Suharto, 162
Sultanate of Patani: alternative histories of, 53–9; glorification of, 37–42, 84–5, 168; *khaek* label and, 140; territory-ceding treaties, 12, 22–3, 48, 165, 199. *See also* Narathiwat province; Pattani province; Yala province
Surayud Chulanont, 36–7, 126

tahann (armed forces): budget increases, 218n7; civilian-based self-defence forces, 68–9; fighting with "ghosts," 16, 143, 175; justified by continued conflict, 115, 175–6; kratom leaf consumption, 138–9, 173; Krue Se mosque massacre, 28; within landscape of violence, 17; militarization of urban space, 46–9, 121–2; military coercion and liberal governance, 126; Muslim boarding school raids, 177–8; public perception of, 95–6; Tak Bai incident and, 35; term usage, 207n16; *waktu tahann* (hours of the army), 67. *See also* militarization and Islamification; state powers
Tak Bai incident (2004): described, 9, 35–7; implication of Muslim schools in, 169, 176–8; reparations for, 78–81; silence surrounding, 94, 95; women's participation in, 170
Talebi, Shahla, 176
talking task industry: *biasa*, 200–3; characterized, 53; conscripts of modernity, 198–200; cultural spectacles, 195–7; development as discourse, 185–6; Growth Triangle development projects, 184–5; Halal Industrial Park, 186–9; loss of local livelihoods, 189–95
Talukhan, Pattani, 186–95
Tambiah, Stanley, 163
Taming of Chance, The (Hacking), 207n19

Taussig, Michael: on act of naming, 32; on civilian support for insurgency, 67–8; on defacement, 85; on Genet's *Prisoner of Love*, 52; on history, 39–40, 201, 226n3; on living in two worlds, 202–3; on mythology and language, 65; on paramilitaries, 188; on philosophy of commodities, 194; on secrecy, 29, 218n2; on state descriptions of violence, 18; on state power, 127–8; on statistical encounters with death, 130; on violence as tourist attraction, 213n19; on violence in Colombia, 7

Tengku Mahayiddin, 33

terror: economy of fear and, 53–4; as means of control, 47; social spaces and, 49; state-created, 124–5. *See also* fear

terrorism. *See* September 11th attacks; war on terror

"terrorology," 154

Thailand: cooperation with foreign powers, 161, 164, 208n1; Growth Triangle development projects, 184–5; identity within modern nation-state, 198–200; military takeover, 24–5; production of otherness, 23–6, 208n4; territory-ceding treaties, 22–3, 48, 165, 199. *See also* historical context; households and marital unions; laughter and cynicism; *mak pasar* (mothers of markets); militarization and Islamification; talking task industry; Thainess (*khwampen* Thai); war on terror

Thai National Reconciliation Commission, 55

Thainess (*khwampen* Thai): degrees of Thainess, 133–4; freedom, 148–54; invention of, 25, 31; kratom leaf consumption and, 137–40; Muslimness, 134–7; race-based political policy, 133–4; repetitive temporality, 154–7; separatism and battles for Islam, 140–7

Thaksin Shinawatra, 15, 35, 126, 145, 164, 200, 208n1, 217n1

Thanet Aphornsuvan, 26, 30, 38

thin thai dee (a region of good people), 31

thin thai ngam (a region of beautiful people), 31

Thiranagama, Sharika, 72

Thommayanti (romance novelist), 55–8

Thongchai Winichakul, 22, 140

threat, temporal dimension of, 103

tom yum restaurants, 101, 182, 191, 202

tradition as obstacle, 148–50

Trang territory, 22–3, 48, 165, 199

Trans-Pacific Partnership Agreement, 160

trauma, 51, 210n4

Trump, Donald, 161

trust and social cohesion, 108–12, 135

truth, 29, 37, 58, 117

Tsing, Anna, 70, 111

Tutu, Desmond, 162

Ulysses (Joyce), 6

unemployment, as tool of the state, 45

United States foreign policy, 158–62. *See also* September 11th attacks; war on terror

"unThainess," 24

Vietnam, 22

Village Development and Self-Defence Volunteers, 67, 68, 69

violence: author's approach to, 10–12; civilian experiences of, 9–10; endemic uncertainty of, 9,

63; as expressions of autonomy, 5–7; Halal Industrial Park and, 195; "insurgency-driven violence," 15–17; law and, 47; modern nation-states and, 13–14; as multifaceted and disordered, 17–20; as part of the ordinary, 8–9, 51–3, 60–1, 105, 118–21, 210n5; social spaces and, 49; temporality of, 154–7; as titillating, 86, 213n19; veiled or misrecognized, 94. *See also* historical context; households and marital unions; laughter and cynicism; *mak pasar* (mothers of markets); militarization and Islamification; talking task industry; Thainess (*khwampen Thai*); war on terror

Wahhabism, 33, 41, 42–5, 143, 144, 164, 166
waktu geriya (hours of the guerrillas), 66–7, 179, 181
war on terror: boarding schools as "dens of terror," 163–6, 176–81; denial of coevalness, 182–3; homogenization, 169–72, 181; humanity as ideological instrument, 159–60; language of, 154–5; in mainstream media, 222n6; "moderate Muslim" states, 161–3; ongoing imperialism, 158–60; struggle for Islam and, 142–5; sustained conflict, 170, 173–6. *See also* ponoks (Muslim boarding schools)
"we" versus "them" divisions, 104–5, 155
Wittgenstein, Ludwig, 65, 80
women: feminist organizations, persecution of, 163; increase in student population, 46; insurgency recruitment, 215n6; lack of media attention, 10–11; "modern" Malay women, 90, 214n1; participation in Tak Bai protest, 170; social violence toward, 94. See also households and marital unions; *mak pasar* (mothers of markets)

Yala province: calls for UN involvement, 34; cultural festivals, 195; ongoing conflict, 8–9; territory-ceding treaties, 22–3, 48, 165, 199
Yingluck Shinawatra, 79, 80, 81, 82, 126–7, 136, 217n1

Zubaida, Sami, 135
Zurbuchen, Mary, 39

Printed and bound by CPI Group (UK) Ltd, Croydon, CR0 4YY
31/08/2025
14727216-0001